THE LIVING WORD
– The Psalms in Everyday Life

Printed by Lightning Source, Milton Keynes, UK

Published by Crossbridge Books
Berrow Green
Martley
Worcester
WR6 6PL
Tel: +44 (0)1886 821128

ISBN 978-0-9561787-9-4

British Library Cataloguing in Publication Data.
A catalogue record for this book is available from
the British Library.

Also by Trevor Dearing:

It's True!
Total Healing
God and Healing of the Mind
Always Here For You
Meditate and Be Made Whole through Jesus Christ
The God of Miracles (with Anne Dearing)

THE LIVING WORD
– THE PSALMS IN EVERYDAY LIFE

REV. TREVOR DEARING, M.A., B.D.

CROSSBRIDGE BOOKS

Dedication

To my wonderful Christian family:

My wife — Anne

Children:
Rebecca Ruth Rachael Philip

Grandchildren:
Mark James David Mark Daniel
Mathew Olivia Jordan

Great-grandchild:
Noah

Acknowledgments

I wish to thank Anne, my wife, for all her encouragement to write this book and her partnership with me in my ministry of spiritual renewal and healing.

Also I wish to thank May Lloyd, Pastor at Stamford Free Church, for finding time in her busy life to type the manuscript.

And Eileen Mohr, my editor and publisher, for all her help in bringing the message of the Book of Psalms to a wide readership.

INTRODUCTION TO THE PSALMS

Here are sacred songs, poems and prayers which originated in Israel's worship and her experience of God. They are traditionally associated with David, and many clearly include references to his own experiences. But they also reflect centuries of individual and corporate responses to God. Human emotions of anger, despair, sadness, guilt, doubt, joy, praise and adoration are expressed. Themes include the Law, Jerusalem and its Temple, Israel's history, the natural world, human suffering and God's justice.

Although these psalms were written many centuries ago and human life has changed in dramatic ways for those of us living in the twenty-first century, yet our *basic* needs and experiences are the same. Like the writers, we are born by the same process of procreation; we live in families and have relations and friends. We also belong to various nations. We need food and drink; we marry and have children, we experience joys and sorrows, life and eventually bereavement and face the prospect of our own death. We experience the horror of war, riches and poverty; we work, rest and sleep. Above all for our study, we face the issue of the meaning and purpose of life itself and our own reason for living. We face, like the psalmists, the ultimate questions of our existence: "Who am I?" "Why am I here?" "Where am I going?" In other words, though human life has changed in many respects through science and technology, basically our lives are the same as in the days of the psalmists, and their utterances apply to human life today. That is why the subtitle to the book can rightly be termed:The Psalms in Everyday Life'.

I have not printed the whole of each psalm in every case, but have especially selected the portions which apply to everyday life and thought; also I have omitted verses from some of the longer psalms for the sake of brevity. The book can be read either as a whole or can be used taking one psalm for every day with my reflections and using this as part of one's daily devotions.

Psalm 1

*Blessed is the man who does not walk in the counsel of the wicked
or stand in the way of sinners or sit in the seat of mockers.
But his delight is in the law of the LORD,
and on his law he meditates day and night.
He is like a tree planted by streams of water,
which yields its fruit in season and whose leaf does not wither.
Whatever he does prospers.
Not so the wicked! They are like chaff that the wind blows away.
Therefore the wicked will not stand in the judgement,
nor sinners in the assembly of the righteous.
For the LORD watches over the way of the righteous,
but the way of the wicked will perish.*

Reflections:

'Blessed'– the word with which the psalm starts means 'happy' and is the key to the theme of the whole utterance. The psalmist is disclosing to us the secret of a happy life.

Firstly: he tells us to be careful in the friends we choose and the company with which we associate, for these will have a formative effect upon our lives.

Secondly: he tells us to give God time and space in our lives by meditating (slow, prayerful reflection) on the Law of God which was the most complete revelation of God's guidance for the way we can live good, wholesome and purposeful lives which were known at that time. The 'Law' for him would mean what we now have as the first five books of our Bible. We can, however, extend this to mean that we should meditate on what we have now as our whole Bible. To do this is to put down the root of our life in God's Word which will give permanent stability to our lives. Also, by the way, the psalmist is not only warning us about the company we keep but also about the literature that we read.

Thirdly: he contrasts all this with the instability and the inevitable consequences of the result of living a life which is out of relationship with God's Word in contrast to the way in which a right relationship with God, based on His Word (His revelation of Himself in the Bible), means that this manner of living is under the watchful eye of God and brings about a life of abiding goodness (see also verse 3).

Psalm 2

Why do the nations conspire and the people plot in vain?
The kings of the earth take their stand
and the rulers gather together against the LORD
and against His Anointed One.
"Let us break their chains," they say, "and throw off their fetters."
The One enthroned in heaven laughs; and the LORD scoffs at them.
Then he rebukes them in his anger
and terrifies them in his wrath, saying,
"I have installed my king on Zion, my holy hill."
I will proclaim the decree of the LORD:
He said to me, "You are my son, today I have become your Father.
Ask of me, and I will make the nations your inheritance,
and the ends of the earth your possession.
You will rule them with an iron sceptre;
you will dash them to pieces like pottery."
Therefore, you kings, be wise; be warned, you rulers of the earth.
Serve the LORD with fear and rejoice with trembling.
Kiss the Son, lest he be angry and you be destroyed in your way,
for his wrath can flare up in a moment.
Blessed are all who take refuge in him.

Reflections:

This is called a 'Messianic' Psalm because it foretells of the coming of the 'Anointed One', the 'Son, The Messiah, whom we know as Jesus Christ.

Unlike Psalm 1 which is personal and appertains to each individual, this psalm addresses all the nations of the world. At the psalmist's time and still today there are what Jesus later called "wars and rumours of wars". All nations on earth today, in their political policies and life have, as it were, "gathered together against the Lord", and in their view, have broken off His chains and thrown off His fetters. However, this has not brought freedom and peace, but instead, bondage to sin and iniquity.

As Christian individuals, living in the sin of the world today with all its murder, killing and torture and with the possibility of mankind being totally destroyed by nuclear weapons, we could be afraid for the future of mankind from which we cannot separate ourselves because our future is interwoven with the future of mankind of which we are a part. Yet, as believers in the all-powerful Sovereignty of God we need not be afraid. The destiny of the world and ourselves within it is in the controlling hands of God, who is supremely more mighty than all the nations put together. So we are optimistic about the future of mankind and look forward to the return of our Lord Jesus Christ to judge mankind and establish His Kingdom of Righteousness. With this in mind the rulers of the nations are called to be 'wise', even now and "to serve the Lord with fear and rejoice with trembling" for "Blessed are all who take refuge in Him."

Psalm 3

(A psalm of David)

O LORD, how many are my foes! How many rise up against me!
Many are saying of me, "God will not deliver him."
But You are a shield around me, O LORD;

You bestow glory on me and lift up my head.
To the LORD I cry aloud, and he answers me from his holy hill.
I lie down and sleep;
I wake again, because the LORD sustains me.
I will not fear the tens of thousands drawn up against me on every side.
Arise, O LORD! Deliver me, O my God!
Strike all my enemies on the jaw; break the teeth of the wicked.
From the LORD comes deliverance.
May your blessing be on your people.

Reflections:

Perhaps we do not ourselves feel "how many are my foes! How many rise up against me!" Yet we remember that at the present time there are Christians who are suffering persecution and even in prison in several countries such as India, all on account of their Christian faith, and we should pray for them daily. We should also remember that our Lord said, "Blessed are you when people insult you, persecute you and falsely say all kinds of evil against you" and that "a man's foes shall be those of his own household". We should thank God that this is not true of us who live, for instance, in England.

However true this may be of us, yet, if we witness boldly and are outspoken about our faith there will be those who oppose us and can even be described as 'enemies of the Christian faith'. At times like this we should rest in our faith in God who is "a shield" around us and will bestow "glory" on us – that is, He will bless us and vindicate us and exonerate us just as Jesus promised us. We need not be afraid.

Perhaps our enemies are actually stress, anxiety and even fear that would keep us awake at night. If we truly trust in God to deliver us from our worst fears, then His promise to us is that we will "lie down and sleep; and awake again because the Lord sustains me".

Christians don't need to have sleepless nights but always, through sublime trust in God they can rest in Him, sleep peacefully and awake truly refreshed.

Psalm 4

(A psalm of David)

Answer me when I call to You, O my righteous God.
Give me relief from my distress;
be merciful to me and hear my prayer.
How long, O men, will you turn my glory into shame?
How long will you love delusions and seek false gods?
Know that the LORD has set apart the godly for himself;
the LORD will hear when I call to him.
In your anger do not sin;
when you are on your beds search your hearts and be silent.
Offer right sacrifices and trust in the LORD.
Many are asking, "Who can show us any good?"
Let the light of your face shine upon us, O LORD.
You have filled my heart with greater joy
than when their grain and new wine abound,
I will lie down and sleep in peace,
for You alone, O LORD, make me dwell in safety.

Reflections:

There are few of us, if any, who will go through our lives without experiencing periods of stress, or even *distress*. This Psalm is addressed especially to us for such times. The psalmist tells us that it is especially at such times that we should pray to God for mercy and relief, knowing that we can be sure that God is with us, that we belong to Him and that He will certainly hear us. We should search our heart, and seek the blessings that come from periods of silence and trust in the Lord. It is then that we shall come through our agony of mind because God will give us *joy* as a gift for which we need not strive.

Once again, as in Psalm 3, we find that lying down and sleeping in peace is assured for us, knowing that the Lord will make us dwell (abide) in safety. So we can find the Lord's presence in time of distress.

Psalm 5

(A psalm of David)

Give ear to my words, O LORD, consider my sighing.
Listen to my cry for help, my King and my God, for to You I
pray.
In the morning, O LORD, You hear my voice;
in the morning I lay my requests before You
and wait in expectation.
You are not a God who takes pleasure in evil;
with You the wicked cannot dwell.
The arrogant cannot stand in your presence;
You hate all who do wrong.
You destroy those who tell lies;
bloodthirsty and deceitful men the LORD abhors.
But I, by your great mercy, will come into your house;
in reverence will I bow down toward your holy temple.
Lead me, O LORD, in your righteousness because of my enemies
– make straight your way before me.
Not a word from their mouth can be trusted;
their heart is filled with destruction.
Their throat is an open grave; with their tongue they speak deceit.
Declare them guilty, O God! Let their intrigues be their downfall.
Banish them for their many sins, for they have rebelled against You.
But let all who take refuge in You be glad; let them ever sing for joy.
Spread your protection over them, that those who rejoice in your name
may rejoice in You.
For surely, O LORD, You bless the righteous;
You surround them with your favour as with a shield.

Reflections:

This is a psalm about prayer for help from God.
Such prayer should be intense – "sighing" – Paul in his Letter to the
Romans writes about praying with "groanings which cannot be uttered"
and says that the Holy Spirit interprets the meaning of such prayer to the
Father.

The psalmist prays in the *morning*. Christians should pray daily, and early morning is surely the best time to pray before the mind is preoccupied with the thoughts and activities of the day. He prays with expectation that his prayer will be answered, just as Jesus subsequently taught us to pray, as recorded in Mark (chapter 11).

The psalmist writes about those who can confidently approach God in prayer. They will not be arrogant nor will they be engaged in wilful sin.

We can come to God when we are in a right relationship with Him through trusting in His mercy (again shown to us in Jesus and especially in His death on the cross).

When we are taking refuge in God we shall, writes the psalmist, be able to be "glad and ever sing with joy", for the Lord will surely bless us and answer our prayer.

Psalm 6

(A psalm of David)

*O LORD, do not rebuke me in your anger
or discipline me in your wrath.
Be merciful to me, LORD, for I am faint;
O LORD, heal me, for my bones are in agony.
My soul is in anguish. How long, O LORD, how long?
Turn, O LORD, and deliver me;
save me because of your unfailing love.
No one remembers You when he is dead.
Who praises You from the grave?
I am worn out from groaning; all night I flood my bed with weeping
and drench my couch with tears.
My eyes grow weak with sorrow; they fail because of all my foes.
Away from me, all you who do evil,
for the LORD has heard my weeping.
The LORD has heard my cry for mercy; the LORD accepts my prayer.
All my enemies will be ashamed and dismayed;
they will turn back in sudden disgrace.*

7

Reflections:

This is a prayer for those who are sick and in physical pain. The psalmist is "faint", his bones in "agony" and his soul in "anguish". He realises that this can be God's disciplining of him but prays that the Lord may deliver him. However, he knows that despite his suffering God's love is unfailing, even though he "floods his bed with tears". He asks God not to let him die but to let him live in communion with Him, and confidently believes that the Lord accepts his prayer and will deliver him from his afflictions of body, mind and spirit. Such should be our belief, attitude and prayer when we are in severe pain. We will do well to react in a similar way, also remembering the words in Exodus 15: 26, "I am the Lord who heals you" and which were wonderfully confirmed by the healing ministry of Jesus.

Psalm 7

(Of David)

O LORD my God, I take refuge in You;
save and deliver me from all who pursue me,
or they will tear me like a lion
and rip me to pieces with no one to rescue me.
O LORD my God, if I have done this
and there is guilt on my hands—
if I have done evil to him who is at peace with me
or without cause have robbed my foe—
then let my enemy pursue and overtake me;
let him trample my life to the ground and make me sleep in the dust.
Arise, O LORD, in your anger;
rise up against the rage of my enemies.
Awake, my God, decree justice.
Let the assembled peoples gather around You.
Rule over them from on high; let the LORD judge the peoples.
Judge me, O LORD, according to my righteousness,
according to my integrity, O Most High.

O righteous God, who searches minds and hearts,
bring to an end the violence of the wicked
and make the righteous secure.
My shield is God Most High, who saves the upright in heart.
God is a righteous judge,
a God who expresses his wrath every day.
If he does not relent, he will sharpen his sword;
he will bend and string his bow.
He has prepared his deadly weapons;
he makes ready his flaming arrows.

He who is pregnant with evil and conceives trouble
gives birth to disillusionment.
He who digs a hole and scoops it out
falls into the pit he has made.
The trouble he causes recoils on himself;
his violence comes down on his own head.
I will give thanks to the LORD because of his righteousness
and will sing praise to the name of the LORD Most High.

Reflections:

Have you ever been the victim of injustice? In other words have you been accused of acting or saying something unworthy of a Christian; something which was sinful, which was slanderous, gossip, something plainly bad and wrong? You know for certain that this is not true and consequently feel distressed or even angry. Most people go through this experience at sometime in their lives and find that endeavouring to defend yourself is to no avail; the injustice continues.

The psalmist depicts such a situation. He writes that if he is, in fact, guilty, then he is prepared to take the consequences, but if in fact he is innocent, then he calls upon God himself to act on his behalf. He commits his cause absolutely into the hand of God who is completely just and righteous in His dealings with men and women. He trusts that God will save and defend him and bring the falsity to 'bounce back' on those w ho perpetrated it. He ends with a prayer of thanksgiving to the God who is righteous, and states that in the face of injustice, which has been committed to God, he will "sing praise to the name of the Lord Most High".

Psalm 8

(A psalm of David)

O LORD, our LORD, how majestic is your name in all the earth!
You have set your glory above the heavens.
From the lips of children and infants You have ordained praise
because of your enemies, to silence the foe and the avenger.
When I consider your heavens, the work of your fingers,
the moon and the stars, which You have set in place,
what is man that You are mindful of him,
the son of man that you care for him?
You have made him a little lower than the heavenly beings
and crowned him with glory and honour.
You made him a ruler over the works of your hands;
and put everything under his feet;
all flocks and herds, and the beasts of the field,
the birds of the air and the fish of the sea,
all that swim the paths of the seas.
O LORD, our LORD, how majestic is your name in all the earth!

Reflections:

Psalm 2 portrayed Man in his standing within the nations of the world; Psalm 8 portrays him within the panorama of the world of nature. God is seen as majestic, transcendent above the universe as the psalmist knew it at that time. We know our universe, in which we live, to be much more vast than his through our research into the dimensions of space, particularly in the last century; therefore our concept of God is that He is incredibly majestic. If, in the light of the psalmist's view of heaven and earth Man seems very small to be the object of God's care, even more so is Man infinitesimally tiny in contrast to our present knowledge of the universe. Yet it is still true that God is "mindful" and caring of and for every individual person. Jesus said that He knows even the number of hairs on each person's head.

10

The psalmist goes on to state that Man is the crown of creation and therefore is to be a steward of its life. This brings us to the point of today's concern that Man, by his activities, is actually ruining God's creation especially through carbon emissions. Every Christian, indeed every *person* living has to share in activities which preserve God's creation, such as where possible recycling their waste, watching their 'carbon footprint' by the low use of energy such as electricity and gas and being behind government's efforts to, as we say, go 'green'. To summarise, we must be good stewards of the world of nature over which God is supremely transcendent and yet has committed to our care.

Psalm 9

(A psalm of David)

I will praise You, O LORD, with all my heart;
I will tell of all your wonders.
I will be glad and rejoice in You;
I will sing praise to your name, O Most High.
My enemies turn back; they stumble and perish before You.
For You have upheld my right and my cause;
You have sat on your throne, judging righteously.
You have rebuked the nations and destroyed the wicked;
You have blotted out their name for ever and ever.
Endless ruin has overtaken the enemy,
You have uprooted their cities;
even the memory of them has perished.
The LORD reigns for ever;
he has established his throne for judgement.
He will judge the world in righteousness;
he will govern the peoples with justice.
The LORD is a refuge for the oppressed,
a stronghold in times of trouble.
Those who know your name will trust in You,
for You, LORD, have never forsaken those who seek You.
Sing praises to the LORD, enthroned in Zion;

11

proclaim among the nations what he has done,
for he who avenges blood will remember;
he does not ignore the cry of the afflicted.
O LORD, see how my enemies persecute me!
Have mercy and lift me up from the gates of death,
that I may declare your praises in the gates of the Daughter of Zion
and there rejoice in your salvation.
The nations have fallen into the pit they have dug;
their feet are caught in the net they have hidden.
The LORD is known by his justice;
the wicked are ensnared by the work of their hands.
The wicked return to the grave, all the nations that forget God.
But the needy will not always be forgotten,
nor the hope of the afflicted ever perish.
Arise, O LORD, let not man triumph;
let the nations be judged in your presence.
Strike them with terror, O LORD; let the nations know they are but men.

Reflections:

This is another psalm about the sovereignty of God. "The Lord reigns for ever; he has established his throne for judgment".

Amidst the international turmoil of our time it needs the exercise of faith to see that this is indeed true. Yet it is a firm Christian belief that God "is known by his justice". What we need to remember is that the Lord God has given human beings a free will; he has not made them as pre-programmed robots or as puppets dangling, as it were, on his fingers, doing and moving exactly as He wills. This has enormous possibilities for good as human beings freely respond to His loving reign. On the contrary, however, it has, as we are all too aware, the possibility that mankind will reject this rule and go its own way with the ever-increasing possibility of chaos, injustice, war and suffering. Yet, Christians believe that despite all the injustice in the world, God has not abdicated. He has not given up His throne to evil. He is still "a refuge for the oppressed and a stronghold in times of trouble" and He has never forsaken those that seek Him; and we believe the words of the old hymn:

God is working His purpose out
 As year succeeds to year …
 …..Nearer and nearer draws the time,
The time that shall surely be,
When the earth shall be filled
 With the glory of God
 As the waters cover the sea.

Psalm 10

Why, O LORD, do You stand far off?
Why do You hide yourself in times of trouble?
In his arrogance the wicked man hunts down the weak,
who are caught in the schemes he devises.
He boasts of the cravings of his heart;
he blesses the greedy and reviles the LORD.
In his pride the wicked does not seek him;
in all his thoughts there is no room for God.
His ways are always prosperous;
he is haughty and your laws are far from him;
he sneers at all his enemies.
He says to himself, "Nothing will shake me;
I'll always be happy and never have trouble."
His mouth is full of curses and lies and threats;
trouble and evil are under his tongue.
He lies in wait near the villages;
from ambush he murders the innocent,
watching in secret for his victims.
He lies in wait like a lion in cover;
he lies in wait to catch the helpless and drags them off in his net.
His victims are crushed, they collapse; they fall under his strength.
He says to himself, "God has forgotten;
he covers his face and never sees."

Arise, LORD! Lift up your hand, O God. Do not forget the helpless.
Why does the wicked man revile God?
Why does he say to himself, "He won't call me to account"?
But You, O God, do see trouble and grief;
You consider it to take it in hand.
The victim commits himself to You;
You are the helper of the fatherless.
Break the arm of the wicked and evil man;
call him to account for his wickedness that would not be found out.

The LORD is King for ever and ever;
the nations will perish from this land.
You hear, O LORD, the desire of the afflicted;
You encourage them, and You listen to their cry,
defending the fatherless and the oppressed,
in order that man, who is of the earth, may terrify no more.

Reflections:

This psalm is a 'heart cry' to God for an answer as to why He hides himself in times of trouble, especially when righteous people are suffering at the hands of the wicked. The psalmist does not really pose an answer and quite frankly there isn't one as long as the petitioner limits himself to the horizons of the present, temporal life which we have on earth. The fact is however, for Christians, that death is not the final and complete end of human life, but that it continues beyond the grave where God's justice is meted out; heaven for the godly and righteous and eternal punishment for the wicked – for those who have lived without thought of or in contempt of God.

'It is given for man once to die
And after death comes the judgment'.

In the meantime, however, we can trust that, as the psalmist says,

"But You, O God, do see trouble and grief; You consider it to take it in hand. The victim commits himself to You; You are the helper of the fatherless… You hear, O Lord, the desire of the afflicted; You encourage them and listen to their cry, defending the fatherless and the oppressed."

Psalm 11

(A psalm of David)

In the LORD I take refuge.
How then can you say to me: "Flee like a bird to your mountain.
For look, the wicked bend their bows;
they set their arrows against the strings
to shoot from the shadows at the upright in heart.
When the foundations are being destroyed,
what can the righteous do?"
The LORD is in his holy temple; the LORD is on his heavenly throne.
He observes the sons of men; his eyes examine them.
The LORD examines the righteous,
but the wicked and those who love violence his soul hates.
On the wicked he will rain fiery coals and burning sulphur;
a scorching wind will be their lot.
For the LORD is righteous, he loves justice;
upright men will see his face.

Reflections:

Ephesians 6 v 12 speaks of our spiritual warfare. Paul writes that "we struggle not against flesh and blood, but against the rulers, against authorities, against the powers of this dark world and against the spiritual forces of evil in the heavenly places." The psalmist writes in verse 16 about "the flaming arrows of the evil one". It is these forces that, as he writes, 'bend their bows; they set their arrows against the strings to shoot from the shadows at the upright in heart' (v 2). Paul says that we should put on the breastplate of righteousness to protect us. The psalmist states that we must not flee from these attacks but take refuge in the Lord "who is on his heavenly throne", emphasising God's power and authority. "He observes the sons of men and examines them" and His wrath is kindled against all that is evil. The psalmist then looks beyond this life to that which is to come and says upright men will see His face. Jesus later said: "Blessed are the pure in heart for they will see God." (Matthew Ch 5 v 8)

Psalm 12

(A psalm of David)

Help, LORD, for the godly are no more;
the faithful have vanished from among men.
Everyone lies to their neighbour;
their flattering lips speak with deception.
May the LORD cut off all flattering lips and every boastful tongue
that says, "We will triumph with our tongues;
we own our lips – who is our master?"
"Because of the oppression of the weak and the groaning of the needy,
I will now arise," says the LORD.
"I will protect them from those who malign them."
And the words of the LORD are flawless,
like silver refined in a furnace of clay, purified seven times.
O LORD, You will keep us safe and protect us from such people for ever.
The wicked freely strut about
when what is vile is honoured among men.

Reflections:

The psalmist has suffered from the use of the tongue. This reminds us, in our everyday lives, to be careful in what we utter from our mouths. Words can be like bullets which can penetrate very deeply. James, in his Letter, warns against the unbridled use of the tongue (James 3 vv 1-10). Words can bring very great blessing, or very deep hurt to the recipient. They can also be used in gossiping to others about a person or persons. Christians should only use words in a positive manner. The psalmist teaches however, that God's Word (We can say those contained in the Bible) are pure and can bless us to the depths of our being. They also can warn us when we would go astray from God's will for us. We can trust, however states the psalmist, in God's protection from the power of evil words spoken against us.

Psalm 13

(A psalm of David)

How long, O LORD? Will You forget me for ever?
How long will You hide your face from me?
How long must I wrestle with my thoughts
and every day have sorrow in my heart?
How long will my enemy triumph over me?
Look on me and answer, O LORD my God.
Give light to my eyes, or I will sleep in death;
My enemy will say, "I have overcome him,"
and my foes will rejoice when I fall.
But I trust in your unfailing love; my heart rejoices in your salvation.
I will sing to the LORD, for he has been good to me.

Reflections:

The psalmist is obviously writing from a state of deep depression. We can all suffer from this at sometime in our lives. He feels that even God has forsaken him; again a state of mind that we can also feel in the depths of our despair. Even people are no help to him, but rather a source of more pain. What answer does he find to this condition? It is to remember what good things God has brought into his life in the past and, despite what he feels, to trust in God's unfailing love and to rejoice in his salvation. This is the answer to any depression into which we may go.

Psalm 14

(A psalm of David)

The fool says in his heart, "There is no God."
They are corrupt, their deeds are vile; there is no one who does good.
The LORD looks down from heaven on the sons of men
to see if there are any who understand, and who seek God.
All have turned aside, they have together become corrupt;
there is no one who does good, not even one.

17

Will evildoers never learn – those who devour my people as men eat
bread and who do not call on the LORD?
There they are, overwhelmed with dread,
for God is present in the company of the righteous.
You evildoers frustrate the plans of the poor,
but the LORD is their refuge.
Oh, that salvation for Israel would come out of Zion!
When the LORD restores the fortunes of his people,
let Jacob rejoice and Israel be glad!

Reflections:

The psalmist scorns those who say "there is no God" and live their lives without any reference to Him, which he states, like today, is the general state of mankind. God, however, is present "in the company of the righteous" – today in the Church. We are reminded of Jesus' words, "where two or three come together in my Name, there am I with them." (Matt 18 v 20) The life of the Christian should therefore consist in gathering together with God's people on a regular basis. When we do this we will find that God is our 'refuge' – being a place not only of safety, but where, as in a fortress, everything that we need has been supplied.

Psalm 15

(A psalm of David)

LORD, who may dwell in your sanctuary?
Who may live on your holy hill?
He whose walk is blameless
and who does what is righteous,
who speaks the truth from his heart
and has no slander on his tongue,

who does his neighbour no wrong
and casts no slur on his fellow-man,
who despises a vile man but honours those who fear the LORD,
who keeps his oath even when it hurts,
who lends his money without usury
and does not accept a bribe against the innocent.
He who does these things will never be shaken.

Reflections:

The psalmist describes those who will live in the constant presence of God in their daily lives. They will live

blamelessly,
righteously,
will always speak the truth,
not slander anyone,
do no wrong to their fellow man,
not cast a slur on their fellow man,
honour those who fear the Lord,
keep their promises even when it means a cost to themselves,
lend money without seeking interest on it,
not accept a bribe.

He concludes: "those who do these things will never be shaken".

All this is a lesson and a challenge to us.

Psalm 16
(Of David)

Keep me safe, O God, for in You I take refuge.
I said to the LORD, "You are my Lord;
apart from You I have no good thing."

19

As for the saints who are in the land, they are the righteous ones
in whom is all my delight.
The sorrows of those will increase of those who run after other gods.
I will not pour out their libations of blood
or take up their names on my lips.
LORD, You have assigned me my portion and my cup;
You have made my lot secure.
The boundary places have fallen for me in a pleasant place;
surely I have a delightful inheritance.
I will praise the LORD, who counsels me;
even at night my heart instructs me.
I have set the LORD always before me.
Because he is at my right hand I will not be shaken.
Therefore my heart is glad and my tongue rejoices;
my body also will rest secure,
Because You will not abandon me to the grave,
nor let your Holy One see decay.
You have made known to me the path of life;
You will fill me with joy in your presence,
with eternal pleasures at your right hand.

Reflections:

This is a psalm about the whole meaning and purpose of human life. It rests in living within belief in God and living the whole of one's life with reference to Him – putting Him first in every decision and every aspect of daily life. In doing this one accepts all the particular circumstances of our lives as appointed by God Himself. The believer also seeks to be instructed by God in his decisions. To live a life which is given to God means that we can be certain that the purpose and the ultimate goal of our life will be to be in His presence in heaven. This is God's revealed plan for those who trust Him, as indeed all of us should on a daily and even moment by moment basis.

Psalm 17

(A psalm of David)

Hear, O LORD, my righteous plea; listen to my cry.
Give ear to my prayer – it does not rise from deceitful lips.
May my vindication come from You;
may your eyes see what is right.
Though You probe my heart and examine me at night,
though You test me, You will find nothing;
I have resolved that my mouth will not sin.
As for the deeds of evil men – by the word of your lips
I have kept myself from the ways of the violent.
My steps have held to your paths, my feet have not slipped.

I call on You, O God, for You will answer me;
give ear to me and hear my prayer.
Show the wonder of your great love, You who save
by your right hand those who take refuge in You from their foes.
Keep me in the apple of your eye;
hide me in the shadow of your wings...

You still the hunger of those You cherish; their sons have plenty,
and they store up wealth for their children,
[15]and I – in righteousness I will see your face;
when I awake, I will be satisfied
with seeing your likeness.

Reflections:

This is a psalm about prayer in which a Christian ought to engage daily. When we pray we should first examine our hearts to make sure that we do not come before the Lord with unconfessed sin in our lives. If there is, then we should trust as the Lord taught us in what we call the 'Lord's Prayer' that we ask God for forgiveness (Matt 6 v 12). Thus the psalmist teaches us that we should do this at the end of every day before we go to sleep. We should make sure that we have kept close to Jesus, and therefore free from the way of the 'violent' and that we have lived "in the ways of the Lord". We can be sure that God will answer our prayers out of His great love for us as we take refuge in Him who keeps us as "the apple of His eye". We can, again as the Lord teaches us in the 'Lord's Prayer', bring our own needs before Him: "give us this day our daily bread". We look forward to life after death with Him when we shall behold His likeness, even in us; "When He appears, we shall be like Him, for we shall see Him as He is" (I John 3 v 2).

Psalm 18

(A psalm of David)

I love You, O LORD, my strength.
The LORD is my rock, my fortress and my deliverer;
my God is my rock, in whom I take refuge. He is my shield
and the horn of my salvation, my stronghold.
I call to the LORD, who is worthy of praise,
and I am saved from my enemies.
The cords of death entangled me;
the torrents of destruction overwhelmed me.
the cords of the grave coiled around me,
the snares of death confronted me.
In my distress I called to the LORD; I cried to God for help.
From his temple he heard my voice;
my cry came before him, into his ears .....
~ ~ ~ ~ ~ ~ ~ ~ ~ ~ ~ ~

[20] The LORD has dealt with me according to my righteousness;
according to the cleanness of my hands
he has rewarded me.
For I have kept the ways of the LORD;
I have not done evil by turning from my God.
All his laws are before me;
I have not turned away from his decrees.
I have been blameless before him
and I have kept myself from sin.
The LORD has rewarded me according to my righteousness,
,   according to the cleanness of my hands in his sight.
To the faithful You show yourself faithful.
To the blameless You show yourself blameless,

22

To the pure You show yourself pure,
but to the crooked You show yourself shrewd.
You save the humble but bring low
those whose eyes are haughty.
You, O LORD, keep my lamp burning;
my God turns my darkness into light.
With your help I can advance against a troop;
with my God I can scale a wall.
As for God, his way is perfect;
the word of the LORD is flawless.
He is a shield for all who take refuge in him.
For who is God besides the LORD?
And who is the Rock except our God?
It is God who arms me with strength
and makes my way perfect.
He makes my feet like the feet of a deer;
he enables me to stand on the heights.
He trains my hands for battle;
my arms can bend a bow of bronze.
You give me your shield of victory, and your right hand sustains me;
You stoop down to make me great.
You broaden the path beneath me,
so that my ankles do not turn over… …

[46]The Lord lives! Praise be to my Rock!
Exalted be God my Saviour!

Reflections:

This is a 'love song' to the Lord; a prayer of thanksgiving. We should always, like the psalmist, really praise God with all our hearts when He has answered our prayer, too, and delivered us from any distress we may have had in our daily lives. God is described by the psalmist as a 'rock' and a 'shield' when we are in trouble of any kind. This applies especially when we have been very near to death itself and when in our distress we have "cried to God for help". We can be sure that whenever we are entangled with drastic problems the Lord will hear us from heaven, His dwelling place. We should always endeavour to live a life which is pleasing to God and not turn away from Him but, as far as

23

possible, be "blameless before Him, for to the faithful He shows Himself faithful; to the blameless He shows Himself blameless; to the pure He shows Himself pure". He saves the humble. God's ways are always perfect. He gives us strength to endure afflictions and He makes our feet like those of a deer, able to stand securely on craggy heights. We can therefore "praise the Lord because He lives" and is like a rock on which we can build our lives. We may want to praise Him with the words: "Exalted be God my Saviour".

Psalm 19

(A psalm of David)

The heavens declare the glory of God;
the skies proclaim the work of his hands.
Day after day they pour forth speech;
night after night they display knowledge.
There is no speech or language
where their voice is not heard.
Their voice goes out into all the earth,
their words to the ends of the world.
~~~~~~~~~~~~~
[7]The law of the LORD is perfect, reviving the soul.
The statutes of the LORD are trustworthy,
making wise the simple.
The precepts of the LORD are right, giving joy to the heart.
The commands of the LORD are radiant,
giving light to the eyes.
The fear of the LORD is pure, enduring for ever.
The ordinances of the LORD are sure,
and altogether righteous.
They are more precious than gold, than much pure gold.
They are sweeter than honey, than honey from the comb.
[11]By them is your servant warned;
in keeping them there is great reward.

Who can discern his errors?

Forgive my hidden faults.
Keep your servant also from wilful sins;
may they not rule over me.
Then will I be blameless,
innocent of great transgression.
May the words of my mouth and the meditation of my heart
be pleasing in your sight,
O LORD, my Rock and my Redeemer.

Reflections:

This psalm really speaks for itself. However, we must realise that human beings could never have known God, His nature and His ways unless He had chosen to reveal Himself – make Himself known to mankind. The ultimate revelation of Himself was and is through actually becoming a man in the person of His Son, the Lord Jesus Christ: "no man has seen God at any time, but God the One and Only, who is at the Father's side has made Him known". (John 1 v 16)

The psalmist, of course, lived before the birth of Christ, but he shares with us the revelation of God in and through the natural world which He Himself has created. He also states that God has revealed Himself through His statutes, precepts and commands which, for us, are written in the Old Testament. The verses from [7]"The law of the Lord is perfect" through to "in keeping them there is great reward" are difficult for most people to accept. They consider rules to be burdensome and preferably broken or circumvented. But it is now more important than ever for such people to understand as the psalmist does, that we will greatly **benefit** from keeping God's laws, since they are given to us to help us avoid the snares and pitfalls so often caused by other people's foolishness or malicious behaviour. However, we can extend this revelation through the written word, to the whole of our Bible.

In response the Psalmist rightly states that God can "discern" his errors and asks God to forgive his "secret" faults. As in Psalm 1 he emphasises the importance of meditation on the nature and Being of God through His written word which should, like prayer, be a daily factor in our devotional life. He asks that this may be pleasing in God's sight, his 'Rock' and his 'Redeemer' and ours too.

25

Psalm 20

(A psalm of David)

May the LORD answer you when you are in distress;
may the name of the God of Jacob protect you.
May he send you help from the sanctuary
and grant you support from Zion.
May he remember all your sacrifices
and accept your burnt offerings.
May he give you the desire of your heart
and make all your plans succeed.
We will shout for joy when you are victorious
and will lift up our banners in the name of our God.
May the LORD grant all your requests.

Now I know that the LORD saves his anointed;
he answers him from his holy heaven
with the saving power of his right hand.
Some trust in chariots and some in horses,
but we trust in the name f the LORD our God.
They are brought to their knees and fall,
but we rise up and stand firm.
O LORD, save the king!
Answer us when we call!

Reflections:

This psalm is in the nature of a prayer for every reader, particularly when he or she is in distress; something which can, at times, be the experience of anyone as they pursue their daily life in the world. It can happen particularly when one faces the loss of a loved one, or has suffered a bitter disappointment. For "help from the sanctuary and grant you support from Zion" (the latter being where God was particularly believed to dwell) we would read: "send you help from the church and from heaven." For "burnt offerings" and "sacrifices" we would consider 'our sacrificial service for the Lord'.

The psalmist then bids us not to put our complete reliance on man's help, but to "trust in the name of the Lord our God".

The Church of England Prayer Book (1662) has taken up the words "Lord (God) save the King (Queen) and answer us when we call" paraphrased as: 'and mercifully hear us when we call upon Thee' into its liturgy for daily use.

Psalm 21

(A psalm of David)

O LORD, the king rejoices in your strength.
How great is his joy in the victories You give!
You have granted him the desire of his heart
and have not withheld the request of his lips.
You welcomed him with rich blessings
and placed a crown of pure gold on his head.
He asked You for life and You gave it to him –
length of days for ever and ever.
Through the victories You gave, his glory is great;
You have bestowed on him splendour and majesty.
Surely You have granted him eternal blessings
and made him glad with the joy of your presence.
For the king trusts in the LORD;
through the unfailing love of the Most High
he will not be shaken.

Reflection

This is a psalm of thanksgiving which we can all utter because He has made us "a kingdom and priests to serve our God" (Rev 1 v 6)

Our thanksgiving will include the joy, trust and unfailing love which we can receive from our gracious Father; and as we also focus on His Son, our Lord Jesus, we have even more to be thankful for.

Psalm 22

(A psalm of David)

My God, my God, why have You forsaken me?
Why are You so far from saving me,
so far from the words of my groaning?
²O my God, I cry out by day, but You do not answer,
by night, and am not silent.
³Yet You are enthroned as the Holy One;
You are the praise of Israel.
⁴In You our fathers put their trust;
they trusted and You delivered them.
⁵They cried to You and were saved;
in You they trusted and were not disappointed.

⁶But I am a worm and not a man,
scorned by men and despised by the people.
⁷All who see me mock me;
they hurl insults, shaking their heads:
⁸"He trusts in the LORD; let the LORD rescue him.
Let him deliver him, since he delights in him."

⁹Yet You brought me out of the womb;
You made me trust in You even at my mother's breast.
¹⁰From birth I was cast upon You;
from my mother's womb You have been my God.
¹¹Do not be far from me,
for trouble is near and there is no one to help.
¹²Many bulls surround me;
strong bulls of Bashan encircle me.
¹³Roaring lions tearing their prey
open their mouths wide against me.
¹⁴I am poured out like water,
and all my bones are out of joint.
My heart has turned to wax;

it has melted away within me.
¹⁵My strength is dried up like a potsherd,
and my tongue sticks to the roof of my mouth;
You lay me in the dust of death.
¹⁶Dogs have surrounded me;
a band of evil men has encircled me,
they have pierced my hands and my feet.
¹⁷I can count all my bones; people stare and gloat over me.
¹⁸They divide my garments among them
and cast lots for my clothing.
¹⁹But You, O LORD, be not far off;
O my Strength, come quickly to help me
²⁰Deliver my life from the sword,
my precious life from the power of the dogs.
²¹Rescue me from the mouth of the lions;
save me from the horns of the wild oxen.

²²I will declare your name to my brothers;
in the congregation I will praise You.
²³You who fear the LORD, praise him!
All you descendants of Jacob, honour him!
Revere him, all you descendants of Israel!
²⁴For he has not despised or disdained
the suffering of the afflicted one;
he has not hidden his face from him
but has listened to his cry for help.

²⁵From You comes the theme of my praise
in the great assembly;
before those who fear You will I fulfil my vows.
²⁶The poor will eat and be satisfied;
they who seek the LORD will praise him –
may your hearts live for ever!
²⁷All the ends of the earth will remember
and turn to the LORD,
and all the families of the nations
will bow down before him,
²⁸for dominion belongs to the LORD
and he rules over the nations.

²⁹All the rich of the earth will feast and worship;
all who go down to the dust will kneel before him –
those who cannot keep themselves alive.
³⁰Posterity will serve him;
future generations will be told about the Lord.
³¹They will proclaim his righteousness to a people yet unborn –
for he has done it.

Reflections:

This psalm is really in essence a prophecy describing in detail how Jesus the Messiah would die (Matt 27 vv 27–56).

vv 1-2 Sin separates us from God and the words "My God, my God, why have You forsaken me?" uttered by Jesus upon the cross are seen by Christians to be the moments when Jesus, who Himself 'had no sin' (2 Cor 5 v 21) was taking upon Himself the punishment for the past, present and future sins of the whole of mankind.

vv 6-8 describe the scorn Jesus endured upon the cross from those who were present at His suffering, and verse 8 depicts the very words used to mock Him and His faith in the Heavenly Father.

vv 14-16 describe the physical suffering of thirst and the nails which pierced His hands and feet.

v 17 describes the nakedness which was probably the most humiliating aspect of a Roman crucifixion.

v 18 describes how the soldiers would cast lots for His clothes.

vv 19-21 describe poetically the feelings Jesus would experience in His supreme agony.

vv 22-24 calls upon mankind to thank Him for His suffering on their behalf because, in fact God accepted His sacrifice of Himself.

vv 25-31 look beyond the cross to His triumph and the way in which "posterity will serve Him and proclaim His righteousness". Every day all the time, Christians are invited to put their trust in His sacrifice for sin and give themselves in thankful service to His kingdom. "For it is by grace you have been saved, through faith – and this not from yourselves, it is the gift of God – not by works, so that no one can boast."(Ephesians 2 v 8-9)

Psalm 23
(A psalm of DavidI

This psalm provides promises for every day of our lives. Probably we never thought about this psalm in this way, even though we say it over and over again.

The LORD is my Shepherd – **Relationship**

I shall not be in want – **Supply**

He makes me lie down in green pastures – **Rest**

He leads me beside quiet waters – **Refreshment**

He restores my soul – **Healing**

He guides me in paths of righteousness – **Guidance**

For His name's sake – **Purpose**

Even though I walk through the valley of the shadow of death – **Testing**

I will fear no evil – **Protection**

For You are with me – **Faithfulness**

Your rod and your staff they comfort me – **Discipline**

You prepare a table before me in the presence of my enemies – **Hope**

You anoint my head with oil – **Consecration**

My cup overflows – **Abundance**

Surely goodness and love will follow me all the days of my life – **Blessing**

And I will dwell in the house of the LORD – **Security**

For ever – **Eternity.**

Psalm 24

(A psalm of David)

¹The earth is the LORD's and everything in it,
the world and all who live in it;
²For he founded it upon the seas
and established it upon the waters.
³Who may ascend the hill of the LORD?
Who may stand in his holy place?
⁴He who has clean hands and a pure heart,
who does not lift up his soul to an idol or swear by what is false.
⁵He will receive blessing from the LORD
and vindication from God his Saviour.
⁶Such is the generation of those who seek him,
who seek your face, O God of Jacob.
⁷Lift up your heads, O you gates;
be lifted up you ancient doors,
that the King of glory may come in.
⁸Who is this King of glory?
The LORD strong and mighty, the LORD mighty in battle.
⁹Lift up your heads, O you gates;
lift them up, you ancient doors, that the King of glory may come in.
¹⁰Who is he, this King of glory?
The LORD Almighty – he is the King of glory.

Reflections:

Verses 1-2 speak of the greatness, power and supremacy of God as seen in Creation.

vv 3-4 and 7-10 speak about entry into the presence of God in prayer and communion with Him as we open the gates of our hearts to let Him into our lives.

v 5 speaks of the spiritual conditions of meeting with God in this way to have "clean hands and a pure heart" – outward and inward purity through being holy as we receive the righteousness of Christ in the presence of God – not to have engaged in wilful sin in actions or thoughts.

The whole psalm speaks about the glory of God in earth, church and our lives; all of which teaching we should take to heart.

Psalm 25

(A psalm of David)

[4]Show me your ways, O LORD, teach me your paths;
[5]guide me in your truth and teach me,
for You are God my Saviour,
and my hope is in You all day long.
[6]Remember, O LORD, your great mercy and love,
for they are from of old.
[7]Remember not the sins of my youth and my rebellious ways;
according to your love remember me, for You are good, O LORD.
[8]Good and upright is the LORD;
therefore he instructs sinners in his ways.
[9]He guides the humble in what is right and teaches them his way.
[10]All the ways of the LORD are loving and faithful
for those who keep the demands of his covenant.
[11]For the sake of your name, O LORD, forgive my iniquity,
though it is great.
[12]Who, then, is the man that fears the LORD?
He will instruct him in the way chosen for him.
[13]He will spend his days in prosperity,
and his descendants will inherit the land.
[14]The Lord confides in those who fear him;
he makes his covenant known to them.
[15]My eyes are ever on the LORD,
for only he will release my feet from the snare.
[16]Turn to me and be gracious to me, for I am lonely and afflicted.
[17]The troubles of my heart have multiplied;
free me from my anguish.

Reflections:

Many a mature adult will look back on their youth and ask God to forgive the sins, activities they were involved in and the things they 'got up to' in their teenage years or early twenties, just as the psalmist did. (v. 7)

The psalmist also asserts that the Lord will "instruct sinners in his ways" and "guide the humble in what is right and teach them his way". (vv 8-9) God has given us a free will and we can conduct our lives ourselves, have our own ambitions, make our own decisions and generally do what we ourselves want to do. However, there is another, the Christian way, to live and that is to commit all of our lives into His hands and live as He has taught us. This way reaches its ultimate expression in following the teaching our Lord has given us about the way to live in what we call "The Sermon on the Mount" (Matthew 5 vv 3-10). To do this is to follow God's instruction and then when, like the psalmist we are lonely and afflicted, in trouble and anguish (v 16-17), we can rely on the Lord to hear us and help us.

Psalm 26

(A psalm of David)

¹Vindicate me, O LORD, for I have led a blameless life;
I have trusted in the LORD without wavering.
²Test me, O LORD, and try me, examine my heart and my mind;
³For your love is ever before me,
and I walk continually in your truth.
⁴I do not sit with deceitful men, nor do I consort with hypocrites;
⁵I abhor the assembly of evildoers and I refuse to sit with the wicked.
⁶I wash my hands in innocence, and go about your altar, O LORD,
⁷proclaiming aloud your praise
and telling of all your wonderful deeds.
⁸I love the house where You live, O LORD,
the place where your glory dwells.
⁹Do not take away my soul along with sinners,
my life with bloodthirsty men,
¹⁰in whose hands are wicked schemes,
whose right hands are full of bribes.
¹¹But I lead a blameless life; redeem me and be merciful to me.

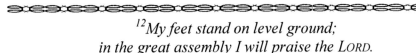

¹²My feet stand on level ground;
in the great assembly I will praise the LORD.

Reflections:

This is a prayer for God to vindicate us when we are being blamed for what we have not done, and when we have "trusted the Lord without wavering" (v 1). Peter in his first Letter states that if we are being punished and know that we have deserved our punishment then we should take it without complaint; but if, like the psalmist, we know that we have done no wrong, then this is "commendable before God". "To this you were called", he writes, "because Christ also suffered for you, leaving an example that you should follow in his steps. He committed no sin and no deceit was found in his mouth. When they hurled their insults at him, he did not retaliate; when he suffered, he made no threats. Instead, he entrusted himself to him who judges justly".
(I Peter 2 vv 19-23) We should do the same!

Psalm 27

(A psalm of David)

¹The LORD is my light and my salvation – whom shall I fear?
The LORD is the stronghold of my life – of whom shall I be afraid?
²When evil men advance against me to devour my flesh,
when my enemies attack me, they will stumble and fall.
³Though an army besiege me, my heart will not fear;
though war break out against me, even then will I be confident.
⁴One thing I ask of the LORD, this is what I seek:
that I may dwell in the house of the LORD all the days of my life,
to gaze upon the beauty of the LORD and to seek him in his temple.
⁵For in the day of trouble he will keep me safe in his dwelling;
he will hide me in the shelter of his tabernacle
and set me high upon a rock.
⁶Then my head will be exalted above the enemies who surround me;
at his tabernacle will I sacrifice with shouts of joy;

I will sing and make music to the LORD.
[7]Hear my voice when I call, O LORD;
be merciful to me and answer me.
[8]My heart says of You, "Seek his face!"
Your face, O LORD, I will seek.
[9]Do not hide your face from me,
do not turn your servant away in anger;
You have been my helper.
Do not reject me or forsake me, O God my Saviour.
[10]Though my father and mother forsake me, the LORD will receive me.
[11]Teach me your way, O LORD;
lead me in a straight path because of my oppressors.
[12]Do not turn me over to the desire of my foes,
for false witnesses rise up against me, breathing out violence.
[13]I am still confident of this:
I will see the goodness of the LORD in the land of the living.
[14]Wait for the LORD;
be strong and take heart and wait for the LORD.

Reflections:

This is a psalm about trusting God when we are in trouble; about having unshakable faith in Him, knowing that nothing can separate us from the love of God (v.3). (Romans 8 vv 35-39) This is true when we make loving and sensing God the priority in all of our life and we are constantly doing this (v.4).   We can know His protection and vindication in any day of trouble (v. 5-6a). This will result in *joy* in the Lord (v. 6b).

The psalmist bids us pray to God in times of trouble (vv 7-9) and assures us of God's constant acceptance of us (vv 10-12) and that we shall see God's goodness, even in this life (v. 13). The psalm teaches us about having enduring patience and waiting for God. "They that wait upon the Lord shall renew their strength", writes Isaiah (Isaiah 40 v 31 KJV). This is when we wait upon Him in expectancy and constancy.

Psalm 28

(A psalm of David)

[1]To You I call, O LORD my Rock;
do not turn a deaf ear to me
for if You remain silent,
I will be like those who have gone down to the pit.
[2]Hear my cry for mercy as I call to You for help,
as I lift up my hands towards your Most Holy Place.
[3]Do not drag me away with the wicked,
with those who do evil, who speak cordially with their neighbours
but harbour malice in their hearts ...
[6]Praise be to the LORD, for he has heard my cry for mercy.
[7]The LORD is my strength and my shield;
my heart trusts in him, and I am helped.
My heart leaps for joy and I will give thanks to him in song.
[8]The LORD is the strength of his people,
a fortress of salvation for his anointed one.
[9]Save your people and bless your inheritance;
be their shepherd and carry them for ever.

Reflections:

This is again a cry for God's help in time of trouble: "Hear my cry for mercy as I call to You for help". The fact that the psalmist states that he is relying solely on God's **mercy** (v 2) is a timely reminder of the Christian teaching, especially that of Paul, that our call upon God cannot be an appeal from any good actions or merit on our part.
(Ephesians 2 v 9 –"not by works, so that no one can boast"). The way into the heart of God is to cast ourselves completely and entirely on His merciful love. Then we shall indeed, like the psalmist, praise the Lord who has heard our cry for mercy. We shall prove that God is our strength in time of trouble, and our hearts will leap for *joy* (v 7). We are reminded of Paul's teaching that we should make our prayers and supplications to God with thanksgiving. (Philippians 4 v 6)

The words 'Save your people
and bless your inheritance' (v. 9) (your people)

have been incorporated into the Book of Common Prayer (1662) for *daily* use.

Psalm 29

(A psalm of David)

¹*Ascribe to the LORD, O mighty ones,*
ascribe to the LORD glory and strength.
²Ascribe to the LORD the glory due to his name;
worship the LORD in the splendour of his holiness.
³The voice of the LORD is over the waters, the God of glory thunders,
the LORD thunders over the mighty waters.
⁴The voice of the LORD is powerful; the voice of the LORD is majestic.
⁵The voice of the LORD breaks the cedars;
the LORD breaks in pieces the cedars of Lebanon.
⁶He makes Lebanon skip like a calf, Sirion like a young wild ox.
⁷The voice of the LORD strikes with flashes of lightning.
⁸The voice of the LORD shakes the desert;
the LORD shakes theDesert of Kadesh.
⁹The voice of the LORD twists the oaks and strips the forests bare.
And in his temple all cry, "Glory!"
¹⁰The LORD sits enthroned over the flood;
the LORD is enthroned as King for ever.
¹¹The LORD gives strength to his people;
the LORD blesses his people with peace.

Reflections:

The psalmist offers an ultimate expression of worship and adoration of God which should be always a part of our daily prayers. He writes: "Ascribe to the Lord glory and strength, ascribe to the Lord the glory due to his name, worship the Lord in the splendour of his holiness" (vv 1-2).

He then draws attention to the power of God's Word, when he utters words from His mouth. We know that the words of the Lord were the instruments of His creation.

He spoke the universe into existence (Gen chapter 1)

He sustains all things by His powerful word (Hebrews 1 v 3)

His word will accomplish all He pleases (Isaiah 55 v 11)

His word effects permanent results (Isaiah 55 v 13b)

His word will never pass away (Matthew 24 v 35)

His word can penetrate to the depth of our being (Hebrews 4 v 12)

Our prayer should be: "Speak, Lord, for Your servant is listening" (1 Samuel 3 v 9)

The psalmist paints a picture of God who is transcendent above all creation, yet gives strength to His people (v 10 -11).

Psalm 30

(A psalm of David)

¹I will exalt You ,O LORD, for You lifted me out of the depths
and did not let my enemies gloat over me.
²O LORD my God, I called to You for help and You healed me.
³O LORD, You brought me up from the grave;
You spared me from going down into the pit.
⁴Sing to the LORD, you saints of his, praise his holy name.
⁵For his anger lasts only a moment, but his favour lasts a lifetime;
weeping may remain for a night, but rejoicing comes in the morning.
⁶When I felt secure I said, "I shall never be shaken."
⁷O LORD, when You favoured me, You made my mountain stand firm;
but when You hid your face, I was dismayed.
⁸To You, O LORD, I called; to the LORD I cried for mercy:
⁹"What gain is there in my destruction,
in my going down into the pit?
Will the dust praise You? Will it proclaim your faithfulness?
¹⁰Hear, O LORD, and be merciful to me; O LORD, be my help."
¹¹You turned my wailing into dancing;
You removed my sackcloth and clothed me with joy,

*¹²that my heart may sing to You and not be silent.
O LORD my God, I will give You thanks for ever.*

Reflections:

The psalmist teaches us how to praise the Lord when He has healed us from sickness, especially when it threatened to be terminal (v 2-3). He praises God because, not only has He healed him, but He has completely turned things round to abundant health; He has brought him to a place of rejoicing (v 5, 11-12). God's anger is but transitory but His favour lasts for a lifetime (v 5).

The psalmist has a very pessimistic view of life after death, as was common in Old Testament times. This has to be contrasted with the Christian's truly optimistic view, for we have a sure and certain hope of everlasting life in Heaven. As we are shown in the Book of Revelation (ch 7 vv 11-17) where it is revealed that God's people engage in continual acts of praise to God and enjoy a condition of perpetual bliss:

¹¹All the angels were standing round the throne and around the elders and the four living creatures. They fell down on their faces before the throne and worshipped God, ¹²saying:

"Amen! Praise and glory and wisdom and thanks and honour and power and strength be to our God for ever and ever. Amen!"

¹³Then one of the elders asked me, "These men in white robes – who are they, and where did they come from?"

¹⁴I answered, "Sir, you know." And he said, 'These are they who have come out of the great tribulation; they have washed their robes and made them white in the blood of the Lamb.

¹⁵Therefore, they are before the throne of God and serve him day and night in his temple; and he who sits upon the throne will spread his tent over them.

¹⁶Never again will they hunger; never again will any thirst. The sun will not beat upon them, nor any scorching heat. ¹⁷For the Lamb at the centre of the throne will be their shepherd; he will lead them to springs of living water.

And God will wipe away every tear from their eyes."

Christians therefore, when they are sick, seek God to heal them but they are not afraid of death. They regard it as the sublime culmination of their life on earth.

Psalm 31

(A psalm of David)

¹In You, O LORD, I have taken refuge;
let me never be put to shame; deliver me in your righteousness.
²Turn your ear to me, come quickly to my rescue;
be my rock of refuge, a strong fortress to save me.
³Since You are my rock and my fortress,
for the sake of your name lead and guide me.
⁴Free me from the trap that is set for me, for You are my refuge.
⁵Into your hands I commit my spirit;
redeem me, O LORD, the God of truth.
⁶I hate those who cling to worthless idols; I trust in the LORD.
⁷I will be glad and rejoice in your love,
for You saw my affliction and knew the anguish of my soul.
⁸You have not handed me over to the enemy
but have set my feet in a spacious place.
⁹Be merciful to me, O LORD, for I am in distress;
my eyes grow weak with sorrow, my soul and my body with grief.
¹⁰My life is consumed by anguish and my years by groaning;
my strength fails because of my affliction, and my bones grow weak.
¹¹Because of all my enemies, I am the utter contempt of my neighbours;
I am a dread to my friends –
those who see me on the street flee from me.
¹²I am forgotten by them as though I were dead;
I have become like broken pottery.
¹³For I hear the slander of many; there is terror on every side;
they conspire against me and plot to take my life.
¹⁴But I trust in You, O LORD; I say, "You are my God."
¹⁵My times are in your hands;

41

deliver me from my enemies and from those who pursue me.
[16]Let your face shine on your servant; save me in your unfailing love.
[17]Let me not be put to shame, O LORD, for I have cried out to You;
but let the wicked be put to shame and lie silent in the grave.
[18]Let their lying lips be silenced, for with pride and contempt
they speak arrogantly against the righteous.
[19]How great is your goodness, which You have stored up
for those who fear You, which You bestow in the sight of men
on those who take refuge in You.
[20]In the shelter of your presence
You hide them from the intrigues of men;
in your dwelling You keep them safe from accusing tongues.
[21]Praise be to the LORD, for he showed his wonderful love to me
when I was in a besieged city.
[22]In my alarm I said, "I am cut off from your sight!"
Yet You heard my cry for mercy when I called to You for help.
[23]Love the LORD, all his saints!
The LORD preserves the faithful, but the proud he pays back in full.
[24]Be strong and take heart, all you who hope in the LORD.

Reflections:

This is another psalm where the psalmist cries out to God in his severe distress from within and from without. It is noticeable, however, that in his dire conditions and situation his faith in God never wavers for a moment. There are some particularly memorable verses in this psalm which are like a treasury of verses that all of us can learn so that we can recall them when our situation is like his. He says of God:

"You are my rock and fortress" (v 3) – an impregnable safe haven.
"You are my God" (v 14).
"My times are in your hands" (v 15). God has complete charge over his ultimate destiny.
"Save me in your unfailing love" (v 16).
"How great is your goodness which You have stored up for those who fear You, which You bestow in the sight of men on those who take refuge in You." (v 19).

He speaks praise to the Lord, for "he showed his wonderful love to me" (v 21).

However, the crux of the psalm lies in the words: "Into your hands I commit my spirit" which were, in fact, the last words which Jesus quoted in His death upon the cross (Luke 23 v 46). They denote entire submission to God the Father and absolute trust in Him.

Psalm 32

(Of David)

¹Blessed is he whose transgressions are forgiven,
whose sins are covered.
²Blessed is the man whose sin the LORD does not count against him
and in whose spirit is no deceit.
³When I kept silent, my bones wasted away
through my groaning all day long.
⁴For day and night your hand was heavy upon me;
my strength was sapped as in the heat of summer.
⁵Then I acknowledged my sin to You and did not cover up my iniquity.
I said, "I will confess my transgressions to the LORD" –
and You forgave the guilt of my sin.
⁶Therefore let everyone who is godly pray to You
while You may be found;
surely when the mighty waters rise, they will not reach him.
⁷You are my hiding place; You will protect me from trouble
and surround me with songs of deliverance.
⁸I will instruct you and teach you in the way you should go;
I will counsel you and watch over you.
⁹Do not be like the horse or the mule, which have no understanding
but must be controlled by bit and bridle or they will not come to you.
¹⁰Many are the woes of the wicked,
but the LORD's unfailing love surrounds the man who trusts in him.

43

¹¹Rejoice in the LORD and be glad, you righteous;
sing, all you who are upright in heart!

Reflections:

This is an expression of the absolute happiness, joy and contentment of one who is unfailingly sure that all his sins have been forgiven, which is echoed in the heart of every Christian because he or she knows that they are completely forgiven by God when they put their trust in His bearing of all their sins by Jesus' perfect sacrifice upon the cross (e.g. Romans 8 vv 1-2). In the psalmist's words, "I acknowledged my sin to You and did not cover up my iniquity. I said, 'I will confess my transgressions to the Lord' and You forgave the guilt of my sin."

John writes in the New Testament: "If we confess our sins, he is faithful and just and will forgive us our sins, and purify us from all unrighteousness." (1 John 1 v 9)

After our sins are forgiven God will be our "hiding place"; He "will protect us from trouble and surround us with songs of deliverance" (v 7).

Then the psalmist is inspired by God to give even more promises for the forgiven person – promises of God's guidance and unfailing love (vv 8-10) and the psalm finishes with a call to rejoice in God who has done, and will do, all this for us (vv 8-11).

Psalm 33

¹Sing joyfully to the LORD, you righteous;
it is fitting for the upright to praise him.
²Praise the LORD with the harp;
make music to him on the ten-stringed lyre.
³Sing to him a new song; play skilfully, and shout for joy.

⁴For the word of the LORD is right and true;
he is faithful in all he does.
⁵The LORD loves righteousness and justice;
the earth is full of his unfailing love.
⁶By the word of the LORD were the heavens made,
their starry host by the breath of his mouth.
⁷He gathers the waters of the seas into jars;
he puts the deep into storehouses.
⁸Let all the earth fear him; let all the people of the world revere him.
⁹For he spoke and it came to be; he commanded and it stood firm.
¹⁰The LORD foils the plans of the nations;
he thwarts the purposes of the peoples.
¹¹But the plans of the LORD stand firm for ever,
the purposes of his heart through all generations.
¹²Blessed is the nation whose God is the LORD,
the people he chose for his inheritance.
¹³From heaven the LORD looks down and sees all mankind;
¹⁴From his dwelling place he watches all who live on earth –
¹⁵He who forms the hearts of all, who considers everything they do.
¹⁶No king is saved by the size of his army;
no warrior escapes by his great strength.
¹⁷A horse is a vain hope for deliverance;
despite its great strength it cannot save.
¹⁸But the eyes of the LORD are on those who fear him,
on those whose hope is in his unfailing love,
¹⁹To deliver him from death and keep them alive in famine.
²⁰We wait in hope for the LORD; he is our help and our shield.
²¹In him our hearts rejoice, for we trust in his holy name.
²²May your unfailing love rest upon us, O LORD,
even as we put our hope in You.

Reflections:

This is a song of praise to God
    "whose word is right and true" (v 4)
    "who created the heavens and the earth" (vv 6-9)
    who thwarts evil amongst the nations and peoples of the earth
    (v 9-10).

The psalmist speaks of the blessing of any nation which acknowledges God's rule over it and which trusts in Him for security from its enemies and puts its hope in Him alone.

Christians, therefore, are bidden in our day to take an active part in politics to whatever extent that they are able and to endeavour through whatever influence they can bring to bear upon the government of their land to see that its laws are subservient to God's law, and they seek to oppose all that is not in accordance with the teaching of the Bible. Their motto, aim and policies are based on the psalmist's words:

"Blessed is the nation whose God is the Lord." (v 12)

Psalm 34

(A psalm of David)

[1] I will extol the LORD at all times;
his praise will always be on my lips.
[2] My soul will boast in the LORD; let the afflicted hear and rejoice.
[3] Glorify the LORD with me; let us exalt his name together.
[4] I sought the LORD and he answered me;
he delivered me from all my fear.
[5] Those who look to him are radiant;
their faces are never covered with shame.
[6] This poor man called and the LORD heard him;
he saved him out of all his troubles.
[7] The angel of the LORD encamps around those who fear him,
and he delivers them.
[8] Taste and see that the LORD is good;
blessed is the man who takes refuge in him.
[9] Fear the LORD, you his saints, for those who fear him lack nothing.
[10] The lions may grow weak and hungry,
but those who seek the LORD lack no good thing.
[11] Come, my children, listen to me;
I will teach you the fear of the LORD.

¹²Whoever of you loves life and desires to see many good days,
¹³keep your tongue from evil and your lips from speaking lies.
¹⁴Turn from evil and do good; seek peace and pursue it.
¹⁵The eyes of the LORD are on the righteous
and his ears are attentive to their cry;
¹⁶The face of the LORD is against those who do evil,
to cut off the memory of them from the earth.
¹⁷The righteous cry out, and the LORD hears them;
he delivers them from all their troubles.
¹⁸The LORD is close to the broken-hearted
and saves those who are crushed in spirit.
¹⁹A righteous man may have many troubles,
but the LORD delivers him from them all.
²⁰He protects all his bones; not one of them will be broken.
²¹Evil will slay the wicked;
the foes of the righteous will be condemned.
²²The LORD redeems his servants;
no one will be condemned who takes refuge in him.

Reflections:

The psalmist calls upon all men and women to join him in praising the Lord for all His goodness and all His mercies for answering the prayers of all who call upon Him. There are many precious verses in this psalm which should be read slowly to appreciate all the promises from God which He has given to all those who love life and desire "to see many good days" (v 12). Amongst the glorious statements are:
"Those who look to him are radiant and their faces are never covered with shame" (v 5)
"The angel of the Lord encamps around those who fear him and he delivers them" (v 7)
"Taste and see that the Lord is good; blessed is the man who takes refuge in him" (v 8)
"The eyes of the Lord are on the righteous and his ears are attentive to their cry" (v 15)
"The righteous cry out and the Lord hears them and delivers them from all their troubles. The Lord is close to the broken-hearted and saves

those who are crushed in spirit". (v 17-18)
"The Lord redeems his servants; no one will be condemned who takes refuge in him." (v 22)

There are conditions attached to these promises, especially in the right use of the tongue (v 12-13), and that we do not engage in anything that is evil (vv 13-14, 16). We must live lives that are pleasing to God every day and engage in good works whenever we can; for this is what is entailed in what the psalmist terms 'being righteous'.

Psalm 35

(A psalm of David)

[10]My whole being will exclaim, "Who is like You, O LORD?
You rescue the poor from those too strong for them,
the poor and needy from those who rob them."
[11]Ruthless witnesses come forward;
they question me on things I know nothing about.
[12]They repay me evil for good and leave my soul forlorn.

[22]O LORD, You have seen this; be not silent.
Do not be far from me, O Lord.
[23]Awake, and rise to my defence! Contend for me, my God and Lord.
[24]Vindicate me in your righteousness, O LORD my God;
do not let them gloat over me.
[25]Do not let them think, "Aha, just what we wanted!"
or say, "We have swallowed him up."
[26]May all who gloat over my distress be put to shame and confusion;
may all who exalt themselves over me
be clothed with shame and disgrace.
[27]May those who delight in my vindication shout for joy and gladness;
may they always say, "The LORD be exalted,
who delights in the well-being of his servant."
[28]My tongue will speak of your righteousness
and of your praises all day long.

Reflections:

I have omitted most of the verses from this psalm because they are sub-Christian. The psalmist seems to have many enemies and prays that God will deal with them in a drastic manner. It is true that as we go through life we cannot please everyone and that there will be people who, for one reason or another, 'fall out' with us even on account of our overt Christian faith.

In my ministry I have had to help in marital and domestic relationships and between children and parents wherein animosity has arisen. However, our Lord's command to the Christian is to "love your enemies and do good to those who hate you" (Luke 6 v 27) and, "You have heard it said 'Love your neighbour and hate your enemy'. But I tell you: Love your enemies and pray for those who persecute you, that you may be children of your Father in heaven. He causes his sun to rise on the evil and the good, and sends rain on the righteous and the unrighteous" (Matthew 5 vv 21-45). However, the psalmist does exclaim of God that He rescues "the poor from those who are too strong for them"(v 10) and asks that those who delight in the vindication of the righteous may "shout for joy and gladness" and that his tongue will speak of God's righteousness and His praises all day long. It is a Christian belief that, in the end, God's will is that good will triumph over evil and righteousness over unrighteousness, and in this promise Christians who have been wronged or badly treated in their relationships can take hope.

Psalm 36
(Of David)

1.   *An oracle is within my heart concerning the sinfulness of the wicked: there I is no fear of God before his eyes.*
2.   *For in his own eyes he flatters himself too much to detect or hate his sin.*
3.   *The words of his mouth are wicked and deceitful;*
     he has ceased to be wise and to do good.
4.   *Even on his bed he plots evil; he commits himself to a sinful course and does not reject what is wrong.*

5.   *Your love, O LORD, reaches to the heavens, your faithfulness to
      the skies.*
6.   *Your righteousness is like the mighty mountains, your justice
      like the great deep. O LORD, You preserve both man and beast.*
7.   *How priceless is your unfailing love! Both high and low among
      men find refuge in the shadow of your wings.*
8.   *They feast on the abundance of your house; You give them drink
      from your river of delights.*
9.   *For with You is the fountain of life; in your light we see light.*
10.   *Continue your love to those who know You, your righteousness
      to the upright in heart.*
11.   *May the foot of the proud not come against me. Nor the hand of
      the wicked drive me away.*
12.   *See how the evildoers lie fallen – thrown down, not able to rise!*

Reflections:

We live in a country (England) where various kinds of crime tend to be
on the increase year after year. We have had to build more prisons for
those convicted of wrongdoing and the numbers in the police force have
needed also to be increased. The numbers attending church services of
most denominations has steadily declined and Sunday Schools for
children have seen rapidly declining numbers. As the psalmist says,
"there is no fear of God" (v 1) and there is no sense of sin or judgement
(v 2) and many people do not reject what is wrong (v 4).

In contrast to all this, the psalmist paints a very wonderful picture of
God. His love reaches to the heavens and His faithfulness to the skies
(v 5). He is a God of righteousness and justice (v 6) and His love is
priceless (v 6-7). He blesses those who do what is right and the
psalmist prays that the words and actions of the wicked will not affect
him in any way, but that God's justice will prevail as he lives his daily
life of being "upright in heart" (v 10).

Psalm 37

(A psalm of David)

[1]Do not fret because of evil men
or be envious of those who do wrong;
[2]for like the grass they will soon wither,
like green plants they will soon die away.
[3]Trust in the LORD and do good;
dwell in the land and enjoy safe pasture.
[4]Delight yourself in the LORD
and he will give you the desires of your heart.
[5]Commit your way to the LORD; trust in him and he will do this:
[6]He will make your righteousness shine like the dawn,
the justice of your cause like the noonday sun.
[7]Be still before the LORD and wait patiently for him;
do not fret when men succeed in their ways,
when they carry out their wicked schemes.
[8]Refrain from anger and turn from wrath;
do not fret — it leads only to evil.
[9]For evil men will be cut off,
but those who hope in the LORD will inherit the land.
[10]A little while, and the wicked will be no more;
though you look for them, they will not be found.
[11]But the meek will inherit the land and enjoy great peace.
[12]The wicked plot against the righteous and gnash their teeth at them;
[13]but the Lord laughs at the wicked, for he knows their day is coming.
[14]The wicked draw the sword and bend the bow
to bring down the poor and needy
to slay those whose ways are upright.
[15]But their swords will pierce their own hearts,
and their bows will be broken.
[16]Better the little that the righteous have
than the wealth of many wicked;
[17]for the power of the wicked will be broken,
but the LORD upholds the righteous.
[18]The days of the blameless are known to the LORD,
and their inheritance will endure for ever.
[19]In times of disaster they will not wither;
in days of famine they will enjoy plenty.

51

20 But the wicked will perish:
The LORD's enemies will be like the beauty of the fields,
they will vanish — vanish like smoke.
21 The wicked borrow and do not repay,
but the righteous give generously;
22 those the LORD blesses will inherit the land,
but those he curses will be cut off.
23 If the LORD delights in a man's way, he makes his steps firm;
24 though he stumble, he will not fall,
for the LORD upholds him with his hand.
25 I was young and now I am old,
yet I have never seen the righteous forsaken
or their children begging bread.
26 They are always generous and lend freely;
their children will be blessed.
27 Turn from evil and do good; then you will dwell in the land for ever.
28 For the LORD loves the just and will not forsake his faithful ones.
They will be protected for ever,
but the offspring of the wicked will be cut off;
29 the righteous will inherit the land and dwell in it for ever.
30 The mouth of the righteous man utters wisdom,
and his tongue speaks what is just.
31 The law of his God is in his heart; his feet do not slip.
32 The wicked lie in wait for the righteous, seeking their very lives;
33 but the LORD will not leave them in their power
or let them be condemned when brought to trial.
34 Wait for the LORD and keep his way.
He will exalt you to inherit the land;
when the wicked are cut off, you will see it.
35 I have seen a wicked and ruthless man flourishing
like a green tree in its native soil,
36 but he soon passed away and was no more;
though I looked for him, he could not be found.
37 Consider the blameless, observe the upright;
there is a future for the man of peace.
38 But all sinners will be destroyed;
the future of the wicked will be cut off.
39 The salvation of the righteous comes from the LORD;

he is their stronghold in time of trouble.
⁴⁰The LORD helps them and delivers them;
he delivers them from the wicked and saves them,
because they take refuge in him.

Reflections:

The psalmist utters many promises to those who live good lives, daily trusting in the Lord.

He will give them the desires of their heart (v 4)

"the meek will inherit the land" (v 11) (see Matthew 5 v 5)

"their inheritance will endure for ever" (v 18)

they will be able to endure hardship (v 19)

the Lord will give him daily security (v 23-24)

the Lord will never forsake those who live good lives (v 28)

He will not leave them in the power of evildoers (v 33-40)

"there is a future for the man of peace" (v 37)

the righteous person will inherit salvation and in the Lord will find security (v 39-40).

The psalmist also states that it is better to have a little in the way of possessions and live a good life than to be wealthy and live in evil ways, for the Lord will himself see that the righteous will always have enough on which to live; but the destiny of the evil man is transitory (v 16-17, 35-36). (See our Lord's teaching in Matthew 6 vv 25-34.)

Psalm 38

(A psalm of David)

¹O LORD, do not rebuke me in your anger
or discipline me in your wrath.
²For your arrows have pierced me,
and your hand has come down upon me.
³Because of your wrath there is no health in my body;
my bones have no soundness because of my sin.
⁴My guilt has overwhelmed me like a burden too heavy to bear.

⁵*My wounds fester and are loathsome because of my sinful folly.*
⁶*I am bowed down and brought very low;*
all day long I go about mourning.
⁷*My back is filled with searing pain; there is no health in my body.*
⁸*I am feeble and utterly crushed; I groan in anguish of heart.*
⁹*All my longings lie open before You, O Lord;*
my sighing is not hidden from You.
¹⁰*My heart pounds, my strength fails me;*
even the light has gone from my eyes.
¹¹*My friends and companions avoid me because of my wounds;*
my neighbours stay far away.
¹²*Those who seek my life set their traps,*
those who would harm me talk of my ruin;
all day long they plot deception.
¹³*I am like a deaf man, who cannot hear,*
like a mute, who cannot open his mouth;
¹⁴*I have become like a man who does not hear,*
whose mouth can offer no reply.
¹⁵*I wait for You, O LORD; You will answer, O Lord my God.*
¹⁶*For I said, "Do not let them gloat*
or exalt themselves over me when my foot slips."
¹⁷*For I am about to fall, and my pain is ever with me.*
¹⁸*I confess my iniquity; I am troubled by my sin.*
¹⁹*Many are those who are my vigorous enemies;*
those who hate me without reason are numerous.
²⁰*Those who repay my good with evil*
slander me when I pursue what is good.
²¹*O LORD, do not forsake me; be not far from me, O my God.*
²²*Come quickly to help me, O Lord my Saviour.*

Reflections:

The psalmist is in **agony** of body, mind and spirit and all this, he feels, is because of his "sinful folly" (v 5) (apparently one specific act or incident). Even his friends have forsaken him (v 11) and he is all alone in his utter misery. It is a fact that **guilt** can play havoc with our minds, bodies and circumstances; it is like a malignant cancer in the very depth of a person's soul and, because our spirit, soul and body all have effects on each other, guilt can issue in depression, panic attacks, ulcers in the stomach and other physical pain. This is especially so when it lurks in the subconscious or unconscious mind. The psalmist expresses urgent petitions for God to forgive him, and the first step towards this happening is when sin is actually confessed (v 18) and brought into the light of God's presence. Our Lord taught about this. He said, "If your eyes are good, your whole body will be full of light. But if your eyes are bad, your whole body will be full of darkness. If then the light within you is darkness, how great is that darkness!" (Matthew 6 v 22-3). The psalmist calls out to God:

"O Lord, do not forsake me; be not far from me, O my God." (v 21)

As Christians it is almost impossible to live our daily lives without sinning in some way against God at some time on our earthly journey and I have had to counsel some who have fallen into adultery or other gross sins. Once again, we can be sure that whereas

"If we claim to be without sin, we deceive ourselves and the truth is not in us. If we confess our sins, he is faithful and just and will forgive us our sins and purify us from all unrighteousness." (I John 1 vv 8-9)

Psalm 39

(A psalm of David)

1   *I said, "I will watch my ways and keep my tongue from sin; I will put a muzzle on my mouth as long as the wicked are in my presence."*

2   *But when I was silent and still, not even saying anything good, my anguish increased.*

3   *My heart grew hot within me, and as I meditated, the fire burned; then I spoke with my tongue:*

4   *"Show me, O LORD, my life's end and the number of my days; let me know how fleeting is my life.*

5   *You have made my days a mere handbreadth; the span of my years is as nothing before You. Each man's life is but a breath.*

6   *Man is a mere phantom as he goes to and fro: He bustles about, but*

only in vain; he heaps up wealth, not knowing who will get it.
7   *"But now, Lord, what do I look for? My hope is in You."*

12 *"Hear my prayer, O LORD, listen to my cry for help; be not deaf to
my weeping. For I dwell with You as an alien, a stranger, as all my
fathers were.*
13 *Look away from me, that I may rejoice again before I depart and
am no more."*

Reflections:

In the last part of this psalm David is still concerned about his sins; he
does not have the reassurance of sins forgiven that we, as Christians,
have. He wants to know what lies ahead of him, especially how much
longer he has to live. He reflects on how transitory human life actually
is and wonders when he, himself, is destined to die. All of us are on a
journey through life and every hour of every day brings us nearer to our
death. Especially as we grow older, the thought of our eventual death is
a thought that is frequently before us. God has given us the capacity to
remember much of our past life and we are aware of our present
existence, but the future is hidden from our eyes.

   This curiosity about the future leads some people to seek an answer
from 'soothsayers' (fortune tellers). Even King Saul in the Old
Testament went to see such a person, known as the 'witch of Endor'
(1 Samuel ch. 28), but consulting such persons is strictly forbidden by
God. (Exodus 22 v 18, Deuteronomy 18 v 10-11, Micah 5 v 12) and
Paul cast an evil spirit out of a young woman who was able to tell
fortunes (Acts 16 v 16-18). Christians always live in the spirit of D. W.
Whittle who wrote:

'I know not what of good or ill
May be reserved for me
Of weary ways or golden days
Before His face I see

*But I know whom I have believed
And am persuaded that He is able
To keep that which I've committed
Unto Him against that day.'* (The time of our death)

He exercises the same faith in the last verse of the hymn:

'I know not when my Lord may come,
I know not how or where
If I shall pass the vale of death
Or meet him in the air. (1 Thess. 4)

But I know whom I have believed.'

Psalm 40
(A psalm of David)

¹I waited patiently for the LORD; he turned to me and heard my cry.
²He lifted me out of the slimy pit, out of the mud and mire;
he set my feet on a rock and gave me a firm place to stand.
³He put a new song in my mouth, a hymn of praise to our God.
Many will see and fear and put their trust in the LORD.
⁴Blessed is the man who makes the LORD his trust,
who does not look to the proud, to those who turn aside to false gods.
⁵Many, O LORD my God, are the wonders You have done.
The things You planned for us no one can recount to You;
were I to speak and tell of them, they would be too many to declare.
⁶Sacrifice and offering You did not desire, but my ears you have
pierced; burnt offerings and sin offerings You did not require.
⁷Then I said, "Here I am, I have come—
it is written about me in the scroll.
⁸I desire to do Your will, O my God; your law is within my heart."
⁹I proclaim righteousness in the great assembly;
I do not seal my lips, as You know, O LORD.
¹⁰I do not hide your righteousness in my heart;
I speak of your faithfulness and salvation.
I do not conceal your love and your truth from the great assembly.
¹¹Do not withhold your mercy from me, O LORD;
may your love and your truth always protect me.

Reflections:

The psalmist waited patiently for the Lord to deliver him from his troubles. This is a lesson every Christian has to learn in his petitions to the Lord; for when we pray His answer is sometimes 'yes', sometimes 'no' and frequently it is 'wait!' God keeps us waiting to test our faith in Him but also because, in His wisdom He knows that it is not the right time to grant our requests. When I was vicar at St Paul's church, Hainault, I had a Church Army sister to assist me (1970-1975). She had a wise saying which during my years of ministry I have proved to be constantly true. It was: "The Lord's timing is always perfect". We must live daily with this faith in God's wisdom.

The psalmist goes on to extol the goodness of God with words like:

"He has put a new song in my mouth; a hymn of praise to our God" (v 3).

He declares that the man who puts his trust in God is "blessed" or "happy". He then goes on to use words which the writer to the Hebrews in the New Testament says is true of Jesus:

"Sacrifice and offerings You did not desire but my ears You have pierced; burnt offerings You did not require.

Then I said, 'Here I am, I have come – it is written of me in the scroll. I desire to do your will, O my God, your law is within my heart." (Hebrews 10 vv 5-10)

That is how Christians have to live – doing, as far as they know it – doing God's will, and seeking to witness to others, with their lives and words, to God's righteousness and faithfulness.

Psalm 41
(A psalm of David)

*[1]Blessed is he who has regard for the weak;
the LORD delivers him in times of trouble.
[2]The LORD will protect him and preserve his life;*

58

he will bless him in the land
and not surrender him to the desire of his foes.
¹²In my integrity You uphold me and set me in your presence for ever.
¹³Praise be to the LORD, the God of Israel,
from everlasting to everlasting.
Amen and amen.

Reflections:

The psalmist paints a picture of how God will reward those who "have regard for the weak". It is an extremely important aspect of the Christian life that we engage in acts of mercy and do good actions to help others in need wherever or whenever we can. Paul in Ephesians states that we are indeed saved from our sins by faith in God's grace in what He has done in reconciling us to Himself by His grace, but he goes on to state that "we are God's workmanship, created in Christ Jesus to do good works, which God prepared in advance for us to do." (Ephesians 2 vv 8-10). James in his Letter declares that, "faith by itself, if not accompanied by action, is dead". (See James 3 vv 14-25)

Jesus Himself said that, at the final judgement, good deeds towards those in need will be brought into account to determine our final destiny. (Matthew 25 vv 31-46) and says that good actions done for such needy people are in fact done for Him Himself. The parable of the 'Good Samaritan' (Luke chapter 10) also shows that love for God should issue in acts of mercy done to our 'neighbour' of whatever nationality, colour or creed he or she may be.

Christians therefore are known by their fruit (Matthew 7) and this fruit is goodness shown in good actions performed in our daily lives.

Psalms 42 and 43

These two psalms were originally one until divided into two later in the Hebrew manuscripts.

Psalm 42

> [1] *As the deer pants for streams of water,*
> *so my soul pants for You, O God.*
> [2] *My soul thirsts for God, for the living God.*
> *When can I go and meet with God?*
> [3] *My tears have been my food day and night,*
> *while men say to me all day long, "Where is your God?"*

[4] *These things I remember as I pour out my soul: how I used to go with the multitude, leading the procession to the house of God, with shouts of joy and thanksgiving among the festive throng.*

> [5] *Why are you downcast, O my soul? Why so disturbed within me?*
> *Put your hope in God, for I will yet praise him,*
> *my Saviour and [6] my God.*
> *My soul is downcast within me; therefore I will remember You*
> *from the land of the Jordan,*
> *the heights of Hermon—from Mount Mizar.*
> [7] *Deep calls to deep in the roar of your waterfalls;*
> *all your waves and breakers have swept over me.*
> [8] *By day the LORD directs his love,*
> *at night his song is with me— a prayer to the God of my life.*
> [9] *I say to God my Rock, "Why have you forgotten me?*
> *Why must I go about mourning, oppressed by the enemy?"*
> [10] *My bones suffer mortal agony as my foes taunt me,*
> *saying to me all day long, "Where is your God?"*
> [11] *Why are you downcast, O my soul? Why so disturbed within me?*
> *Put your hope in God, for I will yet praise him,*
> *my Saviour and my God.*

Psalm 43

¹Vindicate me, O God, and plead my cause against an ungodly nation;
rescue me from deceitful and wicked men.
²You are God my stronghold. Why have You rejected me?
Why must I go about mourning, oppressed by the enemy?
³Send forth your light and your truth, let them guide me;
let them bring me to your holy mountain,
to the place where You dwell.
4Then will I go to the altar of God, to God, my joy and my delight.
I will praise You with the harp, O God, my God.
5Why are you downcast, O my soul? Why so disturbed within me?
Put your hope in God ,for I will yet praise him,
my Saviour and my God.

Reflections:

Here is a man who has had his faith and hope dashed at the depths of his
being. The all-conquering Babylonian army had destroyed nation after
nation in the Middle East, but the psalmist had put his trust in God that
He would never let His Holy Temple be demolished by a heathen army.
The terrible event had happened and the Temple, including the Holy of
Holies where God was deemed supremely to meet with His people
through the His Priest, had been razed to the ground and the heathen
enemies were taunting him all day long with the words: "Where is your
God?" (v 3-10)

In his forlorn state the psalmist remembers with nostalgia the
wonderful day of the past; how he used "to go with the multitude
leading the procession to the house of God with shouts of joy and
thanksgiving among the festive throng." (v 4)

Yet amidst his desperately destroyed faith he urges himself to "Put
your hope in God, for I will yet praise Him, my Saviour and my God."
(Ps 43 v 5)

It is very possible for Christians today to have their faith and hope
dashed until they are so miserable that they appear to be in mourning,
oppressed by the enemy (Satan) with his or her bones "in mortal agony"
(v 9). Then that person needs to look back in their lives on all that s/he

has enjoyed of the blessings of God and say with him: "I will praise Him, my Saviour and my God" (v 11) praying, "Send forth your light and your truth, let them guide me." (Ps 43 v 3)

A Christian's hope is not mere optimism but is based on the way God resurrected Jesus, His Son, after His crucifixion and on our belief with Peter: "In his great mercy He has given us new birth into a living hope through the resurrection of Jesus Christ from the dead" (I Peter 1 v 3).

Psalm 44

¹We have heard with our ears, O God; our fathers have told us
what You did in their days, in days long ago.
²With your hand You drove out the nations and planted our fathers;
You crushed the peoples and made our fathers flourish.
³It was not by their sword that they won the land,
nor did their arm bring them victory;
it was your right hand, your arm, and the light of your face,
for You loved them.
⁴You are my King and my God, who decrees victories for Jacob.
⁵Through You we push back our enemies;
through your name we trample our foes.
⁶I do not trust in my bow, my sword does not bring me victory;
⁷but You give us victory over our enemies,
You put our adversaries to shame.
⁸In God we make our boast all day long,
and we will praise your name for ever.
⁹But now You have rejected and humbled us;
You no longer go out with our armies.
¹⁰You made us retreat before the enemy,
and our adversaries have plundered us.
¹¹You gave us up to be devoured like sheep
and have scattered us among the nations.

[12]*You sold your people for a pittance, gaining nothing from their sale.*
[13]*You have made us a reproach to our neighbours,*
the scorn and derision of those around us.
[14]*You have made us a byword among the nations;*
the peoples shake their heads at us.
[15]*My disgrace is before me all day long,*
and my face is covered with shame
[16]*at the taunts of those who reproach and revile me,*
because of the enemy, who is bent on revenge.
[17]*All this happened to us, though we had not forgotten You*
or been false to your covenant.
[18]*Our hearts had not turned back;*
our feet had not strayed from your path.
[19]*But You crushed us and made us a haunt for jackals*
and covered us over with deep darkness.
[20]*If we had forgotten the name of our God*
or spread out our hands to a foreign god,
[21]*would not God have discovered it,*
since he knows the secrets of the heart?
[22]*Yet for your sake we face death all day long;*
we are considered as sheep to be slaughtered.
[23]*Awake, O Lord! Why do You sleep? Rouse yourself!*
Do not reject us for ever.
[24]*Why do You hide your face and forget our misery and oppression?*
[25]*We are brought down to the dust; our bodies cling to the ground.*
[26]*Rise up and help us; redeem us because of your unfailing love.*

Reflections:

It seems that the psalmist lived at the same time as the writer of psalms 42 and 43. The Babylonian armies had overrun the area that we call the Holy Land and, as was the way in those days, in order to weaken the nation they had conquered, they had scattered the people, especially in this case, they had taken the men to Babylon (v 9-16).

Unlike the author of psalms 42-43 he looks upon this, not as a personal tragedy, but a national one. He does not remember his glorious past, but the past in the way in which Yahweh had acted. He had given His people, the Hebrews, victory over their enemies, especially when He led them, under Joshua, into the Promised Land (v 4-8). The psalmist pleads the innocence of the nation in that it has kept faith with God and not been false to the Covenant He made with Moses (v 17-18). They, therefore, did not deserve punishment; they were innocent of any reason why God should reject them and cause them to flee before their enemy. (v 17-22). Paul quotes verse 22 in Romans 8 v 36 referring to Christians suffering persecution.

Why then, had all this happened? In Hebrews chapter 12 v 6-10, the writer speaks of the 'chastening' which God sometimes inflicts upon people for their eventual good and, in fact, the Old Testament history of the Hebrew nation shows how God chastised people quite often, allowing them to be defeated by their enemies. Job, an individual, suffered greatly, a suffering which was allowed by God, though he pleaded his innocence (Job ch. 1-2 and the whole book of Job). It is possible, therefore, that God not only punishes sin, but sometimes chastises His people, for their spiritual growth and learning. We, as Christians, do not escape such chastisement when God's wisdom sees it to be necessary. We may experience it and learn from it at any time in our normal daily Christian life. Those of us with prophetic insight will also see that God still chastises whole nations as in periods of economic downturn (recession) which we are going through as I write... Oh that England would turn back to God! (See 2 Chronicles 7 v 14.)

Psalm 45

1   *My heart is stirred by a noble theme as I recite my verses for the king; my tongue is the pen of a skilful writer.*

2   *You are the most excellent of men and your lips have been anointed with grace, since God has blessed you for ever.*

3   *Gird your sword upon your side, O mighty one; clothe yourself with splendour and majesty.*

4   *In your majesty ride forth victoriously on behalf of truth, humility and righteousness; let your right hand display awesome deeds.*

5   *Let your sharp arrows pierce the hearts of the king's enemies; let the nations fall beneath your feet.*

6   *Your throne, O God, will last for ever and ever; a sceptre of justice will be the sceptre of your kingdom.*

7   *You love righteousness and hate wickedness; therefore God, your God, has set you above your companions by anointing you with the oil of joy.*

8   *All your robes are fragrant with myrrh and aloes and cassia; from palaces adorned with ivory the music of the strings makes you glad.*

9   *Daughters of kings are among your honoured women; at your right hand is the royal bride in gold of Ophir.*

10 *Listen, O daughter, consider and give ear: Forget your people and your father's house.*

11 *The king is enthralled by your beauty; honour him, for he is your lord.*

12 *The Daughter of Tyre will come with a gift, men of wealth will seek your favour.*

13 *All glorious is the princess within her chamber; her gown is inter-woven with gold.*

14 *In embroidered garments she is led to the king; her virgin companions follow her and are brought to you.*

15 *They are led in with joy and gladness; they enter the palace of the king.*

16 *Your sons will take the place of your fathers; you will make them princes throughout the land.*

17 *I will perpetuate your memory through all generations; therefore the nations will praise you for ever and ever.*

Reflections:

This is called a wedding song by the writer and especially applies to the marriage of a king of Israel. However, Christians would see it as a 'Messianic' psalm foretelling the glorious coronation of our Lord Jesus Christ after His crucifixion, resurrection and ascension into heaven. It foretells the return of the Lord at His 'second coming' to take to Himself His bride, which John in the Book of Revelation sees to be His church. (See Revelation ch. 19)

Psalm 46

¹*God is our refuge and strength,*
an ever-present help in trouble.
²*Therefore we will not fear, though the earth give way*
and the mountains fall into the heart of the sea,
³*though its waters roar and foam*
and the mountains quake with their surging.
⁴*There is a river whose streams make glad the city of God,*
the holy place where the Most High dwells.
⁵*God is within her, she will not fall; God will help her at break of day.*
⁶*Nations are in uproar, kingdoms fall; he lifts his voice, the earth melts.*
⁷*The LORD Almighty is with us; the God of Jacob is our fortress.*
⁸*Come and see the works of the LORD,*
the desolations he has brought on the earth.
⁹*He makes wars cease to the ends of the earth;*
he breaks the bow and shatters the spear, he burns the shields with fire.
¹⁰*"Be still, and know that I am God;*
I will be exalted among the nations, I will be exalted in the earth."
¹¹*The LORD Almighty is with us; the God of Jacob is our fortress.*

Reflections:

This is a psalm wherein the author declares that we can find utter and absolute security in God; no matter what terribly frightening events could take place on the earth's surface; no matter how terrifying are the problems we are facing.

We may find some security in other people, in our passions and financial wellbeing; even in our marriage and in our home; but in the end, it is far better to put our confidence in God alone. God has shown that He is not so transcendent and dwelling in heavenly bliss that He has forsaken us in our troubles; rather He has shown His presence on earth and with us, even though "nations are in uproar and kingdoms fall" (v 6). A very precious verse for us to lay hold of and put into practice is v 10:

"Be still and know that I am God;
I will be exalted among the nations,
I will be exalted in the earth."
And v 11:   "The Lord Almighty is with us;
The God of Jacob is our fortress."

As Martin Luther wrote:

A safe stronghold our God is still
A trusty shield and weapon
He'll help us clear from all the ill
That hath us now o'ertaken.

Psalm 47

[1]*Clap your hands, all you nations;*
shout to God with cries of joy.
[2]*How awesome is the LORD Most High,*
the great King over all the earth!
[3]*He subdued nations under us, peoples under our feet.*
[4]*He chose our inheritance for us, the pride of Jacob, whom he loved.*
[5]*God has ascended amid shouts of joy,*
the LORD amid the sounding of trumpets.
[6]*Sing praises to God, sing praises;*
sing praises to our King, sing praises.
[7]*For God is the King of all the earth; sing to him a psalm of praise.*
[8]*God reigns over the nations; God is seated on his holy throne.*
[9]*The nobles of the nations assemble*
as the people of the God of Abraham,
for the kings of the earth belong to God; he is greatly exalted.

Reflections:

This is a psalm which exudes joy at the sovereignty and reign of God
over all the earth and the nations which dwell on it. We are bidden to

67

shout our praise to God and to clap our hands with happiness, for "the kings of the earth [present-day rulers] belong to God, he is greatly exalted." (v 9) Christians today can, through faith, believe this and proclaim:

> How lovely on the mountains are the feet of him
> Who brings good news, good news,
> Proclaiming peace, announcing news of happiness
> Our God reigns, our God reigns!
>
> (Leonard E Smith Jnr)

And:

> Hallelujah, for the Lord our God
> The Almighty reigns.
> Hallelujah, for the Lord our God
> The Almighty reigns.
> Let us rejoice and be glad
> And give the glory unto Him.
> Hallelujah, for the Lord our God
> The Almighty reigns.
>
> (Dale Garratt)

Psalm 48

> [1]*Great is the LORD, and most worthy of praise,*
> *in the city of our God, his holy mountain.*
> [2]*It is beautiful in its loftiness, the joy of the whole earth.*
> *Like the utmost heights of Zaphon is Mount Zion,*
> *the city of the Great King.*
> [3]*God is in her citadels; he has shown himself to be her fortress.*
> [4]*When the kings joined forces, when they advanced together,*
> [5]*they saw her and were astounded; they fled in terror.*
> [6]*Trembling seized them there, pain like that of a woman in labour.*
> [7]*You destroyed them like ships of Tarshish shattered by an east wind.*
> [8]*As we have heard, so have we seen in the city of the LORD Almighty,*
> *in the city of our God:*
> *God makes her secure for ever.*

⁹*Within your temple, O God, we meditate on your unfailing love.*
¹⁰*Like your name, O God, your praise reaches to the ends of the earth;*
your right hand is filled with righteousness.
¹¹*Mount Zion rejoices, the villages of Judah are glad*
because of your judgments.
¹²*Walk about Zion, go around her, count her towers,*
¹³*consider well her ramparts, view her citadels,*
that you may tell of them to the next generation.
¹⁴*For this God is our God for ever and ever;*
he will be our guide even to the end.

Reflections:

This psalm, no doubt, goes back to the time when Jerusalem, the Holy City, and its temple were intact and the Assyrian armies, who had laid siege to the city, fled and did not conquer it (2 Kings ch 6-7 or 2 Chron 20). It is a psalm which extols the beauty and magnificence of Jerusalem. Christians are today bidden to "pray for the peace of Jerusalem" for "may they prosper who love you" (NKJV) (Psalm 122 v 6) and they sing:

> 'Great is the Lord and greatly to be praised
> In the city of our God
> In the mountain of His holiness
> Beautiful for situation, the joy of the whole earth
> Is Mount Zion on the sides of the north
> The city of the great king
> Is Mount Zion on the sides of the north,
> The city of the great King.'   (Author unknown)

However, we see that the new Jerusalem is a symbol for the Church throughout the world (Rev. 21 v 2). So we are encouraged to pray for the Church worldwide, to envisage the time when it will indeed be "the joy of the whole earth" (v 2), and as we sing about the beauty of Jerusalem, to have prayerful hope that the Church will be cleansed from all unrighteousness and, through faith, become like the bride beautifully prepared for her husband.

Psalm 49

¹*Hear this, all you peoples; listen, all who live in this world,*
²*both low and high, rich and poor alike:*
³*My mouth will speak words of wisdom;*
the utterance from my heart will give understanding.
⁴*I will turn my ear to a proverb; with the harp I will expound my riddle:*
⁵*Why should I fear when evil days come,*
when wicked deceivers surround me—
⁶*those who trust in their wealth and boast of their great riches?*
⁷*No man can redeem the life of another*
or give to God a ransom for him—
⁸*the ransom for a life is costly, no payment is ever enough—*
⁹*that he should live on for ever and not see decay.*
¹⁰*For all can see that wise men die; the foolish and the senseless alike*
perish and leave their wealth to others.
¹¹*Their tombs will remain their houses for ever,*
their dwellings for endless generations,
though they had named lands after themselves.
¹²*But man, despite his riches, does not endure;*
he is like the beasts that perish.
¹³*This is the fate of those who trust in themselves,*
and of their followers, who approve their sayings.
¹⁴*Like sheep they are destined for the grave and death will feed on them.*
The upright will rule over them in the morning;
their forms will decay in the grave, far from their princely mansions.
¹⁵*But God will redeem my life from the grave;*
he will surely take me to himself.   Selah
¹⁶*Do not be overawed when a man grows rich,*
when the splendour of his house increases;
¹⁷*for he will take nothing with him when he dies,*
his splendour will not descend with him.
¹⁸*Though while he lived he counted himself blessed—*
and men praise you when you prosper—
¹⁹*he will join the generation of his fathers,*
who will never see the light of life.
²⁰*A man who has riches without understanding*
is like the beasts that perish.

Reflections:

This is a psalm in which the psalmist meditates on the transitory nature of human life which ends in death for the rich and powerful and for the poor and weak alike. He declares that even riches, however great, cannot save a person from death and, as we say today, "there are no pockets in a shroud", or, as Job said: "Naked I came from my mother's womb, and naked I shall depart" (Job 1 v 21).

In the light of this Christians today must realise and live with the knowledge that they are only stewards of all they have in the realm of time, talents and money for which, in the end, they are responsible to God in their use. For it is He who gave them for use during their life on earth. They seek the meaning and purpose of life in their relationships and service of God and not in seeing how much wealth they can accumulate during their brief sojourn on earth. In the light of this the psalmist finishes with the words:

"A man who has riches without understanding
is like the beasts that perish." (v 20)

Psalm 50

[1]*The Mighty One, God, the LORD, speaks and summons the earth*
from the rising of the sun to the place where it sets.
[2]*From Zion, perfect in beauty, God shines forth.*
[3]*Our God comes and will not be silent;*
a fire devours before him, and around him a tempest rages.
[4]*He summons the heavens above, and the earth,*
that he may judge his people:
[5]*"Gather to me my consecrated ones,*
who made a covenant with me by sacrifice."
[6]*And the heavens proclaim his righteousness, for God himself is judge.*
[7]*"Hear, O my people, and I will speak, O Israel,*
and I will testify against you: I am God, your God.
[8]*I do not rebuke you for your sacrifices or your burnt offerings,*
which are ever before me.

71

⁹I have no need of a bull from your stall or of goats from your pens,
¹⁰for every animal of the forest is mine,
and the cattle on a thousand hills.
¹¹I know every bird in the mountains,
and the creatures of the field are mine.
¹²If I were hungry I would not tell you,
for the world is mine, and all that is in it.
¹³Do I eat the flesh of bulls or drink the blood of goats?
¹⁴Sacrifice thank-offerings to God, fulfil your vows to the Most High,
¹⁵and call upon me in the day of trouble;
I will deliver you, and you will honour me."

²²"Consider this, you who forget God,
or I will tear you to pieces, with none to rescue:
²³He who sacrifices thank-offerings honours me, and he prepares the
way so that I may show him the salvation of God."

Reflections:

After proclaiming the awesomeness of God (vv 1-6) the psalmist dwells on the uselessness of animal sacrifices to satisfy what God requires of men and women, a theme taken up in the New Testament by the writer of the Letter to the Hebrews (ch. 8 vv 6-10). The psalmist states that what is really acceptable to God is a heart and mind set on <u>thanksgiving</u> to God (v 14), then we can call upon God in times of trouble and He will deliver us (v 15).

The Christian life can have no place for being discontented especially in 'grumbling' against the 'lot' God has given us; rather the Christian life should be filled in heart, mind and song, with thanksgiving to God as he or she counts their blessings, especially in what God has done for us in the sacrifice of Christ for our sins and calling us into a relationship of sonship with Him. He has "blessed us in the heavenly realms with every spiritual blessing in Christ" (Ephesians 1 v 3). A worthy Christian hymn which is, in its way, a 'sacrifice of praise' is:

Now thank we all our God
With hearts and hands and voices
Who wondrous things hath done,
In whom His world rejoices.
Who from our mother's arms
Has blessed us on our way
With countless gifts of love,
And still is ours today.   (Martin Rinkart)

Psalm 51
(A psalm of David)

[1]*Have mercy on me, O God, according to your unfailing love;
according to your great compassion blot out my transgressions.*
[2]*Wash away all my iniquity and cleanse me from my sin.*
[3]*For I know my transgressions, and my sin is always before me.*
[4]*Against You, You only, have I sinned
and done what is evil in your sight,
so that You are proved right when You speak
and justified when You judge.*
[5]*Surely I was sinful at birth,
sinful from the time my mother conceived me.*
[6]*Surely You desire truth in the inner parts;
You teach me wisdom in the inmost place.*
[7]*Cleanse me with hyssop, and I will be clean;
wash me, and I will be whiter than snow.*
[8]*Let me hear joy and gladness;
let the bones You have crushed rejoice.*
[9]*Hide your face from my sins and blot out all my iniquity.*
[10]*Create in me a pure heart, O God,
and renew a steadfast spirit within me.*
[11]*Do not cast me from your presence or take your Holy Spirit from me.*
[12]*Restore to me the joy of your salvation
and grant me a willing spirit, to sustain me.*

¹³*Then I will teach transgressors your ways,*
and sinners will turn back to You.
¹⁴*Save me from bloodguilt, O God, the God who saves me,*
and my tongue will sing of your righteousness.
¹⁵*O Lord, open my lips, and my mouth will declare your praise.*
¹⁶*You do not delight in sacrifice, or I would bring it;*
You do not take pleasure in burnt offerings.
¹⁷*The sacrifices of God are a broken spirit;*
a broken and contrite heart, O God,
Youwill not despise.
¹⁸*In your good pleasure make Zion prosper;*
build up the walls of Jerusalem.
¹⁹*Then there will be righteous sacrifices,*
whole burnt offerings to delight You;
then bulls will be offered on your altar.

Reflections:

This is a psalm declaring utmost penitence before God after having committed a grievous sin. It is traditionally attributed to King David when the prophet Nathan came to him after he had committed adultery with Bathsheba and made her pregnant. He had also had her husband killed in battle (2 Samuel chapters 11-12).

David flings himself on the mercy of God for the sin he had deliberately committed. He knows that he is without excuse and hides nothing as he pleads with God for forgiveness. There is no semblance of any deceit; having had his sin exposed to him as he was confronted by the prophet Nathan (2 Samuel 12 vv 1-13). There is now only reality about his wrongdoing. This is how Jesus taught that we should always come to God with our sins, as in the parable of the Pharisee and the tax collector. The latter cried out to God, "Have mercy on me, a sinner" (Luke 18 vv 9-14). When we are real with God in this way, says Jesus, then we will be forgiven.

David asks for a "pure heart" (v 10) and asks that God will restore to him the joy of his salvation (v 12) and subsequently promises that he will then teach transgressors God's ways, so that other sinners will turn back to Him (v 13). So Christians, who know and have experienced God's forgiving love, should likewise share this with others, for "all have all sinned and fall short of the glory of God" (Romans 3 v 23).

He, like other psalmists, states that animal sacrifice does not avail and profoundly says that "the sacrifices of God are a broken spirit" and that God will not despise a "broken and contrite heart" (v 17).

This psalm is thus an utterance which any Christian can take and use in coming before God in penitence.

Psalm 52

(A psalm of David)

¹Why do you boast of evil, you mighty man?
Why do you boast all day long,
you who are a disgrace in the eyes of God?
²Your tongue plots destruction; it is like a sharpened razor,
you who practise deceit.
³You love evil rather than good,
falsehood rather than speaking the truth.
⁴You love every harmful word, O you deceitful tongue!
⁵Surely God will bring you down to everlasting ruin:
He will snatch you up and tear you from your tent;
he will uproot you from the land of the living.
⁶The righteous will see and fear; they will laugh at him, saying,
⁷"Here now is the man who did not make God his stronghold
but trusted in his great wealth and grew strong by destroying others!"
⁸But I am like an olive tree flourishing in the house of God;
I trust in God's unfailing love for ever and ever.
⁹I will praise You for ever for what You have done;
in your name I will hope, for your name is good.
I will praise You in the presence of your saints.

Reflections:

This psalm is again traditionally ascribed to David, which he uttered when Doeg the Edomite had gone to Saul and told him: "David has gone to the house of Ahimelech" – an act of betrayal. (1 Samuel 21 v 7 and chapter 22)

David contrasts the fate of the wicked at the hands of God with that of himself – a righteous and good man. The wicked man loves evil rather than good and speaks falsehood rather than the truth (v 3-4). Such a man will come under the judgment of God. In the days in which we live, the <u>love</u> of God is rightly emphasised; but this has to be balanced with the "<u>wrath</u> of God being revealed from heaven against all the godlessness and wickedness of men who suppress the truth by their wickedness" (Romans 1 v 18) and "The <u>fear</u> of the Lord is the beginning of wisdom" (Proverbs 9 v 10). David goes on to say that trusting in wealth will not in any way insure a wicked person from God's judgment (v 7).

In the New Testament, Jesus Himself speaks of the dangers of wealth turning a person from a right relationship with God and his neighbour. (See the parables of Dives and Lazarus in Luke 16 and the Rich Fool in Luke 12.) Paul, also, in his first letter to Timothy, writes: "Command those who are rich in this present world not to be arrogant nor to put their hope in wealth, which is so uncertain, but to put their hope in God ..." (I Tim 6 v 17). Contrast this with David's picture of himself (vv 8-9). Such teaching helps us, as we are continually assailed by wealthy men and women in the media who turn morality on its head in the very same way as those referred to in verses 3 and 4. It encourages us to get our priorities in the right order as we live our daily lives.

Psalm 53

(Of David)

[1]The fool says in his heart, "There is no God."
They are corrupt, and their ways are vile;
there is no one who does good.
[2]God looks down from heaven on the sons of men
to see if there are any who understand, any who seek God.
[3]Everyone has turned away, they have together become corrupt;
there is no one who does good, not even one.

⁴Will the evildoers never learn—
those who devour my people as men eat bread
and who do not call on God?
⁵There they were, overwhelmed with dread,
where there was nothing to dread.
God scattered the bones of those who attacked you;
you put them to shame, for God despised them.
⁶Oh, that salvation for Israel would come out of Zion!
When God restores the fortunes of his people,
let Jacob rejoice and Israel be glad!

Reflections:

This 'maskil' raises the whole question of belief. Does it matter, in the end, whether we believe in God or not? Does it matter in whom or what we believe? It certainly does. The rise of Nazi power, the holocaust, the Second World War owe their origins to a book written by Hitler — 'Mein Kampf'. He persuaded Germans to believe in the 'master race', in Fascism and the result was devastating beyond description. The 'Cultural Revolution' in China, with its terrible results, especially for Christians, was based on Mao Tse Tung's 'Little Red Book'. The terrorism, including suicide bombers, and the war in Afghanistan come from radical, fundamentalist Muslim belief. The abominable caste system in India is based on Hindu belief. When the psalmist states: "The fool says in his heart, 'There is no God'" (v 1) he means belief in Yahweh, the God who gave the Law and called Himself 'Father'. The result he saw of atheism in his day was "corruption" (v 3) and other negative thought and actions (v 4). It would be an exaggeration in our day to claim that there is no one who does good (v 3) but the whole foundation of Western civilisation is built on Christianity; the demise of this belief in general, can be seen as **the root of** most of our social and moral problems. What is true, as Isaiah (Chapter 53 v 6) wrote of everyone, is the fact that

> "We all, like sheep, have gone astray,
> each of us has turned to his own way;
> and the Lord has laid on him (Jesus)
> the iniquity of us all."

There has never been a time of greater urgency than today, when Christians, in their daily life, should defend and promulgate the

Christian faith. We need, like the psalmist, to pray for the revival of true Christian faith in our land (cf v 6).

Psalm 54
(A psalm of David)

^{1}Save me, O God, by your name; vindicate me by your might.
^{2}Hear my prayer, O God; listen to the words of my mouth.
^{3}Strangers are attacking me;
ruthless men seek my life— men without regard for God.
^{4}Surely God is my help; the Lord is the one who sustains me.

^{6}I will sacrifice a freewill offering to You;
I will praise your name, O LORD, for it is good.
^{7}For he has delivered me from all my troubles.

Reflections:

I have omitted verse 5 because it could never be a Christian's prayer, nor could verse 7b. However, the rest of the psalm is right for Christians to pray, because we should call upon God for help when we are in trouble. It is the right thing to do and to find that God *is* our help and that He does sustain us. It is only when we lack faith in Him that this does not prove to be true. I have met Christians who can pray, for instance, for healing for others but think that it is selfish to ask God for it for themselves. However, this psalm teaches us that 'petition' is a right prayer in which Christians can engage, as our Lord taught us when in His model prayer He urges us to ask God to "give us this day our daily bread" (Matthew 6 v 11). Christian petition also should be balanced, as the psalmist says, with thanksgiving (v 6). Paul taught us in his Letter to the Philippians:

"Do not be anxious about anything, but in everything by prayer and petition, with thanksgiving present your requests to God." (Phil. 4 v 6)

Let us, in our daily lives, follow this teaching about prayer.

Psalm 55

(A psalm of David)

¹Listen to my prayer, O God,
do not ignore my plea;
²hear me and answer me.
My thoughts trouble me and I am distraught
³at the voice of the enemy, at the stares of the wicked;
for they bring down suffering upon me and revile me in their anger.
⁴My heart is in anguish within me; the terrors of death assail me.
⁵Fear and trembling have beset me; horror has overwhelmed me.
I said, "Oh, that I had the wings of a dove!
I would fly away and be at rest—
⁷I would flee far away and stay in the desert;
⁸I would hurry to my place of shelter, far from the tempest and storm."

¹²If an enemy were insulting me, I could endure it;
if a foe were raising himself against me, I could hide from him.
¹³But it is you, a man like myself, my companion, my close friend,
¹⁴with whom I once enjoyed sweet fellowship
as we walked with the throng at the house of God.

¹⁶But I call to God, and the LORD saves me.
¹⁷Evening, morning and noon I cry out in distress,
and he hears my voice.

²²Cast your cares on the LORD and he will sustain you;
he will never let the righteous fall.

Reflections:

I have met many people in my ministry who want to escape from their problems, difficulties and life situations. They would echo the psalmist's cry:

"Oh, that I had the wings of a dove! I would fly away and be at rest. I would flee far away and stay in the desert." (vv 6-7)

This is not the way Christians should think or desire. Rather we should face up to these distressing things and call upon God to give us the strength to endure and be victorious overcomers, even when our "heart is in anguish within us and the terrors of death assail us" (v 4).

As we go through life we may feel very let down by our friends or those whom we have trusted (vv 12-14) and this is particularly hard for us to bear. It is far better to put our absolute trust in God to bring us through our difficulties (vv 17-19) and put into practice the beautiful promise of v 22:

"Cast your cares on the Lord
and he will sustain you; he will
never let the righteous fall."

The promise of Jesus is very apt also, when He said:

"Come to me all you who are weary and burdened and I will give you rest. Take my yoke upon you and learn from me, for I am gentle and humble in heart, and you will find rest for your souls."
(Matt. 11 v 28)

Psalm 56

(A psalm of David)

¹Be merciful to me, O God, for men hotly pursue me;
all day long they press their attack.
²My slanderers pursue me all day long;
many are attacking me in their pride.

80

³*When I am afraid, I will trust in You.*
⁴*In God, whose word I praise, in God I trust; I will not be afraid.*
What can mortal man do to me?
⁵*All day long they twist my words;*
they are always plotting to harm me.
⁶*They conspire, they lurk, they watch my steps, eager to take my life.*
⁷*On no account let them escape;*
in your anger, O God, bring down the nations.
⁸*Record my lament; list my tears on your scroll —*
are they not in your record?
⁹*Then my enemies will turn back when I call for help.*
By this I will know that God is for me.
¹⁰*In God, whose word I praise, in the* LORD, *whose word I praise —*
¹¹*in God I trust; I will not be afraid.*
What can man do to me?
¹²*I am under vows to You, O God;*
I will present my thank-offerings to You.
¹³*For You have delivered me from death and my feet from stumbling,*
that I may walk before God in the light of life.

Reflections:

This psalm is traditionally ascribed to David when the Philistines had seized him in Gath. (1 Sam 21)

These pleas for help are full of the fact that we should not be afraid at what men (or women) can do to us to harm us. Sometimes it can happen during our lifetime that we are subject to gossip and people speaking badly against us. I have known there even to be plots in churches to get rid of a minister or pastor who has served them faithfully but who has crossed one or two of the elders or leaders. Sometimes we can be the objects of vicious attacks upon us. However, as the psalmist says, "What [in the end] can mortal man do to me?" (vv 4, 11) No one can take from us our deep trust in our Lord God, in time or eternity.

At times when we are feeling persecuted, that is the very time when we should put our trust in our Lord God to bring us through what could be to us a time of great stress. The important thing is that we have a good conscience and know we have done no wrong (vv 3, 8). We can then know that "God is for us" (v 9). In God we will trust and not be afraid (v 11) and we will "walk before God in the light of life" (v 13).

As John Bunyan wrote when he was in prison on account of his faith:

> "No foes shall stay his might
> Though he with giants fight
> He will make good his right
> To be a pilgrim.
>
> Since, Lord, Thou dost defend
> Us with Thy Spirit
> We know we at the end
> Shall life inherit.
> Then fancies flee away!
> I'll fear not what men say
> I'll labour night and day
> To be a pilgrim."

Psalm 57

(A psalm of David)

> *¹Have mercy on me, O God, have mercy on me,*
> *for in You my soul takes refuge.*
> *I will take refuge in the shadow of your wings*
> *until the disaster has passed.*
> *²I cry out to God Most High,*
> *to God, who fulfils his purpose for me.*
> *³He sends from heaven and saves me,*
> *rebuking those who hotly pursue me;*
> *God sends his love and his faithfulness.*
> *⁴I am in the midst of lions; I lie among ravenous beasts—*
> *men whose teeth are spears and arrows,*
> *whose tongues are sharp swords.*

⁵Be exalted, O God, above the heavens;
let your glory be over all the earth.
⁶They spread a net for my feet—I was bowed down in distress.
They dug a pit in my path—but they have fallen into it themselves.
⁷My heart is steadfast, O God, my heart is steadfast;
I will sing and make music.
⁸Awake, my soul! Awake, harp and lyre!
I will awaken the dawn.
⁹I will praise You, O Lord, among the nations;
I will sing of You among the peoples.
¹⁰For great is your love, reaching to the heavens;
your faithfulness reaches to the skies.
¹¹Be exalted, O God, above the heavens;
let your glory be over all the earth.

Reflections:

This psalm is traditionally ascribed to David when he fled from Saul into the cave of Adullam. (1 Sam 22)

Once more we have a psalm that bids us to take refuge in God when we are in trouble (v 1). We know that God has a purpose in life for each one of us that nothing will prevent because of His love and faithfulness towards each and every one of us (v 3). We can shout with the psalmist: "Be exalted, O God, above the heavens; let your glory be over all the earth" (vv 5, 11).

The words "My heart is steadfast, O God, my heart is steadfast" (v 7) are echoed in the words of Isaiah: "You will keep in perfect peace him whose mind is steadfast, because he trusts in You" (Isaiah 26 v 3). We, like the psalmist, should praise God for His great love, reaching to the heavens and His faithfulness reaching to the skies (vv 9-10). It is this boundless love, demonstrated in God's giving His only son to die for us (John 3 v 16) and His faithfulness in saving us from our sins (Eph 2 v 8) that we can unreservedly trust.

Psalm 58
(Of David)

1 Do your rulers indeed speak justly? Do you judge uprightly among men?
2 No, in your heart you devise injustice, and your hands mete out violence on the earth.
3 Even from birth the wicked go astray; from the womb they are wayward and speak lies.
4 Their venom is like the venom of a snake, like that of a cobra that has stopped its ears …

Reflections:

This 'miktam' is really sub-Christian and cannot be prayed by those who follow Jesus, who said: "You have heard that it was said, 'Love your neighbour and hate your enemy.' But I tell you: Love your enemies and pray for those who persecute you, that you may be sons of your Father in heaven. He causes the sun to shine on the evil and the good, and sends rain on the righteous and the unrighteous." (Matt 5 v 43-45)

It is, however, true today that there are rulers who are corrupt and vindictive like in Zimbabwe and in other countries of the world, so we must pray that they will be brought down from office and righteous rulers replace them, that there may be true justice in the world and that people may live without fear.

Psalm 59
(A psalm of David)

⁹O my Strength, I watch for You;
You, O God, are my fortress,
¹⁰my loving God.
God will go before me

and will let me gloat over those who slander me.
[11] But do not kill them, O Lord our shield, or my people will forget.
In your might make them wander about, and bring them down.
[12] For the sins of their mouths, for the words of their lips,
let them be caught in their pride.
For the curses and lies they utter,
[13] consume them in wrath, consume them till they are no more.
Then it will be known to the ends of the earth
that God rules over Jacob.
[17] O my Strength, I sing praise to You;
You, O God, are my fortress, my loving God.

Reflections:

The psalmist prays that God will not kill his enemies but will instead triumph over them. He trusts in God to protect him, for "You are my fortress and my loving God" (v 9) and this is repeated in verse 17.

A good commentary on this psalm which Christians can meditate on and take hold of is Martin Luther's hymn:

> A safe stronghold our God is still
> A trusty shield and weapon.
> He'll keep us clear from all the ill
> That hath us now o'ertaken.
> But for us fights the proper Man
> Whom God Himself hath bidden.
> Ask ye, Who is this same?
> Christ Jesus is His Name
> The Lord Sabaoth's Son
> He, and no other one
> Shall conquer in the battle.

85

Psalm 60

(A psalm of David)

⁴*But for those who fear You, You have raised a banner*
to be unfurled against the bow.
⁵*Save us and help us with your right hand,*
that those You love may be delivered.
⁶*God has spoken from his sanctuary:*
"In triumph I will parcel out Shechem
and measure off the Valley of Succoth.
⁷*Gilead is mine, and Manasseh is mine;*
Ephraim is my helmet, Judah my sceptre.
⁸*Moab is my washbasin, upon Edom I toss my sandal;*
over Philistia I shout in triumph."
⁹*Who will bring me to the fortified city? Who will lead me to Edom?*
¹⁰*Is it not You, O God, You who have rejected us*
and no longer go out with our armies?
¹¹*Give us aid against the enemy, for the help of man is worthless.*
¹²*With God we will gain the victory,*
and he will trample down our enemies.

Reflections:

There are times when, in stressful circumstances, everything in our lives seems to be going wrong, so that we may feel that even God has rejected us. This can be especially so when we realise that we engaged in a particular sin or sins and feel that we are in no position to call upon God to help us; that He has rightly rejected us because of our actions or words. Yet the promise of the Scripture is: "If we are faithless, he will remain faithful, for he cannot disown himself." (2 Tim 2 v 13)

A precious verse in this psalm is:
    "But for those who fear You, You have raised a banner to be
    unfurled against the bow" (v 4)
I often sing the chorus:
"He brought us to His banqueting house And his banner over us is love."

86

Psalm 61
(A psalm of David)

¹Hear my cry, O God; listen to my prayer.
²From the ends of the earth I call to You, I call as my heart grows faint;
lead me to the rock that is higher than I.
³For You have been my refuge, a strong tower against the foe.
⁴I long to dwell in your tent for ever
and take refuge in the shelter of your wings.
⁵For You have heard my vows, O God;
You have given me the heritage of those who fear your name.

Reflections:

Here is one who is weary, his heart grows faint (v 2) and in his weariness he calls upon the Lord for strength. He longs to dwell in God's tent (the tabernacle, the place of God's presence) for ever and take refuge in the shelter of God's wings.

A promise to us when we are feeling weary is:
"but those who hope in the Lord
will renew their strength.
They will soar on wings like eagles;
they will run and not grow weary,
they will walk and not be faint." Isaiah 40 v 31.

William Orcutt Cushing takes up this verse in the hymn:

O safe to the rock that is higher than I
My soul in its conflicts and sorrows would fly.
So sinful, so weary, Thine, Thine would I be
Thou blest Rock of Ages, I'm hiding in Thee!

Psalm 62
(A psalm of David)

¹My soul finds rest in God alone; my salvation comes from him.
²He alone is my rock and my salvation;
he is my fortress, I shall never be shaken.

⁵Find rest, O my soul, in God alone; my hope comes from him.
⁶He alone is my rock and my salvation;
he is my fortress, I shall not be shaken.
⁷My salvation and my honour depend on God;
he is my mighty rock, my refuge.
⁸Trust in him at all times, O people; pour out your hearts to him,
for God is our refuge.
⁹Lowborn men are but a breath, the highborn are but a lie;
if weighed on a balance, they are nothing;
together they are only a breath.
¹⁰Do not trust in extortion or take pride in stolen goods;
though your riches increase, do not set your heart on them.
¹¹One thing God has spoken, two things have I heard:
that You, O God, are strong,
and that You, O LORD, are loving.
Surely You will reward each person
according to what he has done.

Reflections:

v 1 "My soul finds rest in God alone"
v 5 "Find rest, O my soul, in God alone".

One is reminded of the words of St Augustine in his 'Confessions': "Thou hast made us for Thyself and our hearts are restless till they rest in Thee". We find our uttermost fulfilment in our deep rest in the heart of God, in the depths of our relationship with Him.

> There is a place of quiet rest
> Near to the heart of God;
> A place where sin cannot molest
> Near to the heart of God.

O Jesus, blest Redeemer,
Sent from the heart of God,
Hold us, who wait before Thee
Near to the heart of God.

(C.B. McAfee)

Vv 7-8 "My salvation and honour depend on God.... Pour out your hearts to Him, for God is our refuge."

We should come before God with real troubles and not in any way in any kind of pretence. We must be utterly open and frank with Him, pouring out to Him our supplications and intercessions.

v 10 "though your riches increase, do not set your heart on them" – we must put our trust in God alone and not in our possessions. We must find absolute security in Him alone, remembering our Lord's words:

"Do not store up for yourselves treasures on earth, where moth and rust destroy, and where thieves break in and steal. But store up for yourselves treasures in heaven, where moth and rust do not destroy and where thieves do not break in and steal. For where your treasure is, there your heart will be also." (Matthew 6 vv 19-21)

Psalm 63

(A psalm of David)

[1]O God, You are my God, earnestly I seek You;
my soul thirsts for You,
my body longs for You, in a dry and weary land where there is no water.
[2]I have seen You in the sanctuary
and beheld your power and your glory.
[3]Because your love is better than life, my lips will glorify You.
[4]I will praise You as long as I live,
and in your name I will lift up my hands.
[5]My soul will be satisfied as with the richest of foods;
with singing lips my mouth will praise You.

89

⁶On my bed I remember You;
I think of You through the watches of the night.
⁷Because You are my help, I sing in the shadow of your wings.
⁸My soul clings to You; your right hand upholds me.

Reflections:

v 1 We, in England, rarely feel intense thirst because, generally, we have water always on hand to drink. However, for those who lived, sometimes in deserts, in the time of the psalmist, the feeling of thirst could be intense, and the psalmist speaks of thirsting for God as in a land where there is no water. Jesus said however, "Blessed are those who hunger and thirst for righteousness, for they will be filled." (Matt 5 v 6)

This longing for God is really for an experience of His presence within and outside our beings which is to some extent satisfied when the Holy Spirit dwells within us. Speaking of the Holy Spirit Jesus said: "He lives with you and will be in you." (John 14 v 17) However, this longing for God will only fully be satisfied when, after this life, we shall be completely and finally in His presence.

v 3 The psalmist's words: "your love is better than life" and because of this "my lips will glorify You" lead us to think that there can surely be no fuller expression of the wonder and riches of the experiencing of God's love than is expressed in these words.

v 6 "On my bed I will remember You". Brother Lawrence wrote a booklet on 'The Practice of the Presence of God' which is the practice of the psalmist.

v 8 "clinging" on to God is a beautiful expression of our life with Him when all else seems to be transient and unstable.

The whole of verses 1-8 is a rich expression of a Christian's daily experience of God's love and our dependence on Him.

Psalm 64
(A psalm of David)

¹Hear me, O God, as I voice my complaint;
protect my life from the threat of the enemy.
²Hide me from the conspiracy of the wicked,
from that noisy crowd of evildoers.

⁹All mankind will fear; they will proclaim the works of God
and ponder what he has done.
¹⁰Let the righteous rejoice in the LORD and take refuge in him;
let all the upright in heart praise him!

Reflection:

This psalm portrays a <u>living</u> God who is active in the world and affairs of men and especially of individuals who trust Him for protection and vindication. I was once taught what was called the 'God is dead' Theology which stated that there was a god but for all practical purposes he might as well not exist, for he never does anything in any way in the world, amongst mankind and never interferes in any way with what is happening in world affairs, the law of nature, or individual lives. These three short lines of verse 9 expose the erroneous nature of this fallacy:

"All mankind will fear;
They will proclaim the works of the Lord
And ponder what he has done."

Psalm 65
(A psalm of David)

¹Praise awaits You, O God, in Zion;
to You our vows will be fulfilled.
²O You who hear prayer,
to You all men will come.
³When we were overwhelmed by sins,
You forgave our transgressions.
⁴Blessed are those You choose
and bring near to live in your courts!
We are filled with the good things of your house, of your holy temple.
⁵You answer us with awesome deeds of righteousness,
O God our Saviour,
the hope of all the ends of the earth and of the farthest seas,
⁶who formed the mountains by your power,
having armed yourself with strength,
⁷who stilled the roaring of the seas, the roaring of their waves,
and the turmoil of the nations.
⁸Those living far away fear your wonders;
where morning dawns and evening fades
You call forth songs of joy.
⁹You care for the land and water it; You enrich it abundantly.
The streams of God are filled with water
to provide the people with grain, for so You have ordained it.
¹⁰You drench its furrows and level its ridges;
You soften it with showers and bless its crops.
¹¹You crown the year with your bounty,
and your carts overflow with abundance.
¹²The grasslands of the desert overflow;
the hills are clothed with gladness.
¹³The meadows are covered with flocks
and the valleys are mantled with grain;
they shout for joy and sing.

Reflections:

This is a prayer which Christians can utter to God in its entirety. It sees
God as the One who forgives transgressions and fills His people with

good things (v 1-4). It then goes on to say that this great Creator God who formed the mountains, the seas and the waves, is not only present in Zion (Jerusalem) but also to those who are "far away". Even they shall see God at work in "mighty wonders" and wherever morning dawns and the evening fades He will call forth "songs of joy" (v 5-8). Then come these particular verses which are often recited or sung at Christian Harvest Thanksgiving services: v 9-13. It is God who sends the rain or the streams to water the land (even drench it) and causes crops to grow. At harvest time He crowns the year with His goodness and the grasslands and the desert overflow with His bounty. It is a good thing for Christians not to take their food for granted but to realise that:

> We plough the fields and scatter
> The good seed on the land,
> But it is fed and watered
> By God's Almighty hand.
> All good gifts around us
> Are sent from heaven above
> Then thank he Lord, O thank the Lord
> For all His love.
>
> (Matthias Claudius)

And to sing:

> To Thee O God our hearts we raise
> In hymns of adoration.
> To Thee bring sacrifice of praise
> With shouts of exultation.
> Bright robes of gold the fields adorn,
> The hills with joy are ringing;
> The valleys stand so thick with corn
> That even they are singing.
>
> (William Chatterton Dix)

However, amidst the plenty of the Western world Christians' heart, prayers and actions must go out to the millions of people on earth who cannot really sing these songs, or echo the words of the psalmist because they are hungry and some even starving to death. Christians must urge their governments to give bountiful aid to these people and support all charitable agencies which are working to relieve poverty and burdens of unjust debt amongst the nations so that in their day, may it be soon, the words of Psalm 65 will really be the refrain of everyone.

Psalm 66

¹Shout with joy to God, all the earth!
²Sing the glory of his name; make his praise glorious!
³Say to God, "How awesome are your deeds!
So great is your power that your enemies cringe before You.
⁴All the earth bows down to You; they sing praise to You,
they sing praise to your name."
⁵Come and see what God has done,
how awesome his works on man's behalf!
⁶He turned the sea into dry land,
they passed through the waters on foot—
come, let us rejoice in him.
⁷He rules for ever by his power, his eyes watch the nations—
let not the rebellious rise up against him.
⁸Praise our God, O peoples, let the sound of his praise be heard;
⁹he has preserved our lives and kept our feet from slipping.
¹⁰For You, O God, tested us; You refined us like silver.
¹¹You brought us into prison and laid burdens on our backs.
¹²You let men ride over our heads; we went through fire and water,
but You brought us to a place of abundance.
¹³I will come to your temple with burnt offerings
and fulfil my vows to You—
¹⁴vows my lips promised and my mouth spoke when I was in trouble.
¹⁵I will sacrifice fat animals to You and an offering of rams;
I will offer bulls and goats.
¹⁶Come and listen, all you who fear God;
let me tell you what he has done for me.
¹⁷I cried out to him with my mouth; his praise was on my tongue.

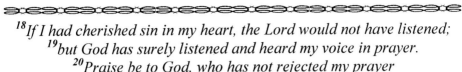

[18]If I had cherished sin in my heart, the Lord would not have listened;
[19]but God has surely listened and heard my voice in prayer.
[20]Praise be to God, who has not rejected my prayer
or withheld his love from me!

Reflections:

This is a psalm full of praise for what God has done in the past: for the Hebrew nation as a whole and for the individual in particular. As the psalmist bids his readers to "shout for joy" (v 1) and declares: "How awesome are your deeds! So great is your power" (v 3) we may want to join him in praise. And we can be glad that He rules for ever by His power and that his eyes "watch the nations" (v 7). He declares that God may let his people go through times of testing (v 11,12a), but this is a refining and purifying process (v 10). In the light of all this the psalmist promises to God that he will fulfil his vows and offer sacrifices of thanksgiving (v 13-15). He states that if he had cherished sin in his heart God would not have listened to his prayers — but God has indeed listened and heard his prayer (v 18-19).

All this teaches us that in our daily lives, when we are in any kind of trouble and when things seem to be going adversely for us, then it is good to look back at God's abundant blessings upon us in the past and realise that, although He may be permitting us to go through a time of trial, yet He has not changed His nature or His love and care for us, but we can take heart, for he will bring us through our difficulties to a place of blessing again in our lives. It is important however for us not to harbour any known sin in our lives but to make sure as far as possible that our lives are pure and good in His sight.

Psalm 67

[1]May God be gracious to us and bless us
and make his face shine upon us,
[2]that your ways may be known on earth,
your salvation among all nations.

³May the peoples praise You, O God; may all the peoples praise You.
        ⁴May the nations be glad and sing for joy,
    for You rule the peoples justly and guide the nations of the earth.

⁵May the peoples praise You, O God; may all the peoples praise You.
⁶Then the land will yield its harvest, and God, our God, will bless us.
        ⁷God will bless us, and all the ends of the earth will fear him.

Reflections:

This psalm is a prayer to God for Him to bless our lives. The Christian is a blessed man or woman because of his or her relationship with God at depth and we should always realise that, in our daily lives, we are a blessed people, or especially a blessed person. Through the testimony of God's people, He will make His ways known upon earth and His salvation among the nations (v 2). The psalmist calls upon all the peoples of the earth to praise the Lord (v 3) because God's rule is always just and we know that God inhabits the praises of His people. He will bless not only us but our land, and through His people's witness to His justice "all the ends of the earth will fear Him" (v 6-7).

Psalm 68
(A psalm of David)

¹May God arise, may his enemies be scattered;
        may his foes flee before him.
²As smoke is blown away by the wind, may You blow them away;
    as wax melts before the fire, may the wicked perish before God.
        ³But may the righteous be glad and rejoice before God;
            may they be happy and joyful.
        ⁴Sing to God, sing praise to his name,
        extol him who rides on the clouds—
    his name is the LORD — and rejoice before him.

[5]*A father to the fatherless, a defender of widows,*
is God in his holy dwelling.
[6]*God sets the lonely in families,*
he leads forth the prisoners with singing;
but the rebellious live in a sun-scorched land.

[7]*When You went out before your people, O God,*
when You marched through the wasteland,
[8]*the earth shook, the heavens poured down rain*
before God, the One of Sinai, before God, the God of Israel.
[9]*You gave abundant showers, O God;*
You refreshed your weary inheritance.
[10]*Your people settled in it,*
and from your bounty, O God, You provided for the poor.

[11]*The Lord announced the word,*
and great was the company of those who proclaimed it:
[12]*"Kings and armies flee in haste;*
in the camps men divide the plunder.
[13]*Even while you sleep among the campfires,*
the wings of my dove are sheathed with silver,
its feathers with shining gold."
[14]*When the Almighty scattered the kings in the land,*
it was like snow fallen on Zalmon.
[15]*The mountains of Bashan are majestic mountains;*
rugged are the mountains of Bashan.
[16]*Why gaze in envy, O rugged mountains,*
at the mountain where God chooses to reign,
where the LORD himself will dwell for ever?
[17]*The chariots of God are tens of thousands*
and thousands of thousands;
the Lord has come from Sinai into his sanctuary.
[18]*When You ascended on high, You led captives in your train;*
You received gifts from men, even from the rebellious—
that You, O LORD God, might dwell there.

[19]*Praise be to the Lord, to God our Saviour,*
who daily bears our burdens.

²⁰Our God is a God who saves;
*from the Sovereign L*ORD *comes escape from death.*

²⁴Your procession has come into view, O God,
the procession of my God and King into the sanctuary.
²⁵In front are the singers, after them the musicians;
with them are the maidens playing tambourines.
²⁶Praise God in the great congregation;
*praise the L*ORD *in the assembly of Israel.*
²⁷There is the little tribe of Benjamin, leading them,
there the great throng of Judah's princes,
and there the princes of Zebulun and of Naphtali.
²⁸Summon your power, O God;
show us your strength, O God, as You have done before.
²⁹Because of your temple at Jerusalem kings will bring You gifts.
³⁰Rebuke the beast among the reeds,
the herd of bulls among the calves of the nations.
Humbled, may it bring bars of silver.
Scatter the nations who delight in war.
³¹Envoys will come from Egypt; Cush will submit herself to God.

³²Sing to God, O kingdoms of the earth, sing praise to the Lord,
³³to him who rides the ancient skies above,
who thunders with mighty voice.
³⁴Proclaim the power of God, whose majesty is over Israel,
whose power is in the skies.
³⁵You are awesome, O God, in your sanctuary;
the God of Israel gives power and strength to his people.
Praise be to God!

Reflections:

The Christian can pray with the psalmist that "God may arise and his enemies be scattered" (v 1) for he longs to see the reign of God established on the earth. He may also pray that those who follow God's laws will, in contrast to the wicked, be "righteous and glad and rejoice before God and be happy and joyful" (v 3). Christians also certainly believe that God is a "father to the fatherless, a defender of widows" and "sets the lonely in families" (v 5-6). The Christian will support all the efforts of governments to help the needy and underprivileged to have social justice and better lives.

V 11. "The Lord announced the word and great was the company of those who proclaimed it" is taken up in Handel's oratorio, 'The Messiah' to speak of Christian evangelists and missionaries taking the gospel of the Lord Jesus Christ to all mankind. Christians should pray for all those in this day who are doing God's work in this way.

V 18. "When You ascended on high You led captives in your train and received gifts from men" is taken up by Paul in his Letter to the Ephesians to be a prophecy of the ascension of the Lord Jesus Christ into heaven and from there to distribute the gifts of the Holy Spirit to members of His Church (Ephesians 4 vv 7-8).

V 19 speaks of God who bears our burdens as Jesus Himself said He would (Matthew 11 v 28) and because of the resurrection of the Lord Jesus Christ there comes to the Christian "escape from death" (v 20).

V 24-27 sees a great living procession of praise by God's people in which, where they are organised today Christians should take part, especially on Good Friday when united churches' processions are still common as an act of witness.

V 30 Christians can still pray that God will scatter the nations that delight in war and join with the psalmist in the promises of vv 32-35.

Psalm 69
(A psalm of David)

¹Save me, O God, for the waters have come up to my neck.
²I sink in the miry depths, where there is no foothold.
I have come into the deep waters; the floods engulf me.
³I am worn out calling for help; my throat is parched.
My eyes fail, looking for my God.

99

[4]*Those who hate me without reason outnumber the hairs of my head;*
many are my enemies without cause, those who seek to destroy me.
I am forced to restore what I did not steal.
[5]*You know my folly, O God; my guilt is not hidden from You.*
[6]*May those who hope in You not be disgraced because of me,*
O Lord, the LORD Almighty;
may those who seek You not be put to shame because of me,
O God of Israel.
[7]*For I endure scorn for your sake, and shame covers my face.*
[8]*I am a stranger to my brothers, an alien to my own mother's sons;*
[9]*for zeal for your house consumes me,*
and the insults of those who insult You fall on me.
[10]*When I weep and fast, I must endure scorn;*
[11]*when I put on sackcloth, people make sport of me.*
[12]*Those who sit at the gate mock me,*
and I am the song of the drunkards.
[13]*But I pray to You, O LORD, in the time of your favour;*
in your great love, O God, answer me with your sure salvation.
[14]*Rescue me from the mire, do not let me sink;*
deliver me from those who hate me, from the deep waters.
[15]*Do not let the floodwaters engulf me or the depths swallow me up*
or the pit close its mouth over me.
[16]*Answer me, O LORD, out of the goodness of your love;*
in your great mercy turn to me.
[17]*Do not hide your face from your servant;*
answer me quickly, for I am in trouble.
[18]*Come near and rescue me; redeem me because of my foes.*
[19]*You know how I am scorned, disgraced and shamed;*
all my enemies are before You.
[20]*Scorn has broken my heart and has left me helpless;*
I looked for sympathy, but there was none,
for comforters, but I found none.
[21]*They put gall in my food*
and gave me vinegar for my thirst.

[29]*I am in pain and distress; may your salvation, O God, protect me.*
[30]*I will praise God's name in song*
and glorify him with thanksgiving.

[31]This will please the LORD more than an ox,
more than a bull with its horns and hoofs.
[32]The poor will see and be glad—
you who seek God, may your hearts live!
[33]The LORD hears the needy and does not despise his captive people.
[34]Let heaven and earth praise him,
the seas and all that move in them,
[35]for God will save Zion and rebuild the cities of Judah.
Then people will settle there and possess it;
[36]the children of his servants will inherit it,
and those who love his name will dwell there.

Reflections:

The psalmist is in deep distress. He likens himself to a man who is being sucked deeper and deeper into a bog or quicksand. His feet cannot find anything solid and secure on which to place them; there is nothing on which he can stand and which will prevent him from being sucked deeper and deeper into the mire. V 1-2. In his dire distress he calls out for God to help and deliver him. In times of wellbeing our prayers can be formal and cursory but when we are in distress like the psalmist, our prayers are an agonising cry from the heart to God for deliverance. These are the sort of prayers which really reach into the heart of God and find an answer from His love and power.

Much in this psalm is prophetic of the life and agonising death on the cross and the sufferings of the Lord Jesus. For instance v 9 "for the zeal of your house consumes me" is quoted by John in his Gospel in his account of the 'cleansing of the temple' by our Lord Jesus Christ. In chapter 2 v 17 it is stated that, "His disciples remembered that it is written, 'Zeal for your house will consume me'." And so we see that the verse is prophetic.

V 20-21: "Scorn has broken my heart and has left me helpless, I looked for sympathy but there was none, for comforters but I found none. They put gall in my food and gave me vinegar for my thirst" is also prophetic and actually happened to Jesus as He was dying on the cross (see Matthew 27 v 48, Mark 15 v 36, Luke 23 v 36, John 19 v 29-30).

The psalm concludes with praise to God, despite the psalmist's pain and distress (v 29-30). To praise God when all is well with us is a fitting act of worship, but it is even more acceptable to God to praise Him when we are suffering. What we are in fact saying is: "O God, despite my pain and terrible distress, You are worthy of my praise." This is a sort of vote of confidence in the love and power of God "whose love is as great as his power and neither knows measure nor end" (Charles Wesley).

Psalm 70

(A Psalm of David)

[1]Hasten, O God, to save me;
O LORD, come quickly to help me.
[2]May those who seek my life be put to shame and confusion;
may all who desire my ruin be turned back in disgrace.
[3]May those who say to me, "Aha! Aha!" turn back
because of their shame.
[4]But may all who seek You rejoice and be glad in You;
may those who love your salvation always say,
"Let God be exalted!"
[5]Yet I am poor and needy; come quickly to me, O God.
You are my help and my deliverer;
O LORD, do not delay.

Reflections:

This is another 'heart cry' to God for help. It is a prayer of contrasts: that one's persecutors may be put to shame (v 2-3) and yet all who truly seek God may rejoice and be glad in Him; and those, like Christians, who love His salvation may say, "Let God be exalted" (v 4).

The psalmist is experiencing delay from God to answer his prayers for deliverance and it is true to our experience that God may keep us waiting before He actually meets our need. This He does because:

The timing is not right in His eyes to answer our prayer immediately or

He is testing our faith in Him to keep and help us.

He is teaching us the Christian virtue of patience which, when exercised, is well pleasing in His sight and deepens our relationship with Him.

Psalm 71

[1]In You, O LORD, I have taken refuge; let me never be put to shame.
[2]Rescue me and deliver me in your righteousness;
turn your ear to me and save me.
[3]Be my rock of refuge, to which I can always go;
give the command to save me,
for You are my rock and my fortress.
[4]Deliver me, O my God, from the hand of the wicked,
from the grasp of evil and cruel men.
[5]For You have been my hope, O Sovereign LORD,
my confidence since my youth.
[6]From birth I have relied on You;
You brought me forth from my mother's womb.
I will ever praise You.
[7]I have become like a portent to many, but You are my strong refuge.
[8]My mouth is filled with your praise,
declaring your splendour all day long.
[9]Do not cast me away when I am old;
do not forsake me when my strength is gone.
[10]For my enemies speak against me;
those who wait to kill me conspire together.
[11]They say, "God has forsaken him;
pursue him and seize him, for no one will rescue him.
[12]Be not far from me, O God;
come quickly, O my God, to help me.
[13]May my accusers perish in shame;
may those who want to harm me be covered with scorn and disgrace.

¹⁴*But as for me, I will always have hope;*
I will praise You more and more.
¹⁵*My mouth will tell of your righteousness,*
of your salvation all day long, though I know not its measure.
¹⁶*I will come and proclaim your mighty acts, O Sovereign LORD;*
I will proclaim your righteousness, yours alone.
¹⁷*Since my youth, O God, You have taught me,*
and to this day I declare your marvellous deeds.
¹⁸*Even when I am old and grey, do not forsake me, O God,*
till I declare your power to the next generation,
your might to all who are to come.
¹⁹*Your righteousness reaches to the skies, O God,*
You who have done great things.
Who, O God, is like You?
²⁰*Though You have made me see troubles, many and bitter,*
You will restore my life again;
from the depths of the earth You will again bring me up.
²¹*You will increase my honour and comfort me once again.*
²²*I will praise You with the harp for your faithfulness, O my God;*
I will sing praise to You with the lyre, O Holy One of Israel.
²³*My lips will shout for joy when I sing praise to You—*
I, whom You have redeemed.
²⁴*My tongue will tell of your righteous acts all day long,*
for those who wanted to harm me
have been put to shame and confusion.

Reflections:

David praises the Lord God for His faithfulness to him throughout the whole of his life, from being born, as a child and throughout his youth. (vv 5,6,17). Now when he is "old and grey" he asks God not to forsake him, but to be his refuge and strength in his old age. God is his rock and his fortress even now (v 3). He states that from birth he relied on God (v 6) and that God has been his confidence since his youth (v 5). Now his strength is gone because of his age; but he will always have hope in God and praise Him "more and more" (v 14). He wants to hand on his testimony to God's faithfulness to the next generation (v 18). Though his life has not been without troubles yet he has been restored; God will increase his honour and comfort him once again (v 21). The

whole psalm rings with praise to God. He would today sing with
sincerity the words of the hymn:

> Great is Thy faithfulness, O God my Father,
> There is no shadow of turning with Thee,
> All I have needed Thy hand hath provided
> Great is Thy faithfulness, Lord unto me.
>
> *T O Chisholm*

It is my experience, throughout a very long ministry, that there are
those who start off as Christians with great enthusiasm, especially when
they are young, but do not have the will to continue their faith
throughout the whole of their lives. Our Lord foretold this in the
parable of the sower and his seed (Matthew 13). Jesus said that it is the
person who "stands firm to the end" who will be saved. (Matthew 10 v
22) It is wonderful today to hear the testimonies of elderly people who
have proved God's faithfulness throughout a long life. It is because the
torch of the Gospel has been handed on from one generation to another
that the Christian faith is now known by people, throughout the world,
even after two thousand years since the birth of our Saviour.

Psalm 72

> [1]*Endow the king with your justice, O God,*
> *the royal son with your righteousness.*
> [2]*He will judge your people in righteousness,*
> *your afflicted ones with justice.*
> [3]*The mountains will bring prosperity to the people,*
> *the hills the fruit of righteousness.*
> [4]*He will defend the afflicted among the people*
> *and save the children of the needy; he will crush the oppressor.*
> [5]*He will endure as long as the sun, as long as the moon,*
> *through all generations.*

105

⁶He will be like rain falling on a mown field,
like showers watering the earth.
⁷In his days the righteous will flourish;
prosperity will abound till the moon is no more.
⁸He will rule from sea to sea
and from the River to the ends of the earth.
⁹The desert tribes will bow before him
and his enemies will lick the dust.
¹⁰The kings of Tarshish and of distant shores
will bring tribute to him;
the kings of Sheba and Seba will present him gifts.
¹¹All kings will bow down to him and all nations will serve him.
¹²For he will deliver the needy who cry out,
the afflicted who have no one to help.
¹³He will take pity on the weak and the needy
and save the needy from death.
¹⁴He will rescue them from oppression and violence,
for precious is their blood in his sight.
¹⁵Long may he live! May gold from Sheba be given him.
May people ever pray for him and bless him all day long.
¹⁶Let grain abound throughout the land;
on the tops of the hills may it sway.
Let its fruit flourish like Lebanon;
let it thrive like the grass of the field.
¹⁷May his name endure for ever; may it continue as long as the sun.
All nations will be blessed through him,
and they will call him blessed.
¹⁸Praise be to the LORD God, the God of Israel,
who alone does marvellous deeds.
¹⁹Praise be to his glorious name for ever;
may the whole earth be filled with his glory. Amen and Amen.

²⁰This concludes the prayers of David son of Jesse.

Reflections:

This is again a 'Messianic' psalm foretelling the rule of Jesus as supreme king over all mankind; now in the hearts and lives of believers and ultimately at His triumphal return at the end of the Ages, when all who do not acknowledge His rule will be banished into a lost eternity.

The hallmarks of Jesus' reign are "righteousness" and "justice" (vv 1-2). Supreme, however, are His concern and care for the afflicted, the needy and their children (v 12, v 4) the weak and the oppressed (vv 12-14). At His 'Second Coming' in glory the "whole earth" will be "filled with His glory" (v 19).

In the New Testament all this is portrayed in our Lord's foretelling of what will happen at the Final Judgment of all mankind (Matthew 25 vv 31-46). Once more the King's concern for the hungry, the thirsty, those who are too poor to have adequate clothing, the sick and the prisoners is revealed.

In our present time it is not enough for a person to accept Jesus as Saviour (Ephesians 1 v 7) but also all believers need to crown Him as King and Lord of their lives. They will then, in the present day, show their concern and action for the needy as portrayed in the picture of their King. Also such submission to His Lordship will issue in lives of obedience to Him. The writer to the Hebrews says that "Jesus is the source of eternal salvation for all who obey Him" (Hebrews 5 v 9). Jesus said that all who hear His words and obey them are like a man who built his house upon a rock so that it will be able to withstand any assault upon it (Matthew 7 vv 24-27).

Psalm 73

¹Surely God is good to Israel, to those who are pure in heart.
²But as for me, my feet had almost slipped;
I had nearly lost my foothold.
³For I envied the arrogant when I saw the prosperity of the wicked.
⁴They have no struggles; their bodies are healthy and strong.
⁵They are free from the burdens common to man;
they are not plagued by human ills.
⁶Therefore pride is their necklace;
they clothe themselves with violence.

⁷From their callous hearts comes iniquity;
the evil conceits of their minds know no limits.
⁸They scoff, and speak with malice;
in their arrogance they threaten oppression.
⁹Their mouths lay claim to heaven,
and their tongues take possession of the earth.
¹⁰Therefore their people turn to them
and drink up waters in abundance.
¹¹They say, "How can God know?
Does the Most High have knowledge?"
¹²This is what the wicked are like—
always carefree, they increase in wealth.
¹³Surely in vain have I kept my heart pure;
in vain have I washed my hands in innocence.
¹⁴All day long I have been plagued;
I have been punished every morning.
¹⁵If I had said, "I will speak thus,"
I would have betrayed your children.
¹⁶When I tried to understand all this, it was oppressive to me
¹⁷till I entered the sanctuary of God;
then I understood their final destiny.
¹⁸Surely You place them on slippery ground;
You cast them down to ruin.
¹⁹How suddenly are they destroyed,
completely swept away by terrors!
²⁰As a dream when one awakes, so when You arise, O Lord,
You will despise them as fantasies.
²¹When my heart was grieved and my spirit embittered,
²²I was senseless and ignorant; I was a brute beast before You.
²³Yet I am always with You; You hold me by my right hand.
²⁴You guide me with your counsel,
and afterward You will take me into glory.
²⁵Whom have I in heaven but You?
And earth has nothing I desire besides You.

²⁶My flesh and my heart may fail,
but God is the strength of my heart
and my portion for ever.

²⁷Those who are far from You will perish;
You destroy all who are unfaithful to You.
²⁸But as for me, it is good to be near God.
I have made the Sovereign LORD my refuge;
I will tell of all your deeds.

Reflections:

The psalmist is perplexed at the wellbeing and prosperity of those who have no thought or acknowledgement of God or any relationship with Him whilst he, himself, a man who is a God-fearer, is "plagued"; and "punished" (vv 1-14). He cannot understand this (v 16). However, in contrast to himself he believes that the "godless" have no real or permanent security (vv 18-20). He then castigates himself for having such thoughts about the situation (vv 21-22) and sees that he himself is very blessed and secure through having a relationship with God, and ends by saying: "But as for me, it is good to be near God. I have made the Sovereign Lord my refuge. I will tell of all your deeds" (v 28).

The problem of the suffering of the righteous in contrast to the wellbeing of those who have no thought of God does arise quite often in the minds of believers today, but the security derived from wealth is fickle compared to that derived from a relationship with God. The attitude of the Christian towards wealth should be one of detachment. God may, in His sovereignty, grant riches and wellbeing to some of His children but they should regard this as incomparable to the spiritual riches (see Ephesians 1 v 3) they have through their relationship with God, which is all that really matters from the perspectives of life within the kingdom of God. Wealthy Christians should be pleased to be generous givers — to God's work through His Church and also through the many aid charities helping those in need.

Psalm 74

[1]*Why have You rejected us for ever, O God?*
Why does your anger smoulder against the sheep of your pasture?
[2]*Remember the people You purchased of old,*
the tribe of your inheritance, whom You redeemed—
Mount Zion, where You dwelt.
[3]*Turn your steps toward these everlasting ruins,*
all this destruction the enemy has brought on the sanctuary.
[4]*Your foes roared in the place where You met with us;*
they set up their standards as signs.
[5]*They behaved like men wielding axes*
to cut through a thicket of trees.
[6]*They smashed all the carved panelling with their axes and hatchets.*
[7]*They burned your sanctuary to the ground;*
they defiled the dwelling place of your Name.
[8]*They said in their hearts, "We will crush them completely!"*
They burned every place where God was worshipped in the land.
[9]*We are given no miraculous signs; no prophets are left,*
and none of us knows how long this will be.
[10]*How long will the enemy mock You, O God?*
Will the foe revile your name for ever?
[11]*Why do You hold back your hand, your right hand?*
Take it from the folds of your garment and destroy them!
[12]*But You, O God, are my king from of old;*
You bring salvation upon the earth.
[13]*It was You who split open the sea by your power;*
You broke the heads of the monster in the waters.
[14]*It was You who crushed the heads of Leviathan*
and gave him as food to the creatures of the desert.
[15]*It was You who opened up springs and streams;*
You dried up the ever-flowing rivers.
[16]*The day is yours, and yours also the night;*
You established the sun and moon.
[17]*It was You who set all the boundaries of the earth;*
You made both summer and winter.
[18]*Remember how the enemy has mocked You, O LORD,*
how foolish people have reviled your name.

¹⁹Do not hand over the life of your dove to wild beasts;
do not forget the lives of your afflicted people for ever.
²⁰Have regard for your covenant,
because haunts of violence fill the dark places of the land.
²¹Do not let the oppressed retreat in disgrace;
may the poor and needy praise your name.
²²Rise up, O God, and defend your cause;
remember how fools mock You all day long.
²³Do not ignore the clamour of your adversaries,
the uproar of your enemies, which rises continually.

Reflections:

This psalm, like Psalms 42 and 43, was written after the Babylonian armies had invaded Jerusalem and razed the city and the temple to the ground in 586BC. The way they ruthlessly destroyed the temple, including the Holy of Holies, is graphically described by the psalmist in verses 4-7. This caused him to cry out: "How long will the enemy mock You, O God? Will the foe revile your name for ever? Why do You hold back your hand, your right hand? Take it from the folds of your garment and destroy them!" (vv 10-11).

In contrast to the apparent ineptitude of the Almighty the psalmist begins to recite the mighty works of God in Israel's history (vv 13-17). He then utters a heartfelt prayer that God will not forget the lives of His afflicted people for ever (v 19) and asks God to rise up and defend His cause (v 22).

In the face of much that happens in the world today, such as torture, war and destruction perpetrated by those who do not acknowledge the existence of the God and Father of our Lord Jesus Christ, Christians today may have the same kind of thoughts as the psalmist; yet their faith is based upon all that God has done in the life, ministry, death and resurrection of the Messiah, Jesus, in the first century AD.

The Christian looks, with the eye of faith, to the mighty acts of God and believes that He will, in the end, triumph over all His foes. As Peter writes, God "in His great mercy has given us new birth into a living hope, through the resurrection of Jesus Christ from the dead" (1 Peter 1 v 3).

Psalm 75

[1] We give thanks to You, O God,
we give thanks, for your Name is near;
men tell of your wonderful deeds.
[2] You say, "I choose the appointed time; it is I who judge uprightly.
[3] When the earth and all its people quake,
it is I who hold its pillars firm.
[4] To the arrogant I say, 'Boast no more,'
and to the wicked, 'Do not lift up your horns.
[5] Do not lift your horns against heaven;
do not speak with outstretched neck.' "
[6] No one from the east or the west or from the desert can exalt a man.
[7] But it is God who judges:
He brings one down, he exalts another.
[8] In the hand of the LORD is a cup
full of foaming wine mixed with spices;
he pours it out, and all the wicked of the earth
drink it down to its very dregs.
[9] As for me, I will declare this for ever;
I will sing praise to the God of Jacob.
[10] I will cut off the horns of all the wicked,
but the horns of the righteous will be lifted up.

Reflections:

This is a psalm which declares the Sovereignty of God over all human history, past and present and future. The psalmist gives God thanks for all His wondrous deeds in the past (as recorded in the Old Testament history of the Hebrews) (v 1). He states that it is God who chooses His appointed time to act in righteous judgment in the present (v 2). In the light of this, believers can be confident about God's future vindication of His perfect will of righteousness on the earth. God is warning the arrogant who defy Him (vv 4-5), the symbol of "lifting up the horn" expressing a defiant attitude of boasting in one's own strength rather than being dependent on God.. It is God, he declares, who judges men and women and will lift up the "horns" of the righteous (vv 6-10), in other words, they will find strength in the righteousness of God.

Christians today live with basically the same faith as the psalmist and do all they can to live good lives which are pleasing to God, but they are immeasurably privileged in comparison, having their Saviour Jesus with them constantly to help. They can be reassured that the God of the past history of the Hebrews will choose His own time to bring an end to wickedness and exalt all that is in accordance with His perfect will.

Psalm 76

[1]In Judah God is known; his name is great in Israel.
[2]His tent is in Salem, his dwelling place in Zion.
[3]There he broke the flashing arrows,
the shields and the swords, the weapons of war.
[4]You are resplendent with light,
more majestic than mountains rich with game.
[5]Valiant men lie plundered, they sleep their last sleep;
not one of the warriors can lift his hands.
[6]At your rebuke, O God of Jacob, both horse and chariot lie still.
[7]You alone are to be feared.
Who can stand before You when You are angry?
[8]From heaven You pronounced judgment,
and the land feared and was quiet—
[9]when You, O God, rose up to judge,
to save all the afflicted of the land.
[10]Surely your wrath against men brings You praise,
and the survivors of your wrath are restrained.
[11]Make vows to the LORD your God and fulfil them;
let all the neighbouring lands bring gifts to the One to be feared.
[12]He breaks the spirit of rulers;
he is feared by the kings of the earth.

Reflections:

Christians certainly believe from the teaching of the Bible that God is love (See John 3 v 16). However, this love can easily be reckoned to be a sign of weakness; a sort of sloppy, sentimental emotion which means that human beings can do whatever they like and God will overlook sinful actions, even evil ones, God being powerless to act with any sort of judgment or punishment for the perpetrators. However, the Bible also teaches us about God's wrath. So Paul writes that "the wrath of God is being revealed from heaven against all the godlessness and wickedness of men who suppress the truth by their wickedness" (Rom 1 v 18) and that "those who do such things deserve death" (Rom 1 v 32). So the psalmist teaches that it is not nations who are "superpowers" having great armies that are ultimately to be feared, but God Himself, even saying that, in the face of human power, "Surely your wrath against men brings You praise, and the survivors of your wrath are restrained" (v 10). Much of the rise of rampant social and other evils of our time can be accounted for in that human beings, especially in the West, have lost any fear of God. Christians should live with deep reverence and teach others the fact that there is a rightful fear of God whose judgment will surely be manifest and even the most powerful nations, being human, will be brought to account. "Just as man is destined to die once and after that to face judgment" (Hebrews 9 v 27).

Psalm 77

[1]I cried out to God for help; I cried out to God to hear me.
[2]When I was in distress, I sought the Lord;
at night I stretched out untiring hands
and my soul refused to be comforted.

[3]I remembered You, O God, and I groaned;
I mused, and my spirit grew faint.
[4]You kept my eyes from closing; I was too troubled to speak.
[5]I thought about the former days, the years of long ago;
[6]I remembered my songs in the night.
My heart mused and my spirit enquired:
[7]"Will the Lord reject for ever?
Will he never show his favour again?

⁸Has his unfailing love vanished for ever?
Has his promise failed for all time?
⁹Has God forgotten to be merciful?
Has he in anger withheld his compassion?"

¹⁰Then I thought, "To this I will appeal:
the years of the right hand of the Most High."
¹¹I will remember the deeds of the LORD;
yes, I will remember your miracles of long ago.
¹²I will meditate on all your works
and consider all your mighty deeds.
¹³Your ways, O God, are holy.
What god is so great as our God?
¹⁴You are the God who performs miracles;
You display your power among the peoples.
¹⁵With your mighty arm You redeemed your people,
the descendants of Jacob and Joseph.
¹⁶The waters saw You, O God, the waters saw You and writhed;
the very depths were convulsed.
¹⁷The clouds poured down water,
the skies resounded with thunder; your arrows flashed back and forth.
¹⁸Your thunder was heard in the whirlwind,
your lightning lit up the world; the earth trembled and quaked.
¹⁹Your path led through the sea,
your way through the mighty waters,
though your footprints were not seen.
²⁰You led your people like a flock
by the hand of Moses and Aaron.

Reflections:

Once more we have a psalmist who is in deep distress. We are not told just what his troubles are but they are overwhelming him and he is finding no answer to his prayers. It is easy when we are in such distress as was this psalmist, to let our problems overwhelm us and take over all our thinking so that they are like a dark cloud overshadowing our whole life. However, the psalmist does the right thing; he dwells on the great, miraculous deeds which God did in the past. Surely such a God who intervenes in history and individual human lives can help him.

Christians believe in an all-powerful God of love whose purposes for the world and individuals cannot in the end be thwarted. Are you being overwhelmed by anxiety and fear? If so, meditate on the greatness of God, who does not dwell in tranquil bliss without any care for His children, but who does intervene in human life to bring His purposes to pass – He will do so for you.

Psalm 78

[1]O my people, hear my teaching; listen to the words of my mouth.
[2]I will open my mouth in parables,
I will utter hidden things, things from of old—
[3]what we have heard and known, what our fathers have told us.
[4]We will not hide them from their children;
we will tell the next generation the praiseworthy deeds of the LORD,
his power, and the wonders he has done.
[5]He decreed statutes for Jacob and established the law in Israel,
which he commanded our forefathers to teach their children,
[6]so the next generation would know them,
even the children yet to be born,
and they in turn would tell their children.
[7]Then they would put their trust in God
and would not forget his deeds but would keep his commands.
[8]They would not be like their forefathers—
a stubborn and rebellious generation,
whose hearts were not loyal to God,
whose spirits were not faithful to him.
[9]The men of Ephraim, though armed with bows,
turned back on the day of battle;
[10]they did not keep God's covenant and refused to live by his law.
[11]They forgot what he had done, the wonders he had shown them.
[12]He did miracles in the sight of their fathers
in the land of Egypt, in the region of Zoan.

116

¹³He divided the sea and led them through;
he made the water stand firm like a wall.
¹⁴He guided them with the cloud by day
and with light from the fire all night.
¹⁵He split the rocks in the desert
and gave them water as abundant as the seas;
¹⁶he brought streams out of a rocky crag
and made water flow down like rivers.
¹⁷But they continued to sin against him,
rebelling in the desert against the Most High.
¹⁸They wilfully put God to the test
by demanding the food they craved.
¹⁹They spoke against God, saying,
"Can God spread a table in the desert?
²⁰When he struck the rock, water gushed out,
and streams flowed abundantly.
But can he also give us food? Can he supply meat for his people?"
²¹When the LORD heard them, he was very angry;
his fire broke out against Jacob, and his wrath rose against Israel,
²²for they did not believe in God or trust in his deliverance.
²³Yet he gave a command to the skies above
and opened the doors of the heavens;
²⁴he rained down manna for the people to eat,
he gave them the grain of heaven.
²⁵Men ate the bread of angels;
he sent them all the food they could eat.
²⁶He let loose the east wind from the heavens
and led forth the south wind by his power.
²⁷He rained meat down on them like dust,
flying birds like sand on the seashore.
²⁸He made them come down inside their camp, all around their tents.
²⁹They ate till they had more than enough,
for he had given them what they craved.
³⁰But before they turned from the food they craved,
even while it was still in their mouths,
³¹God's anger rose against them;
he put to death the sturdiest among them,
cutting down the young men of Israel.
³²In spite of all this, they kept on sinning;

117

in spite of his wonders, they did not believe.
³³So he ended their days in futility and their years in terror.
³⁴Whenever God slew them, they would seek him;
they eagerly turned to him again.
³⁵They remembered that God was their Rock,
that God Most High was their Redeemer.
³⁶But then they would flatter him with their mouths,
lying to him with their tongues;
³⁷their hearts were not loyal to him,
they were not faithful to his covenant.
³⁸Yet he was merciful; he forgave their iniquities
and did not destroy them.
Time after time he restrained his anger
and did not stir up his full wrath.
³⁹He remembered that they were but flesh,
a passing breeze that does not return.
⁴⁰How often they rebelled against him in the desert
and grieved him in the wasteland!
⁴¹Again and again they put God to the test;
they vexed the Holy One of Israel.
⁴²They did not remember his power—
the day he redeemed them from the oppressor,
⁴³the day he displayed his miraculous signs in Egypt,
his wonders in the region of Zoan.
⁴⁴He turned their rivers to blood;
they could not drink from their streams.
⁴⁵He sent swarms of flies that devoured them,
and frogs that devastated them.
⁴⁶He gave their crops to the grasshopper, their produce to the locust.
⁴⁷He destroyed their vines with hail and their sycamore-figs with sleet.
⁴⁸He gave over their cattle to the hail,
their livestock to bolts of lightning.
⁴⁹He unleashed against them his hot anger,
his wrath, indignation and hostility—a band of destroying angels.
⁵⁰He prepared a path for his anger;
he did not spare them from death but gave them over to the plague.
⁵¹He struck down all the firstborn of Egypt,
the firstfruits of manhood in the tents of Ham.

⁵²*But he brought his people out like a flock;*
he led them like sheep through the desert.
⁵³*He guided them safely, so they were unafraid;*
but the sea engulfed their enemies.
⁵⁴*Thus he brought them to the border of his holy land,*
to the hill country his right hand had taken.
⁵⁵*He drove out nations before them*
and allotted their lands to them as an inheritance;
he settled the tribes of Israel in their homes.
⁵⁶*But they put God to the test and rebelled against the Most High;*
they did not keep his statutes.
⁵⁷*Like their fathers they were disloyal and faithless,*
as unreliable as a faulty bow.
⁵⁸*They angered him with their high places;*
they aroused his jealousy with their idols.
⁵⁹*When God heard them, he was very angry;*
he rejected Israel completely.
⁶⁰*He abandoned the tabernacle of Shiloh,*
the tent he had set up among men.
⁶¹*He sent the ark of his might into captivity,*
his splendour into the hands of the enemy.
⁶²*He gave his people over to the sword;*
he was very angry with his inheritance.
⁶³*Fire consumed their young men,*
and their maidens had no wedding songs;
⁶⁴*their priests were put to the sword,*
and their widows could not weep.
⁶⁵*Then the Lord awoke as from sleep,*
as a man wakes from the stupor of wine.
⁶⁶*He beat back his enemies; he put them to everlasting shame.*
⁶⁷*Then he rejected the tents of Joseph,*
he did not choose the tribe of Ephraim;
⁶⁸*but he chose the tribe of Judah, Mount Zion, which he loved.*
⁶⁹*He built his sanctuary like the heights,*
like the earth that he established for ever.
⁷⁰*He chose David his servant and took him from the sheep pens;*
⁷¹*from tending the sheep he brought him*
to be the shepherd of his people Jacob,
of Israel his inheritance.

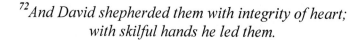

⁷²And David shepherded them with integrity of heart;
with skilful hands he led them.

Reflections:

The psalmist writes of all the great miracles God performed to get His people from slavery in Egypt into the land of Canaan – the 'promised land' where He meted out portions for each tribe to settle and so it became their 'homeland'. However the psalmist also intersperses these great events with their faithlessness and even rebelliousness against God and the punishments which ensued. The Christian rejoices in God's mighty actions for His then chosen people the Jews. However, for a Christian, God has done something even greater in procuring a salvation which embraces all people of all races who will receive it. This greater act, which created a "new covenant" (or agreement) with the human race for all time, was His sending His Son Jesus Christ into the world to die upon the Cross and atone for all the sins of mankind, "for God did not send His Son into the world to condemn the world, but to save the world through him" (John 3 v 17). Jesus, on the eve of His crucifixion, had a last supper with His disciples and, as He broke the bread and poured out the wine said: "This is my blood of the covenant which is poured out for many for the forgiveness of sins" (Matthew 26 v 28). As Christians we remember this, God's supreme act for mankind every time we celebrate Holy Communion. As we eat the bread and drink the wine we also reaffirm, through faith, our acceptance of what God has done in Christ and renew our promises to be obedient to Him. However, Christians, like the Jews of old, do sin and fall short of their part of the 'bargain' to live holy and blameless lives. Some, at times, even rebel against God and reject the offer of His great love. Yet, in this New Covenant, there is *always* a way back into a right relationship with God through repentance and trust. It is always true that as Paul declares to Timothy, "Here is a trustworthy saying:

> If we died with him
> we will also live with him;
> if we endure
> we will also reign with him.
> If we disown him
> He will also disown us;

if we are faithless
He will remain faithful,
for he cannot disown himself." (2 Tim 2 vv 11-13)

Psalm 79

¹O God, the nations have invaded your inheritance;
they have defiled your holy temple,
they have reduced Jerusalem to rubble.
²They have given the dead bodies of your servants
as food to the birds of the air,
the flesh of your saints to the beasts of the earth.
³They have poured out blood like water all around Jerusalem,
and there is no one to bury the dead.
⁴We are objects of reproach to our neighbours,
of scorn and derision to those around us.
⁵How long, O LORD? Will You be angry for ever?
How long will your jealousy burn like fire?
⁶Pour out your wrath on the nations that do not acknowledge You,
on the kingdoms that do not call on your name;
⁷for they have devoured Jacob and destroyed his homeland.
⁸Do not hold against us the sins of the fathers;
may your mercy come quickly to meet us, for we are in desperate need.
⁹Help us, O God our Saviour, for the glory of your name;
deliver us and forgive our sins for your name's sake.
¹⁰Why should the nations say, "Where is their God?"
Before our eyes, make known among the nations
that You avenge the outpoured blood of your servants.
¹¹May the groans of the prisoners come before You;
by the strength of your arm preserve those condemned to die.
¹²Pay back into the laps of our neighbours seven times
the reproach they have hurled at You, O Lord.
¹³Then we your people, the sheep of your pasture,
will praise You for ever;
from generation to generation we will recount your praise.

Reflections:

Once more we are confronted with the cries of a devout Hebrew lamenting over the destruction of Jerusalem by a heathen army. He brings before God, not only the knocked down buildings which have been reduced to rubble, but also the terrible suffering of the people at the hands of the enemy and he calls out to God for vengeance.

The desire for vengeance on those who have made us suffer is not a Christian desire but the Bible is not silent about the fact that God will avenge his people when they have been made to suffer unjustly. There are thirty-four references to 'vengeance' in the Old Testament, and the most significant is Deuteronomy 32 v 35: " 'It is mine to avenge; I will repay', says the Lord". This was clearer in the King James translation: " 'Vengeance is mine' saith the Lord, 'I will repay'." But in the more complete revelation of God's character in the New Testament there is, as one would expect, fewer references to this act of revenge; nevertheless it is there. Paul gives the Christian attitude towards it in Romans 12 vv 18-21 when he writes, "If it is possible, as far as depends on you, live at peace with everyone. Do not take revenge, my friends, but leave room for God's wrath, for it is written: 'It is mine to avenge; I will repay,' says the Lord. .... Do not be overcome by evil, but overcome evil with good." As the psalmist says, God is glorified when good triumphs over evil.

Psalm 80

¹Hear us, O Shepherd of Israel, You who lead Joseph like a flock;
You who sit enthroned between the cherubim, shine forth
²before Ephraim, Benjamin and Manasseh.
Awaken your might; come and save us.
³Restore us, O God; make your face shine upon us,
that we may be saved.
⁴O LORD God Almighty, how long will your anger smoulder
against the prayers of your people?

[5]*You have fed them with the bread of tears;*
You have made them drink tears by the bowlful.
[6]*You have made us a source of contention to our neighbours,*
and our enemies mock us.
[7]*Restore us, O God Almighty; make your face shine upon us,*
that we may be saved.

[8]*You brought a vine out of Egypt;*
You drove out the nations and planted it.
[9]*You cleared the ground for it, and it took root and filled the land.*
[10]*The mountains were covered with its shade,*
the mighty cedars with its branches.
[11]*It sent out its boughs to the Sea, its shoots as far as the River.*
[12]*Why have You broken down its walls*
so that all who pass by pick its grapes?
[13]*Boars from the forest ravage it*
and the creatures of the field feed on it.
[14]*Return to us, O God Almighty! Look down from heaven and see!*
Watch over this vine,
[15]*the root your right hand has planted,*
the son you have raised up for yourself.
[16]*Your vine is cut down, it is burned with fire;*
at your rebuke your people perish.
[17]*Let your hand rest on the man at your right hand,*
the son of man You have raised up for yourself.
[18]*Then we will not turn away from You;*
revive us, and we will call on your name.
[19]*Restore us, O LORD God Almighty;*
make your face shine upon us, that we may be saved.

Reflections:

This psalm is a prayer for restoration. It is about God restoring the
fortunes of His people from the terrible fate which they have suffered.
In the time of Jesus when God's people were under the rule and
dominion of the Romans the people looked for a Messiah who would
restore Israel to be free and indeed to rule the earth. Perhaps we can see
a prophecy about this in verses 17-18: "Let your hand rest on the man at
your right hand, the son of man You have raised up for yourself. Then

123

we will not turn away from You; revive us, and we will call upon your name."

Before the ascension the disciples said to the resurrected Jesus, who they believed would indeed free them from the Romans, "Lord, are you at this time going to restore the kingdom to Israel?" (Acts 1 v 6). Jesus did not answer this question in a direct way but said that something even more important was going to happen as an act of God, in that the disciples would receive power very soon, when they would be baptised in the Holy Spirit (Acts 1 v 5,8). Christianity is not basically about political rule but is about God's action deep within the spirit of man. It is about spiritual restoration to a status with God which man had before his fall from grace (Genesis 3) and his subsequent alienation from God. Jesus announced at the beginning of His ministry that the kingdom of God was at hand (Mark 1). This is shown in the New Testament to be a spiritual kingdom which can be experienced by all who repent and are 'born again' (John 3).

It is also true that when even a Christian falls away from God through sin, no person is beyond the possibility of restoration to being a child of God.

Psalm 81

1Sing for joy to God our strength;
shout aloud to the God of Jacob!
2Begin the music, strike the tambourine,
play the melodious harp and lyre.
3Sound the ram's horn at the New Moon,
and when the moon is full, on the day of our Feast;
4this is a decree for Israel, an ordinance of the God of Jacob.
5He established it as a statute for Joseph
when he went out against Egypt,
where we heard a language we did not understand.
6He says, "I removed the burden from their shoulders;
their hands were set free from the basket.

⁷In your distress you called and I rescued you,
I answered you out of a thundercloud;
I tested you at the waters of Meribah.
⁸"Hear, O my people, and I will warn you—
if you would but listen to me, O Israel!
⁹You shall have no foreign god among you;
you shall not bow down to an alien god.
¹⁰I am the LORD your God, who brought you up out of Egypt.
Open wide your mouth and I will fill it.
¹¹"But my people would not listen to me; Israel would not submit to me.
¹²So I gave them over to their stubborn hearts
to follow their own devices.
¹³"If my people would but listen to me, if Israel would follow my ways,
¹⁴how quickly would I subdue their enemies
and turn my hand against their foes!
¹⁵Those who hate the LORD would cringe before him,
and their punishment would last for ever.
¹⁶But you would be fed with the finest of wheat;
with honey from the rock I would satisfy you."

Reflections:

This psalm begins with joyous praise to God. It is not the psalmist alone who echoes praise. He calls upon all his people to do the same with music, the tambourine, the harp, the lyre and ram's horn. It seems that the Jewish people kept special festivals of praise at every new moon (v 3). Throughout the Old Testament it is apparent that, except for the Solemn Day of Atonement the Hebrew people loved their festivals when they joined together to praise the Lord, even, as in this psalm, in times of adversity. The early Christians followed this tradition as they met together for worship even in the face of persecution like that under Emperor Nero. John Wesley stated that the Bible knows nothing of solitary religion. In the Old Testament God called together a people, the Hebrews, to praise Him and in the New Testament, a new people of all languages and nationalities to continue these acts of praise as they met together. Praise to God echoes throughout the Bible. Praise, especially in times of adversity for Christians, whether corporately or as individuals is a vote of confidence in God. It is an act of faith. It creates faith. It re-focuses the souls and spirits of God's people away from their problems to God, the source of deliverance. It brings worshippers closer to the heart of God who "inhabits the praises of His people" (Psalm 22 v 3). God responds in miraculous power to the voices of praise, for instance in the case of Paul and Silas incarcerated in Philippi jail (Acts 16). Let us, with the psalmist, praise the Lord!

Psalm 82

[1]God presides in the great assembly;
he gives judgment among the "gods":
[2]"How long will you defend the unjust
and show partiality to the wicked?
[3]Defend the cause of the weak and fatherless;
maintain the rights of the poor and oppressed.
[4]Rescue the weak and needy;
deliver them from the hand of the wicked.
[5]"They know nothing, they understand nothing.
They walk about in darkness;
all the foundations of the earth are shaken.
[6]"I said, 'You are "gods"; you are all sons of the Most High.'
[7]But you will die like mere men; you will fall like every other ruler."
[8]Rise up, O God, judge the earth,
for all the nations are your inheritance.

Reflections:

Here Jehovah God is portrayed in His heavenly realm with all the other so-called gods being governed and ruled by Him. They are all called upon to "maintain the rights of the poor and oppressed" (v 3) and to rescue the weak and needy from the hand of the wicked (v 4). In the New Testament we see also that there are spiritual beings inhabiting the spiritual realm beyond human senses. There are angels and archangels who are good and "principalities, powers and demons" which are evil and bent on harming human beings. Paul in Ephesians (chapter 6) says that our struggle on earth is "not against flesh and blood, but against the rulers, against the authorities, against the powers of this dark world and against the spiritual forces of evil in the heavenly realms"(v 12). He calls upon Christians to put on "the whole armour of God" to assist them. However, Christians will be victorious because their Lord Jesus Christ is "far above all rule and authority, power and dominion and every title that can be given, not only in the present age but also in the one to come. And God placed all things under his feet and appointed him to be head over everything for the church" (Eph 1 vv 21-22).

Psalm 83

[1]*O God, do not keep silent; be not quiet, O God, be not still.*
[2]*See how your enemies are astir, how your foes rear their heads.*
[3]*With cunning they conspire against your people;*
they plot against those You cherish.
[4]*"Come," they say, "let us destroy them as a nation,*
that the name of Israel be remembered no more."
[5]*With one mind they plot together;*
they form an alliance against You—
[6]*the tents of Edom and the Ishmaelites, of Moab and the Hagrites,*
[7]*Gebal, Ammon and Amalek, Philistia, with the people of Tyre.*
[8]*Even Assyria has joined them*
to lend strength to the descendants of Lot.
[9]*Do to them as You did to Midian,*
as You did to Sisera and Jabin at the river Kishon,
[10]*who perished at Endor and became like refuse on the ground.*
[11]*Make their nobles like Oreb and Zeeb,*
all their princes like Zebah and Zalmunna,
[12]*who said, "Let us take possession of the pasturelands of God."*
[13]*Make them like tumbleweed, O my God, like chaff before the wind.*
[14]*As fire consumes the forest or a flame sets the mountains ablaze,*

> ¹⁵*so pursue them with your tempest*
> *and terrify them with your storm.*
> ¹⁶*Cover their faces with shame*
> *so that men will seek your name, O LORD.*
> ¹⁷*May they ever be ashamed and dismayed;*
> *may they perish in disgrace.*
> ¹⁸*Let them know that You, whose name is the LORD—*
> *that You alone are the Most High over all the earth.*

Reflections:

The psalmist cries out to God to vindicate Himself and His people against all those who are enemies of His people. He states that powerful, evil nations have even formed a conspiracy to overthrow God's chosen people (v 5-8). He is expressing the question of the perennial mystery which has been asked by God's people throughout the ages. God's people know that He is Sovereign and Almighty yet evil still rears its ugly head even against the righteous and the good. In the New Testament, after stating the way in which God has exalted and appointed His Son, Jesus, above angels and all creatures, the writer to the Hebrews has to say, "Yet at present we do not see everything subject to Him" (Jesus) (chap 2 v 8b) yet still we "see Jesus, who was made a little lower than the angels, now crowned with glory and honour" (Heb. 2 v 9). In the Revelation of St John the Divine, the writer speaks of the "end time" battle between Christ and all evil, especially the devil, and declares that those who "had been slain because of the word of God and the testimony they had maintained … called out with a loud voice, 'How long, Sovereign Lord, holy and true, until you judge the inhabitants of the earth and avenge our blood?' " (Rev 6 vv 9-10). St Paul also cries out in his time: "Come, O Lord!" (1Cor 16 v 22). All this teaches us that Christians today, in the face of all that is evil in the world and in some cases persecution, must keep the vision of the final triumph of their Lord ever before their eyes and persevere in faith and in hope of their Lord's future triumph.

Psalm 84

[1]How lovely is your dwelling place, O LORD Almighty!
[2]My soul yearns, even faints, for the courts of the LORD;
my heart and my flesh cry out for the living God.
[3]Even the sparrow has found a home,
and the swallow a nest for herself,
where she may have her young—
a place near your altar, O LORD Almighty, my King and my God.
[4]Blessed are those who dwell in your house;
they are ever praising You.
[5]Blessed are those whose strength is in You,
who have set their hearts on pilgrimage.
[6]As they pass through the Valley of Baca,
they make it a place of springs;
the autumn rains also cover it with pools.
[7]They go from strength to strength,
till each appears before God in Zion.
[8]Hear my prayer, O LORD God Almighty;
listen to me, O God of Jacob.
[9]Look upon our shield, O God;
look with favour on your anointed one.
[10]Better is one day in your courts than a thousand elsewhere;
I would rather be a doorkeeper in the house of my God
than dwell in the tents of the wicked.
[11]For the LORD God is a sun and shield;
the LORD bestows favour and honour;
no good thing does he withhold from those whose walk is blameless.
[12]O LORD Almighty, blessed is the man who trusts in You.

Reflections:

The psalmist extols the magnificence and splendour of the temple, which, before it was finally destroyed by the Romans in AD64 was the centre, the focal point of Jewish worship. The psalmist loves the temple as the place where God was deemed to have made His Presence and where worshippers could be certain to meet with Him. It was a place of pilgrimage and the place where the sacrifices ordained by God through

Moses were constantly offered. Perhaps the psalmist's love for the Temple is nowhere better portrayed than in his words, "Better is one day in your courts than a thousand elsewhere" (v 10).

In later New Testament times, when they no longer had a temple, the Jews worshipped in synagogues which sprang up in every town and village where there were ten or more male Jews in the Roman Empire. Christians attended temple worship (see Acts 3 where Peter and John are going there) and also preached in the synagogues.

In the first three centuries after Christ, Christians had no place of worship for themselves but met in believers' homes and in the catacombs.

Church buildings are now revered by many Christians as places of worship for themselves and as helps to the devotional life, but they have learnt what Paul said as recorded in Acts 17: "The God who made the world and everything in it is the Lord of heaven and earth and does not live in temples built by hands" (v 24) and that "he is not far from each one of us" (v 27). Jesus promised that "where two or three come together in my name, there am I with them" (Matt 18 v 20). This is perhaps the simplest and ultimate description of a Christian church.

Psalm 85

¹You showed favour to your land, O LORD;
You restored the fortunes of Jacob.
²You forgave the iniquity of your people
and covered all their sins.
³You set aside all your wrath and turned from your fierce anger.
⁴Restore us again, O God our Saviour,
and put away your displeasure toward us.
⁵Will You be angry with us for ever?
Will You prolong your anger through all generations?
⁶Will You not revive us again, that your people may rejoice in You?
⁷Show us your unfailing love, O LORD, and grant us your salvation.

⁸I will listen to what God the LORD will say;
he promises peace to his people, his saints—
but let them not return to folly.
⁹Surely his salvation is near those who fear him,
that his glory may dwell in our land.
¹⁰Love and faithfulness meet together;
righteousness and peace kiss each other.
¹¹Faithfulness springs forth from the earth,
and righteousness looks down from heaven.
¹²The LORD will indeed give what is good,
and our land will yield its harvest.
¹³Righteousness goes before him
and prepares the way for his steps.

Reflections:

This psalmist, though living centuries before Jesus Christ, has never-theless a Christian concept of the nature of God. He is a God who:

> Forgives sin (v 2);
> Sets aside his wrath (v 3)
> Promises peace to His people (v 8)
> Saves those who fear Him (v 9)
> In Him (seen supremely in the life, teaching, death and resur-rection of Jesus Christ) love and faithfulness meet together (v 10)
> His righteousness (integrity) and subsequent demand of right living have "kissed each other" (v 10)
> Is faithful (v 11)
> And supremely good and will give good things to His children (v 12)
> Has commanded righteousness to go before Him (v 13).

No wonder he prays that God will revive His people's love, faith and trust in Him, so that His people may rejoice in Him (v 6). In the face of a massive falling away from God in the Western world, God's people also today, urgently pray for revival.

131

Psalm 86
(A prayer of David)

[1]*Hear, O* L[ORD], *and answer*
me, for I am poor and needy.
[2]*Guard my life, for I am devoted to You.*
You are my God; save your servant who trusts in You.
[3]*Have mercy on me, O Lord, for I call to You all day long.*
[4]*Bring joy to your servant, for to You, O Lord, I lift up my soul.*
[5]*You are forgiving and good, O Lord,*
abounding in love to all who call to You.
[6]*Hear my prayer, O* L[ORD]*; listen to my cry for mercy.*
[7]*In the day of my trouble I will call to You,*
for You will answer me.
[8]*Among the gods there is none like You, O Lord;*
no deeds can compare with yours.
[9]*All the nations You have made*
will come and worship before You, O Lord;
they will bring glory to your name.
[10]*For You are great and do marvellous deeds;*
You alone are God.
[11]*Teach me your way, O* L[ORD]*, and I will walk in your truth;*
give me an undivided heart, that I may fear your name.
[12]*I will praise You, O Lord my God, with all my heart;*
I will glorify your name for ever.
[13]*For great is your love toward me;*
You have delivered me from the depths of the grave.
[14]*The arrogant are attacking me, O God;*
a band of ruthless men seeks my life—men without regard for You.
[15]*But You, O Lord, are a compassionate and gracious God,*
slow to anger, abounding in love and faithfulness.
[16]*Turn to me and have mercy on me;*
grant your strength to your servant
and save the son of your maidservant.

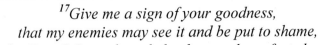

¹⁷Give me a sign of your goodness,
that my enemies may see it and be put to shame,
for You, O LORD, have helped me and comforted me.

Reflections:

David portrays a right belief, attitude and faith in God which should be an example, even today, of believers' prayers to God when they are being overwhelmed by trouble.

V.1	He acknowledges that he is poor and needy (humility).
V.2	He prays that God will guard his life because he is devoted to Him.
V.2	He trusts in God.
V.3	He prays for mercy and persists in prayer without giving up.
V.4	He prays for a restoration of joy in his life as he lifts up his soul to God.
V.5	He prays to God who he knows is forgiving and abounding in love.
V.7	In his day of trouble, he does not wallow in self-pity, or resentment towards God but believes implicitly that God will answer his prayer.
V. 9-10	He believes in a big God who has made all nations, who will come to bring glory to His name, whose deeds are great and marvellous.
V.11	He prays that he will live a life that is pleasing to God.
V.12	His prayer is filled with praise of a God who is (v15) compassionate and gracious, slow to anger and abounding in love and faithfulness.

May we all believe in the God of David (i.e. our Father in Jesus) and pray like him when we are in trouble.

133

Psalm 87

¹He has set his foundation on the holy mountain;
²the LORD loves the gates of Zion more than all the dwellings of Jacob.
³Glorious things are said of you, O city of God:
⁴"I will record Rahab and Babylon among those who acknowledge
me—Philistia too, and Tyre, along with Cush—
and will say, 'This one was born in Zion'."
⁵Indeed, of Zion it will be said,
"This one and that one were born in her,
and the Most High himself will establish her."
⁶The LORD will write in the register of the peoples:
"This one was born in Zion."
⁷As they make music they will sing,
"All my fountains are in you."

Reflections:

We have seen that a psalmist extolled the glories of the Jewish Temple (Psalm 84). In this psalm the writer extols the glory of the whole city of Zion, which is now called Jerusalem, which was first captured and made the capital by King David. He exclaims that it is an enormous privilege actually to be born there. It is still regarded as the most holy city on earth by both Jews and Christians and is much revered by Muslims. However, we can see deeper significance here when we remember that Zion, or Jerusalem, is used in the New Testament as a figure representing the Church (e.g. Rev 21 v 2) which in turn gives us deeper understanding of many Old Testament passages.

The best commentary on this psalm is to be found in the Christian hymn:

> Glorious things of thee are spoken,
> Zion, city of our God.
> He whose word cannot be broken
> Formed thee for his own abode:
> On the rock of ages founded,
> What can shake thy sure repose?
> With salvation's wall surrounded,

Thou may'st smile at all thy foes.

See, the streams of living waters,
Springing from eternal love,
Well supply thy sons and daughters,
And all fear of want remove:
Who can faint while such a river
Ever flows their thirst to assuage –
Grace which like the Lord, the giver
Never fails from age to age?

Blest inhabitants of Zion,
Washed in the Redeemer's blood,
Jesus, whom their souls rely on,
Makes them kings and priests to God.
'Tis His love His people raises
Over self to reign as kings;
And, as priests, His solemn praises
Each for a thank-offering brings.

Saviour, since of Zion's city
I, through grace, a member am,
Let the world deride or pity,
I will glory in Thy name:
Fading is the worldling's pleasure,
All his boasted pomp and show;
Solid joys and lasting pleasure,
None but Zion's children know.

For Christians the city of Zion typifies and signifies the privileges and security of the Christian Church for those who belong to it.

Psalm 88

¹*O LORD, the God who saves me, day and night I cry out before You.*
²*May my prayer come before You; turn your ear to my cry.*
³*For my soul is full of trouble and my life draws near the grave.*
⁴*I am counted among those who go down to the pit;*
I am like a man without strength.
⁵*I am set apart with the dead, like the slain who lie in the grave,*
whom You remember no more, who are cut off from your care.
⁶*You have put me in the lowest pit, in the darkest depths.*
⁷*Your wrath lies heavily upon me;*
You have overwhelmed me with all your waves.
⁸*You have taken from me my closest friends*
and have made me repulsive to them.
I am confined and cannot escape;
⁹*my eyes are dim with grief.*
I call to You, O LORD, every day;
I spread out my hands to You.
¹⁰*Do You show your wonders to the dead?*
Do those who are dead rise up and praise You?
¹¹*Is your love declared in the grave, your faithfulness in Destruction?*
¹²*Are your wonders known in the place of darkness,*
or your righteous deeds in the land of oblivion?
¹³*But I cry to You for help, O LORD;*
in the morning my prayer comes before You.
¹⁴*Why, O LORD, do You reject me and hide your face from me?*
¹⁵*From my youth I have been afflicted and close to death;*
I have suffered your terrors and am in despair.
¹⁶*Your wrath has swept over me; your terrors have destroyed me.*
¹⁷*All day long they surround me like a flood;*
they have completely engulfed me.
¹⁸*You have taken my companions and loved ones from me;*
the darkness is my closest friend.

Reflections:

Here is a psalmist who is very ill and unlike the writer of psalm 86, he has completely lost faith in God. He has, in fact, been on the verge of death even from his youth (v 15). In his despair he paints a picture of the Hebrew belief in life-after-death. The belief in the Old Testament, with few exceptions, was that at death a person descended into a shadowy underworld named in the Hebrew Sheol or Hades. The psalmist states that in this condition of existence:

V.10   God's wonders cannot be seen
V.10   the dead cannot praise God
V.11   they cannot apprehend God's love or faithfulness
V.12   they cannot know His righteous deeds
        It is a place of darkness (v12).

What a contrast to the promises given by Jesus for example as recorded in John's gospel chapter 14:
"Do not let your hearts be troubled. Trust in God, trust also in me. In my Father's house are many rooms; if it were not so, I would have told you. I am going there to prepare a place for you. And if I go and prepare a place for you, I will come back and take you to be with me that you also may be where I am." (verses 1-3)
Or that portrayed in Revelation 21 vv 3,4:
"And I heard a loud voice from the throne saying, 'Now the dwelling of God is with men, and he will live with them. They will be his people, and God himself will be with them and be their God. He will wipe every tear from their eyes. There will be no more death or mourning or crying or pain, for the old order of things has passed away'."

The Christian confidently believes with Paul in his Letter to the Philippians, chapter 1 verses 20-24:
"I eagerly expect and hope that I will in no way be ashamed, but will have sufficient courage so that now as always Christ will be exalted in my body, whether by life or by death. For to me, to live is Christ and to die is gain. If I am to go on living in the body, this will mean fruitful labour for me. Yet what shall I choose? I do not know! I am torn between the two. I desire to depart and be with Christ, which is better by far; but it is more necessary for you that I remain in the body."

And as Christians confidently sing:

137

1. "For ever with the Lord!"
   Amen! so let it be,
   Life from the dead is in that word,'
   'Tis immortality.
   Here in the body pent,
   Absent from Him, I roam;
   Yet nightly pitch my moving tent
   A day's march nearer home.

2. My Father's house on high,
   Home of my soul, how near
   At times to faith's foreseeing eye
   Thy golden gates appear!
   Ah, then my spirit faints
   To reach the land I love,
   The bright inheritance of saints,
   Jerusalem above!

3. "For ever with the Lord!"
   Father, if 'tis Thy will,
   The promise of that faithful word
   E'en here to me fulfil.
   Be Thou at my right hand,
   Then can I never fail.
   Uphold Thou me, and I shall stand;
   Fight Thou, and I'll prevail.

4. So when my latest breath
   Shall rend the veil in twain,
   By death I shall escape from death
   And life eternal gain.
   Knowing as I am known,
   How shall I love that word!
   And oft repeat before the throne,
   "For ever with the Lord!"

(James Montgomery)

Psalm 89

[1]I will sing of the LORD's great love for ever;
with my mouth I will make your faithfulness known
through all generations.
[2]I will declare that your love stands firm for ever,
that You established your faithfulness in heaven itself.
[3]You said, "I have made a covenant with my chosen one,
I have sworn to David my servant,
[4]'I will establish your line for ever
and make your throne firm through all generations'."
[5]The heavens praise your wonders, O LORD,
your faithfulness too, in the assembly of the holy ones.
[6]For who in the skies above can compare with the LORD?
Who is like the LORD among the heavenly beings?
[7]In the council of the holy ones God is greatly feared;
he is more awesome than all who surround him.
[8]O LORD God Almighty, who is like You?
You are mighty, O LORD, and your faithfulness surrounds You.
[9]You rule over the surging sea;
when its waves mount up, You still them.
[10]You crushed Rahab like one of the slain;
with your strong arm You scattered your enemies.
[11]The heavens are yours, and yours also the earth;
You founded the world and all that is in it.
[12]You created the north and the south;
Tabor and Hermon sing for joy at your name.
[13]Your arm is endued with power;
your hand is strong, your right hand exalted.
[14]Righteousness and justice are the foundation of your throne;
love and faithfulness go before You.
[15]Blessed are those who have learned to acclaim You,
who walk in the light of your presence, O LORD.
[16]They rejoice in your name all day long;
they exult in your righteousness.
[17]For You are their glory and strength,
and by your favour You exalt our horn.
[18]Indeed, our shield belongs to the LORD,
our king to the Holy One of Israel.

[19]Once You spoke in a vision,
to your faithful people You said:
"I have bestowed strength on a warrior;
I have exalted a young man from among the people.
[20]I have found David my servant;
with my sacred oil I have anointed him.
[21]My hand will sustain him; surely my arm will strengthen him.
[22]No enemy will subject him to tribute;
no wicked man will oppress him.
[23]I will crush his foes before him and strike down his adversaries.
[24]My faithful love will be with him,
and through my name his horn will be exalted.
[25]I will set his hand over the sea, his right hand over the rivers.
[26]He will call out to me, 'You are my Father,
my God, the Rock my Saviour.'
[27]I will also appoint him my firstborn,
the most exalted of the kings of the earth.
[28]I will maintain my love to him for ever,
and my covenant with him will never fail.
[29]I will establish his line for ever,
his throne as long as the heavens endure.

[30]"If his sons forsake my law and do not follow my statutes,
[31]if they violate my decrees and fail to keep my commands,
[32]I will punish their sin with the rod, their iniquity with flogging;
[33]but I will not take my love from him,
nor will I ever betray my faithfulness.
[34]I will not violate my covenant or alter what my lips have uttered.
[35]Once for all, I have sworn by my holiness—
and I will not lie to David—
[36]that his line will continue for ever
and his throne endure before me like the sun;
[37]it will be established for ever like the moon,
the faithful witness in the sky."

[38]But You have rejected, You have spurned,
You have been very angry with your anointed one.
[39]You have renounced the covenant with your servant

and have defiled his crown in the dust.
⁴⁰You have broken through all his walls
and reduced his strongholds to ruins.
⁴¹All who pass by have plundered him;
he has become the scorn of his neighbours.
⁴²You have exalted the right hand of his foes;
You have made all his enemies rejoice.
⁴³You have turned back the edge of his sword
and have not supported him in battle.
⁴⁴You have put an end to his splendour
and cast his throne to the ground.
⁴⁵You have cut short the days of his youth;
You have covered him with a mantle of shame.
⁴⁶How long, O LORD ? Will you hide yourself for ever?
How long will your wrath burn like fire?
⁴⁷Remember how fleeting is my life.
For what futility You have created all men!
⁴⁸What man can live and not see death,
or save himself from the power of the grave?
⁴⁹O Lord, where is your former great love,
which in your faithfulness You swore to David?
⁵⁰Remember, Lord, how your servant has been mocked,
how I bear in my heart the taunts of all the nations,
⁵¹the taunts with which your enemies have mocked, O LORD,
with which they have mocked every step of your anointed one.

⁵²Praise be to the LORD for ever!
Amen and Amen.

Reflections:

This psalm is again about the nature of God, but goes on to state how believers should relate to God on a daily basis and the consequences if they do not. So God is a person of great love and faithfulness (vv 1-2). He is sovereign over all He has created in heaven and earth (vv 5-13). Righteousness and justice are the attributes by which He rules (v 14). In the light of this, "Blessed are those who have learned to acclaim You", to acknowledge the greatness and everlasting love of God and live daily experiences of His presence with them. Believers rejoice in

141

His name all the day long and delight in His right dealings with them. God is their constant glory and strength as they experience His favour. He is also a shield and defence against anything or anybody who would hurt them (vv 15-17).

The psalmist regards what he has learnt about King David as the model for believers to follow and the blessings of God they will know if they live like him (vv 19-24). David was regarded as the ideal king by the Jews and the promise was that the Messiah, when he came, would be a descendant of his. So Matthew in his gospel sets out that Jesus was a direct descendant of David. In Mark's Gospel Blind Bartimaeus cries out "Jesus, Son of David, have mercy on me!" (Mark 10 v 47). However, if the Jewish people disobey God they will be punished by Him and become a prey to their enemies. This is what happened in the psalmist's time and he cries out for God's mercy: "How long, O Lord? Will You hide yourself for ever? How long will your wrath burn like fire?" (v 46) but the psalmist, in the end, praises God who will indeed, once more restore His people as He will any believer who repents of sin and turns back to daily obey God's commandments.

Psalm 90

¹Lord, You have been our dwelling place throughout all generations.
²Before the mountains were born
or You brought forth the earth and the world,
from everlasting to everlasting You are God.
³You turn men back to dust,
saying, "Return to dust, O sons of men."
⁴For a thousand years in your sight
are like a day that has just gone by, or like a watch in the night.
⁵You sweep men away in the sleep of death;
they are like the new grass of the morning—
⁶though in the morning it springs up new,
by evening it is dry and withered.

*⁷We are consumed by your anger
and terrified by your indignation.
⁸You have set our iniquities before You,
our secret sins in the light of your presence.
⁹All our days pass away under your wrath;
we finish our years with a moan.
¹⁰The length of our days is seventy years—
or eighty, if we have the strength;
yet their span is but trouble and sorrow,
for they quickly pass, and we fly away.
¹¹Who knows the power of your anger?
For your wrath is as great as the fear that is due You.
¹²Teach us to number our days aright,
that we may gain a heart of wisdom.
¹³Relent, O LORD! How long will it be?
Have compassion on your servants.
¹⁴Satisfy us in the morning with your unfailing love,
that we may sing for joy and be glad all our days.
¹⁵Make us glad for as many days as You have afflicted us,
for as many years as we have seen trouble.
¹⁶May your deeds be shown to your servants,
your splendour to their children.
¹⁷May the favour of the Lord our God rest upon us;
establish the work of our hands for us;
yes, establish the work of our hands.*

Reflections:

The psalmist paints a picture of the eternity of God as against the transitory life of human beings.

The eternity of God is proclaimed in verses 1-2: "Before the mountains were born or You brought forth the earth and the world, from everlasting to everlasting You are God" and "a thousand years in your sight are like a day that has just gone by or like a watch in the night" (v 4). In contrast, "All our days pass away under your wrath... the length of our days is seventy years – or eighty, if we have the strength; yet their span is but trouble and sorrow, for they quickly pass, and we fly away" (v 10).

The psalmist has observed the average lifespan in his time to be 70-

143

80 years. However, it may be worth noting that some Biblical scholars interpret Genesis 6 v 3 as meaning that God is saying that the lifespan of mankind will be 120 years. This is also the number given by anatomical scientists as being the lifespan to be expected, considering all aspects of man's physiology.

The eternity of God as declared here is perhaps reminiscent of Jesus Christ in addressing the seven churches, where He confirms: " 'I am the Alpha and the Omega' says the Lord God, 'who is and was and is to come, the Almighty' " (Revelation 1 v 8) and specifically referring to Himself in chapter 22 verse 13.

In the light of this contrast, the psalmist prays that God would teach us "to number our days aright, that we may gain a heart of wisdom" (v 12). The psalmist sets the perspective in which every believer should live every day.

As Charles Wesley taught the Methodists to sing:

How happy every child of grace,
Who knows his sins forgiven!
'The earth,' he cries, 'is not my place,
I seek my place in heaven.'

A stranger in the world below,
I calmly sojourn here;
Its evils in a moment end,
Its joys are seen as past.
But oh, the bliss to which I tend
Eternally shall last.

Psalm 91

[1] He who dwells in the shelter of the Most High
will rest in the shadow of the Almighty.
[2] I will say of the LORD, "He is my refuge and my fortress,
my God, in whom I trust."
[3] Surely he will save you from the fowler's snare
and from the deadly pestilence.
[4] He will cover you with his feathers,
and under his wings you will find refuge;
his faithfulness will be your shield and rampart.
[5] You will not fear the terror of night,
nor the arrow that flies by day,
[6] nor the pestilence that stalks in the darkness,
nor the plague that destroys at midday.
[7] A thousand may fall at your side, ten thousand at your right hand,
but it will not come near you.
[8] You will only observe with your eyes
and see the punishment of the wicked.
[9] If you make the Most High your dwelling—
even the LORD, who is my refuge—
[10] then no harm will befall you,
no disaster will come near your tent.
[11] For he will command his angels concerning you
to guard you in all your ways;
[12] they will lift you up in their hands,
so that you will not strike your foot against a stone.
[13] You will tread upon the lion and the cobra;
you will trample the great lion and the serpent.
[14] "Because he loves me," says the LORD, "I will rescue him;
I will protect him, for he acknowledges my name.
[15] He will call upon me, and I will answer him;
I will be with him in trouble, I will deliver him and honour him.
[16] With long life will I satisfy him and show him my salvation."

145

Reflections:

This psalm is all about the security of a believer who trusts in the Lord. Security is one of the most important factors and is basic to human need from early childhood into old age. The psalmist's message is that this can only ultimately be found in God.

The Almighty and the Most High are ancient titles for God in Hebrew thought. In verse 2 God is likened to a refuge; a fortress which is impregnable. In verse 4 He is likened to an eagle protecting its young ones in its wings. In verse 4 there is also the use of angels to protect us. This is a celestial bodyguard around the believer which will carry him above the rock-strewn road of life.

We will be protected from hidden dangers (the snare of the trapper) or deadly diseases or demons. Nothing, like sunstroke, shall overwhelm us. God is seen to be the effective answer to all fear, whether rational or irrational. However intense the battle, however long the list of casualties, the believer will survive unscathed, especially when God's judgment falls on the wicked, the believer will look on, unharmed.

From verse 14 the psalmist presents promises inspired by God. Security is for those whose faith clings to God, for the one whose heart finds security in God's heart, and its intimate knowledge of God's nature and power. God will be with such a one and fend off trouble and will rescue his life as he is lifted beyond danger. Long life is promised to him — eternity — as God answers his prayers. What an everyday security is promised in this psalm!

Psalm 92

¹It is good to praise the LORD
and make music to your name, O Most High,
²to proclaim your love in the morning
and your faithfulness at night,
³to the music of the ten-stringed lyre and the melody of the harp.
⁴For You make me glad by your deeds, O LORD;
I sing for joy at the works of your hands.

⁵How great are your works, O LORD, how profound your thoughts!
⁶The senseless man does not know, fools do not understand,
⁷that though the wicked spring up like grass
and all evildoers flourish, they will be for ever destroyed.
⁸But You, O LORD, are exalted for ever.
⁹For surely your enemies, O LORD,
surely your enemies will perish; all evildoers will be scattered.
¹⁰You have exalted my horn like that of a wild ox;
fine oils have been poured upon me.
¹¹My eyes have seen the defeat of my adversaries;
my ears have heard the rout of my wicked foes.
¹²The righteous will flourish like a palm tree,
they will grow like a cedar of Lebanon;
¹³planted in the house of the LORD,
they will flourish in the courts of our God.
¹⁴They will still bear fruit in old age,
they will stay fresh and green,
¹⁵proclaiming, "The LORD is upright;
he is my Rock, and there is no wickedness in him."

Reflections:

In Psalm 90 we see the finitude of man contrasted with the eternity of God. In this psalm the instability and fickleness of all that is evil and wicked is set against the powerful goodness of God and the blessings of living a righteous (or good) life.

The wicked are senseless (v 6) and though they may have some success and prosperity it is only transitory (vv 6-7). God's enemies will perish and be scattered (v 9) whereas the believers will be exalted and blessed. The righteous will have stability in their lives like a deep-rooted tree and will experience successful living even in old age as they proclaim the goodness of God and the fact that there is no wickedness in Him (vv 12-16).

Music was seen by the Jewish people as the ideal vehicle with which to offer praise (vv 1-4) and this tradition has been continued to the present day in Christian worship in songs like:

Now thank we all our God
With hearts and hands and voices,
Who wondrous things hath done,
In whom his world rejoices;
Who, from our mothers' arms,
Hath blessed us on our way
With countless gifts of love
And still is ours today.

O may this bounteous God
Through all our lives be near us
With ever-joyful hearts
And blessed peace to cheer us;
And keep us in His grace
And guide us when perplexed,
And free us from all ills
In this world and the next.

All praise and thanks to God
The Father now be given,
The Son, and Him who reigns
With them in highest heaven;
The one eternal God,
Whom earth and heaven adore,
For thus it was, is now,
And shall be evermore.

(Martin Rinckart).

Psalm 93

[1]The LORD reigns, he is robed in majesty;
the LORD is robed in majesty and is armed with strength.
The world is firmly established; it cannot be moved.
[2]Your throne was established long ago;
You are from all eternity.

148

³The seas have lifted up, O LORD,
the seas have lifted up their voice;
the seas have lifted up their pounding waves.
⁴Mightier than the thunder of the great waters,
mightier than the breakers of the sea—
the LORD on high is mighty.
⁵Your statutes stand firm;
holiness adorns your house for endless days, O LORD.

Reflections:

The psalmist proclaims the unending rule of God, His throne and the stability of the world which He has created (vv 1-3). His power is seen to be far beyond that of the waves, even when a ferocious storm is raging. Similarly the statutes of the Lord are impregnable, and His holiness is a changeless adornment.

This is the faith of a believer in times which may be good or bad. God remains the same! This can be found to be expressed in the hymn:

Abide with me, fast falls the eventide.
The darkness deepens, Lord with me abide;
When other helpers fail and comforts flee,
Help of the helpless, oh abide with me.

Swift to its close ebbs out life's little day,
Earth's joys grow dim, its glories pass away;
Change and decay in all around I see,
O Thou who changest not, abide with me.
I need Thy presence every passing hour,
What but Thy grace can foil the tempter's power?
Who like Thyself my guide and stay can be?
Through cloud and sunshine, O abide with me.

I fear no foe, with Thee at hand to bless;
Ills have no weight and tears no bitterness;
Where, death, thy sting? Where, grave, thy victory?
I triumph still if Thou abide with me.

Hold Thou Thy cross before my closing eyes,
Shine through the gloom and point me to the skies;
Heaven's morning breaks and earth's vain shadows flee;
In life, in death, O Lord, abide with me.

(H. F Lyte)

Psalm 94

¹O LORD, the God who avenges,
O God who avenges, shine forth.
²Rise up, O Judge of the earth;
pay back to the proud what they deserve.
³How long will the wicked, O LORD,
how long will the wicked be jubilant?
⁴They pour out arrogant words; all the evildoers are full of boasting.
⁵They crush your people, O LORD; they oppress your inheritance.
⁶They slay the widow and the alien; they murder the fatherless.
⁷They say, "The LORD does not see; the God of Jacob pays no heed."
⁸Take heed, you senseless ones among the people;
you fools, when will you become wise?
⁹Does he who implanted the ear not hear?
Does he who formed the eye not see?
¹⁰Does he who disciplines nations not punish?
Does he who teaches man lack knowledge?
¹¹The LORD knows the thoughts of man;
he knows that they are futile.
¹²Blessed is the man You discipline, O LORD,
the man You teach from your law;
¹³You grant him relief from days of trouble,
till a pit is dug for the wicked.
¹⁴For the LORD will not reject his people;
he will never forsake his inheritance.
¹⁵Judgment will again be founded on righteousness,
and all the upright in heart will follow it.

[16]Who will rise up for me against the wicked?
Who will take a stand for me against evildoers?
[17]Unless the LORD had given me help,
I would soon have dwelt in the silence of death.
[18]When I said, "My foot is slipping,"
your love, O LORD, supported me.
[19]When anxiety was great within me,
your consolation brought joy to my soul.
[20]Can a corrupt throne be allied with You—
one that brings on misery by its decrees?
[21]They band together against the righteous
and condemn the innocent to death.
[22]But the LORD has become my fortress,
and my God the rock in whom I take refuge.
[23]He will repay them for their sins
and destroy them for their wickedness;
the LORD our God will destroy them.

Reflections:

This psalm raises the whole problem as to why there is so much suffering in the world, especially when good men and women suffer at the hands of the evil and wicked. This is also a problem posed in the prophecy of Habakkuk, who asks of God, "… Why then do You tolerate the treacherous? Why are You silent while the wicked swallow up those more righteous than themselves?" (Hab 1 v 13). The psalmist and the prophet can find no ultimate answer to this question. The psalmist is sure that the suffering of the righteous does not pass by the knowledge of God (vv 8-9). He can see that through such suffering the Lord is disciplining His people (v 10 and v 12). Such discipline is taught in the New Testament by the writer of the Letter to the Hebrews. He writes: "My son, do not make light of the Lord's discipline … because the Lord disciplines those he loves … endure hardship as discipline … God disciplines us for our good that we may share in his holiness" (see Hebrews chap 12 vv 5-12).

The psalmist is confident that, in the end, "the Lord will not reject his people; he will never forsake his inheritance." In the meantime the Lord gives His help (v 17) and God's love supports him. When anxiety is great within him the Lord's consolation brings joy to his soul (vv 17-19).

We can learn the lessons of the psalmist when we are going through trouble or even persecution from unbelievers in our daily lives.

Psalm 95

[1]Come, let us sing for joy to the LORD;
let us shout aloud to the Rock of our salvation.
[2]Let us come before him with thanksgiving
and extol him with music and song.
[3]For the LORD is the great God,
the great King above all gods.
[4]In his hand are the depths of the earth,
and the mountain peaks belong to him.
[5]The sea is his, for he made it, and his hands formed the dry land.
[6]Come, let us bow down in worship,
let us kneel before the LORD our Maker;
[7]for he is our God and we are the people of his pasture,
the flock under his care.
Today, if you hear his voice,
[8]do not harden your hearts as you did at Meribah,
as you did that day at Massah in the desert,
[9]where your fathers tested and tried me,
though they had seen what I did.
[10]For forty years I was angry with that generation;
I said, "They are a people whose hearts go astray,
and they have not known my ways."
[11]So I declared on oath in my anger,
"They shall never enter my rest."

Reflections:

This psalm is a call to worship the Lord God who is the Rock of our salvation, supreme in heaven and earth and the creator of the mountains and the seas. The psalmist reminds us that we are His people, "the people of his pasture and the flock under his care" (vv 1-7).

He then continues by urging God's people not to disobey His voice as they did in the desert at Meribah and Massah when they complained that God was not providing for their needs. On that occasion God spoke to the people through Moses and in the Old Testament he continues to speak to His people through those especially chosen by Him to be prophets. However, in the New Testament the writer of the Letter to the Hebrews states, "In the past God spoke to our forefathers through the prophets ... but in these last days he has spoken to us by his Son, [Jesus] whom he appointed heir of all things and through whom he made the universe" (chap 1 vv1-2) and he quotes this psalm, warning listeners not to harden their hearts as they did in the rebellion (chap 3 vv 14-15). So, as Christians, we hear God's voice through the words and works of Jesus. To 'harden one's heart' means to rebel against God's words and to completely ignore them.

We can, however, go further than even 'Hebrews' teaches, for God in these days will speak to each one of us individually in our daily lives (See Jeremiah 31 vv 33-34). We pray with the hymn writer: "Master, speak, Thy servant heareth,/ waiting for Thy gracious word" (Frances Ridley Havergal). When we hear, let us obey, and align our will with His, as Mary did when she said, "May it be to me as you have said." (Luke 1 v 38).

Psalm 96

¹Sing to the LORD a new song;
sing to the LORD, all the earth.
²Sing to the LORD, praise his name;
proclaim his salvation day after day.

*3Declare his glory among the nations,
his marvellous deeds among all peoples.
4For great is the LORD and most worthy of praise;
he is to be feared above all gods.
5For all the gods of the nations are idols,
but the LORD made the heavens.
6Splendour and majesty are before him;
strength and glory are in his sanctuary.
7Ascribe to the LORD, O families of nations,
ascribe to the LORD glory and strength.
8Ascribe to the LORD the glory due his name;
bring an offering and come into his courts.
9Worship the LORD in the splendour of his holiness;
tremble before him, all the earth.
10Say among the nations, "The LORD reigns."
The world is firmly established, it cannot be moved;
he will judge the peoples with equity.
11Let the heavens rejoice, let the earth be glad;
let the sea resound, and all that is in it;
12let the fields be jubilant, and everything in them.
Then all the trees of the forest will sing for joy;
13they will sing before the LORD, for he comes,
he comes to judge the earth.
He will judge the world in righteousness
and the peoples in his truth.*

Reflections:

This psalm is another call to worship the Lord God. The psalmist calls upon all heavens and earth to praise Him (vv 1-2, 4, 11-13). Especially he calls upon the "families of the nations" to worship the Lord "in the splendour of his holiness" (v 7). It is this holiness of God which makes people tremble (v 9). The psalmist does even more than call God's people to worship Him. They are to **proclaim** God's glory amongst the nations — they are to engage in witnessing to all mankind the glory of God (v 3). There is also to be a **response** to God's glory and holiness; people are to bring an offering to His courts (the temple). The New Testament teaches that since Jesus died upon the cross, making a perfect sacrifice to God, animal sacrifices no longer suffice or are required by

God (see Hebrews chapters 8-10). Christians are now required daily to offer their whole beings to God as a '*living sacrifice*' in response to all He has done for us in saving us from our sins, through Jesus Christ (Romans 12 v 1). Finally the psalmist states that God will come, in the end, to judge mankind. This judgment for Christians is in, through and by Jesus Christ (Matt chap 25 vv 31-46).

Psalm 97

¹The LORD reigns, let the earth be glad;
let the distant shores rejoice.
²Clouds and thick darkness surround him;
righteousness and justice are the foundation of his throne.
³Fire goes before him and consumes his foes on every side.
⁴His lightning lights up the world; the earth sees and trembles.
⁵The mountains melt like wax before the LORD,
before the Lord of all the earth.
⁶The heavens proclaim his righteousness,
and all the peoples see his glory.

⁷All who worship images are put to shame,
those who boast in idols—worship him, all you gods!
⁸Zion hears and rejoices and the villages of Judah are glad
because of your judgments, O LORD.
⁹For You, O LORD, are the Most High over all the earth;
You are exalted far above all gods.
¹⁰Let those who love the LORD hate evil,
for he guards the lives of his faithful ones
and delivers them from the hand of the wicked.
¹¹Light is shed upon the righteous
and joy on the upright in heart.
¹²Rejoice in the LORD, you who are righteous,
and praise his holy name.

Reflections:

The psalmist proclaims the absolute sovereignty of God in heaven and earth (vv 1,7,9). He also paints a picture of His awesomeness (v 2-5). These attributes of God can be seen in the heavens (v 6). The people of God rejoice in this truth about the nature of God because He is actually ***their*** God whom they can love (v 10). Knowledge of Him demands hating all that is evil (v 10) because God delivers and vindicates all that is good (vv 10-12). Knowledge that we have of this our God will in fact guard and guide our everyday lives.

Psalm 98

¹Sing to the LORD a new song, for he has done marvellous things;
his right hand and his holy arm have worked salvation for him.
²The LORD has made his salvation known
and revealed his righteousness to the nations.
³He has remembered his love
and his faithfulness to the house of Israel;
all the ends of the earth have seen the salvation of our God.
⁴Shout for joy to the LORD, all the earth,
burst into jubilant song with music;
⁵make music to the LORD with the harp,
with the harp and the sound of singing,
⁶with trumpets and the blast of the ram's horn—
shout for joy before the LORD, the King.
⁷Let the sea resound, and everything in it,
the world, and all who live in it.
⁸Let the rivers clap their hands,
let the mountains sing together for joy;
⁹let them sing before the LORD, for he comes to judge the earth.
He will judge the world in righteousness
and the peoples with equity.

Reflections:

The psalmist declares that God is the Saviour of His people through
"his right hand and his holy arm" (v 1). He has provided this salvation
from all that would assail his people and made it known to the ends of
the earth (vv 2-3). The psalmist calls all peoples of the earth to worship
this saving God with harps, singing, trumpets and horns. They are to
shout for joy before the Lord, the King (v 4-6). The creation itself is
bidden to join in this praise because God will judge mankind with
scrupulous fairness. Christians, in fact, know of a greater salvation than
ever the psalmist could have conceived, even though spiritually
receptive men such as this psalmist saw Israel as within God's timing,
i.e. poised between God's past and His future. It would be that wrought
in the life, death and resurrection of God's Son, Jesus Christ which
annuls the power of sin and brings believers peace with God (see
Romans 8). This is a cause for praise every day of a believer's life on
earth and, after that, in heaven.

Psalm 99

¹The LORD reigns, let the nations tremble;
he sits enthroned between the cherubim,
let the earth shake.
²Great is the LORD in Zion; he is exalted over all the nations.
³Let them praise your great and awesome name—
he is holy.
⁴The King is mighty, he loves justice—
You have established equity;
in Jacob You have done what is just and right.
⁵Exalt the LORD our God and worship at his footstool;
he is holy.

⁶Moses and Aaron were among his priests,
Samuel was among those who called on his name;
they called on the LORD and he answered them.
⁷He spoke to them from the pillar of cloud;
they kept his statutes and the decrees he gave them.
⁸O LORD our God, You answered them;
You were to Israel a forgiving God,
though You punished their misdeeds.
⁹Exalt the LORD our God
and worship at his holy mountain,
for the LORD our God is holy.

Reflections:

Here the psalmist exalts Zion (Jerusalem) and the temple, which was evidently still standing when he wrote. He conceives the Lord as sovereign and holy and that He dwells in the temple, between the cherubim (v 1). He calls all nations to worship Him. The psalmist reminds his hearers that the Lord spoke to Israel through Moses, Aaron and Samuel and they kept His statutes. God is acknowledged as a forgiving God, although He punishes people for their misdeeds.

We have seen this picture of the supremacy of God before in the psalms. What it means for us is that we should give Him the utmost and first priority in all that concerns our daily lives.

Psalm 100

¹Shout for joy to the LORD, all the earth.
²Worship the LORD with gladness;
come before him with joyful songs.
³Know that the LORD is God.
It is he who made us, and we are his;
we are his people, the sheep of his pasture.

158

⁴Enter his gates with thanksgiving and his courts with praise;
give thanks to him and praise his name.
⁵For the LORD is good and his love endures for ever;
his faithfulness continues through all generations.

Reflections:

This, like psalm 95, is a call to worship God, indeed to shout for joy and worship Him with gladness and joyful songs (v 1). There is nothing morbid about worshipping the true God both then and now. The psalmist reiterates the statement that God is like a shepherd and we are His sheep (See psalm 23) and that because of this we should praise Him and thank Him for all His goodness, His love and His faithfulness.
As Charles Wesley taught Methodists to sing:

> Thou Shepherd of Israel, and mine,
> The joy and desire of my heart,
> For closer communion I pine,
> I long to reside where Thou art.
> The pasture I languish to find
> Where all, who their Shepherd obey
> Are fed, on Thy bosom reclined
> And screened from the heat of the day.
>
> 'Tis there, with the lambs of Thy flock,
> There only I covet to rest,
> To lie at the foot of the rock,
> Or rise to be hid in Thy breast.

Psalm 101
(A psalm of David)

¹I will sing of your love and justice;
to You, O LORD, I will sing praise.
²I will be careful to lead a blameless life—
when will You come to me?
I will walk in my house with blameless heart.

³I will set before my eyes no vile thing.
The deeds of faithless men I hate; they will not cling to me.
⁴Men of perverse heart shall be far from me;
I will have nothing to do with evil.
⁵Whoever slanders his neighbour in secret,
him will I put to silence;
whoever has haughty eyes and a proud heart,
him will I not endure.
⁶My eyes will be on the faithful in the land,
that they may dwell with me;
he whose walk is blameless will minister to me.
⁷No one who practises deceit will dwell in my house;
no one who speaks falsely will stand in my presence.
⁸Every morning I will put to silence all the wicked in the land;
I will cut off every evildoer from the city of the LORD.

Reflections:

This is a psalm of King David about how he pledges to live and reign as King in relation to God.

v.1. He will sing about God's love and justice.

v.2. He will be careful to lead a blameless life.

v.3. He will set no vile thing before his eyes and the deeds of faithless men will not be allowed to cling to him.

v.4. Men of perverse heart will be far from him and he will have nothing to do with evil.

v.5. He will put to silence all who slander their neighbours and he will not endure proud and haughty people.

v.6. He will look upon and have fellowship with the faithful and those who live blamelessly.

v.7. No one who practises deceit will dwell in his house and no one who speaks lies will stand in his presence.

v.8. As king he will put to silence all the wicked in the land and cut off evildoers from the city of the Lord (Jerusalem).

Verses 1-4 are applicable to Christians. In our everyday life we should live like this. Verses 5-7 need to be interpreted by Christians basically as opportunities for prayer. Under the New Covenant we are called upon to reach out in love to those who flout God's laws, but in such a way that we do not join them in sinful behaviour. In many cases the best way to help them is to pray regularly for them.

Psalm 102

¹Hear my prayer, O LORD; let my cry for help come to You.
²Do not hide your face from me when I am in distress.
Turn your ear to me; when I call, answer me quickly.
³For my days vanish like smoke;
my bones burn like glowing embers.
⁴My heart is blighted and withered like grass;
I forget to eat my food.
⁵Because of my loud groaning I am reduced to skin and bones.
⁶I am like a desert owl, like an owl among the ruins.
⁷I lie awake; I have become like a bird alone on a roof.
⁸All day long my enemies taunt me;
those who rail against me use my name as a curse.
⁹For I eat ashes as my food and mingle my drink with tears
¹⁰because of your great wrath,
for You have taken me up and thrown me aside.
¹¹My days are like the evening shadow; I wither away like grass.
¹²But You, O LORD, sit enthroned for ever;
your renown endures through all generations.
¹³You will arise and have compassion on Zion,
for it is time to show favour to her;
the appointed time has come.
¹⁴For her stones are dear to your servants;
her very dust moves them to pity.

¹⁵The nations will fear the name of the L<small>ORD</small>,
all the kings of the earth will revere your glory.
¹⁶For the L<small>ORD</small> will rebuild Zion and appear in his glory.
¹⁷He will respond to the prayer of the destitute;
he will not despise their plea.
¹⁸Let this be written for a future generation,
that a people not yet created may praise the L<small>ORD</small>:

¹⁹"The L<small>ORD</small> looked down from his sanctuary on high,
from heaven he viewed the earth,
²⁰to hear the groans of the prisoners
and release those condemned to death."

²¹So the name of the L<small>ORD</small> will be declared in Zion
and his praise in Jerusalem
²²when the peoples and the kingdoms assemble to worship the L<small>ORD</small>.
²³In the course of my life he broke my strength; he cut short my days.
²⁴So I said: "Do not take me away, O my God, in the midst of my days;
your years go on through all generations.
²⁵In the beginning You laid the foundations of the earth,
and the heavens are the work of your hands.
²⁶They will perish, but You remain;
they will all wear out like a garment.
Like clothing You will change them and they will be discarded.
²⁷But You remain the same, and your years will never end.
²⁸The children of your servants will live in your presence;
their descendants will be established before You."

Reflections:

This psalm is entitled "A prayer of an afflicted man when he is faint and pours out his lament before the Lord."

Verses 1-11 describe the terrible depths into which he has fallen. He is suffering in body, mind and spirit, and his enemies taunt him. This reminds us of the sufferings of Job and in our ministry of healing my wife Anne and myself have met many people who are in the same terrible state as the psalmist.

His tone changes from verse 12 when he meditates on the fact that the Lord sits "enthroned for ever" and God's renown "endures through all generations".   He has faith to believe that God is a God of compassion   (v 13) and that He is able to restore the fortunes of Zion; also that all nations will one day fear the name of the Lord and revere His glory   (vv 13-15). God can be trusted to respond to the prayer of the destitute (v. 17).

The psalmist wants this truth about God's love, compassion and power to be passed down to all generations as he asserts the unchangeable nature of God and that this is above and beyond the transitory nature of His creation (vv 18-28).

We do well to meditate on all these truths about God when affliction visits us and we can trust that God will answer our prayer and listen to our cries for help.

Psalm 103
(A psalm of David)

¹Praise the LORD, O my soul;
all my inmost being, praise his holy name.
²Praise the LORD, O my soul, and forget not all his benefits—
³who forgives all your sins
and heals all your diseases,
⁴who redeems your life from the pit
and crowns you with love and compassion,
⁵who satisfies your desires with good things
so that your youth is renewed like the eagle's.

⁶The LORD works righteousness
and justice for all the oppressed.

⁷He made known his ways to Moses, his deeds to the people of Israel:
⁸The LORD is compassionate and gracious,
slow to anger, abounding in love.
⁹He will not always accuse, nor will he harbour his anger for ever;

163

¹⁰*he does not treat us as our sins deserve*
or repay us according to our iniquities.
¹¹*For as high as the heavens are above the earth,*
so great is his love for those who fear him;
¹²*as far as the east is from the west,*
so far has he removed our transgressions from us.
¹³*As a father has compassion on his children,*
so the LORD *has compassion on those who fear him;*
¹⁴*for he knows how we are formed, he remembers that we are dust.*
¹⁵*As for man, his days are like grass,*
he flourishes like a flower of the field;
¹⁶*the wind blows over it and it is gone,*
and its place remembers it no more.
¹⁷*But from everlasting to everlasting*
the LORD*'s love is with those who fear him,*
and his righteousness with their children's children—
¹⁸*with those who keep his covenant*
and remember to obey his precepts.
¹⁹*The* LORD *has established his throne in heaven,*
and his kingdom rules over all.
²⁰*Praise the* LORD, *you his angels,*
you mighty ones who do his bidding, who obey his word.
²¹*Praise the* LORD, *all his heavenly hosts,*
you his servants who do his will.
²²*Praise the* LORD, *all his works*
everywhere in his dominion.

Praise the LORD, *O my soul.*

Reflections:

This psalm is a magnificent expression of praise to the Lord which arises from our inmost being. Like David, we should also praise the Lord from the depths of our hearts because:

v 3.   He forgives all our sins (v 3), removing them from us as far as the east is from the west (v 12).

v 3.   He heals all our diseases

v 4.   He saves us from early death

v 5.   He satisfies our desires with good things, so that our youth is renewed like the eagle's.

v 6.   He works righteousness and justice for all who are oppressed.

v 8-13. He is compassionate and gracious, slow to anger and abounding in love, especially to His children who fear Him.

vv 14-17. He remembers our weakness and finitude in His dealings with us and His love is also with those who fear Him.

v 19.   He is sovereign over all.

Like David we should, in the words of the Church of England Prayer Book "with angels and archangels and all the company of heaven, we praise Thy holy name" (vv 20-22). When we do so, visualising the innumerable saints and angels in Heaven and joining with them to praise God, we may sometimes find ourselves lifted up in a wonderful way as we experience the Divine presence.

Psalm 104

¹Praise the LORD, O my soul.
O LORD my God, You are very great;
You are clothed with splendour and majesty.

²He wraps himself in light as with a garment;
he stretches out the heavens like a tent
³and lays the beams of his upper chambers on their waters.
He makes the clouds his chariot and rides on the wings of the wind.
⁴He makes winds his messengers, flames of fire his servants.
⁵He set the earth on its foundations; it can never be moved.

⁶You covered it with the deep as with a garment;
the waters stood above the mountains.
⁷But at your rebuke the waters fled,
at the sound of your thunder they took to flight;

⁸*they flowed over the mountains, they went down into the valleys,*
to the place You assigned for them.
⁹*You set a boundary they cannot cross;*
never again will they cover the earth.
¹⁰*He makes springs pour water into the ravines;*
it flows between the mountains.
¹¹*They give water to all the beasts of the field;*
the wild donkeys quench their thirst.
¹²*The birds of the air nest by the waters;*
they sing among the branches.
¹³*He waters the mountains from his upper chambers;*
the earth is satisfied by the fruit of his work.
¹⁴*He makes grass grow for the cattle,*
and plants for man to cultivate—
bringing forth food from the earth:
¹⁵*wine that gladdens the heart of man,*
oil to make his face shine, and bread that sustains his heart.
¹⁶*The trees of the LORD are well watered,*
the cedars of Lebanon that he planted.
¹⁷*There the birds make their nests;*
the stork has its home in the pine trees.
¹⁸*The high mountains belong to the wild goats;*
the crags are a refuge for the conies.
¹⁹*The moon marks off the seasons,*
and the sun knows when to go down.
²⁰*You bring darkness, it becomes night,*
and all the beasts of the forest prowl.
²¹*The lions roar for their prey and seek their food from God.*
²²*The sun rises, and they steal away;*
they return and lie down in their dens.
²³*Then man goes out to his work, to his labour until evening.*

²⁴*How many are your works, O LORD! In wisdom You made them all;*
the earth is full of your creatures.
²⁵*There is the sea, vast and spacious,*
teeming with creatures beyond number—
living things both large and small.
²⁶*There the ships go to and fro,*
and the leviathan, which You formed to frolic there.

[27]*These all look to You to give them their food at the proper time.*
[28]*When You give it to them, they gather it up;*
when you open your hand, they are satisfied with good things.
[29]*When You hide your face, they are terrified;*
when You take away their breath, they die and return to the dust.
[30]*When You send your Spirit, they are created,*
and You renew the face of the earth.
[31]*May the glory of the LORD endure for ever;*
may the LORD rejoice in his works—
[32]*he who looks at the earth, and it trembles,*
who touches the mountains, and they smoke.
[33]*I will sing to the LORD all my life;*
I will sing praise to my God as long as I live.
[34]*May my meditation be pleasing to him,*
as I rejoice in the LORD.
[35]*But may sinners vanish from the earth and the wicked be no more.*

Praise the LORD, O my soul.

Praise the LORD. / Hallelujah.

Reflections:

The psalmist paints a wonderful picture of God's awesomeness, that greatness, His sovereignty and His power in relation to and as shown by all that He has created.

vv 1-4. He is clothed with splendour and majesty as seen in the heavens, the clouds and the wind.

vv 5-9. He has created the earth and given it absolute stability; this includes the seas and the rivers in their rightful place.
vv 10-18 He gives water to drink to all His creatures and trees in which the birds can nest. This water is basic to producing grass and man's food.

vv 19-23. He has created the sun and moon and determined when each shall give light for beasts and men to use.

167

vv 24-26. The psalmist marvels at the sea and all that goes on in it.

vv 27-30. God provides food for all He has created and is sovereign over life and death.

The psalmist declares that because of all these wonderful works of God he will sing to the Lord all his life and he will also meditate and rejoice (vv 31-35). The psalm ends with: "Hallelujah", which is translated in most Bibles as "Praise the Lord". I have added the Hebrew version here and in subsequent instances, as for many readers the word "Hallelujah" holds special significance.

All this is also indeed material for Christians to engage in fruitful praise and meditation, as for instance we find in John Keble's hymn:

> There is a book who runs may read,
> Which heavenly truth imparts,
> And all the lore its scholars need,
> Pure eyes and Christian hearts.
> The works of God above, below,
> Within us and around,
> Are pages in that book, to show
> How God Himself is found.
>
> The glorious sky, embracing all,
> Is like the Maker's love,
> Wherewith encompassed, great and small
> In peace and order move.
>
> One Name above all glorious names,
> With its ten thousand tongues
> The everlasting sea proclaims,
> Echoing angelic songs.

Two worlds are ours; 'tis only sin
Forbids us to descry
The mystic heaven and earth within,
Plain as the sea and sky.

Thou who hast given me eyes to see
And love this sight so fair,
Give me a heart to find out Thee
And read Thee everywhere.

Psalm 105

¹Give thanks to the LORD, call on his name;
make known among the nations what he has done.
²Sing to him, sing praise to him; tell of all his wonderful acts.
³Glory in his holy name;
let the hearts of those who seek the LORD rejoice.
⁴Look to the LORD and his strength;
seek his face always.
⁵Remember the wonders he has done,
his miracles, and the judgments he pronounced,
⁶O descendants of Abraham his servant,
O sons of Jacob, his chosen ones.
⁷He is the LORD our God; his judgments are in all the earth.
⁸He remembers his covenant for ever,
the word he commanded, for a thousand generations,
⁹The covenant he made with Abraham,
the oath he swore to Isaac.
¹⁰He confirmed it to Jacob as a decree,
to Israel as an everlasting covenant:
¹¹ "To you I will give the land of Canaan
as the portion you will inherit. "

[12]When they were but few in number,
few indeed, and strangers in it,
[13]they wandered from nation to nation,
from one kingdom to another.
[14]He allowed no one to oppress them;
for their sake he rebuked kings:
[15]"Do not touch my anointed ones; do my prophets no harm."
[16]He called down famine on the land
and destroyed all their supplies of food;
[17]and he sent a man before them— Joseph, sold as a slave.
[18]They bruised his feet with shackles, his neck was put in irons,
[19]till what he foretold came to pass,
till the word of the LORD proved him true.
[20]The king sent and released him,
the ruler of peoples set him free.
[21]He made him master of his household,
ruler over all he possessed,
[22]to instruct his princes as he pleased and teach his elders wisdom.

[23]Then Israel entered Egypt;
Jacob lived as an alien in the land of Ham.
[24]The LORD made his people very fruitful;
he made them too numerous for their foes,
[25]whose hearts he turned to hate his people,
to conspire against his servants.
[26]He sent Moses his servant, and Aaron, whom he had chosen.
[27]They performed his miraculous signs among them,
his wonders in the land of Ham.
[28]He sent darkness and made the land dark—
for had they not rebelled against his words?
[29]He turned their waters into blood, causing their fish to die.
[30]Their land teemed with frogs,
which went up into the bedrooms of their rulers.
[31]He spoke, and there came swarms of flies,
and gnats throughout their country.
[32]He turned their rain into hail,
with lightning throughout their land;
[33]he struck down their vines and fig trees
and shattered the trees of their country.

³⁴*He spoke, and the locusts came, grasshoppers without number;*
³⁵*they ate up every green thing in their land,*
ate up the produce of their soil.
³⁶*Then he struck down all the firstborn in their land,*
the first fruits of all their manhood.

³⁷*He brought out Israel, laden with silver and gold,*
and from among their tribes no one faltered.
³⁸*Egypt was glad when they left,*
because dread of Israel had fallen on them.
³⁹*He spread out a cloud as a covering,*
and a fire to give light at night.
⁴⁰*They asked, and he brought them quail*
and satisfied them with the bread of heaven.
⁴¹*He opened the rock, and water gushed out;*
like a river it flowed in the desert.
⁴²*For he remembered his holy promise*
given to his servant Abraham.
⁴³*He brought out his people with rejoicing,*
his chosen ones with shouts of joy;
⁴⁴ *he gave them the lands of the nations,*
and they fell heir to what others had toiled for—
⁴⁵*that they might keep his precepts and observe his laws.*

Praise the LORD. / Hallelujah.

Reflections:

This psalm describes all the wonders that God performed to bring His people from being 'nobodies' – 'wanderers' – into the promised land of Canaan. The psalmist bids all God's people to recall all that God did for His people and make it known to all the nations of the earth. God, the psalmist declares, did all this to be faithful to His covenant and the promise He made to Abraham – God will always keep His covenant and His promises, of that we can be as sure of in our day as was the psalmist.

What is different, however, for Christians is that God made a New Covenant with people of all nations through His Son Jesus Christ to bring us from being 'lost' to knowing His protection and guidance; to bring us to the promised eternal destination of which Canaan is but a shadow. This is well expressed in Charles Wesley's hymn:

None is like Jeshurun's God,
So great, so strong, so high;
Lo! He spreads His wings abroad,
He rides upon the sky.
Israel is His first-born son;
God, the almighty God, is thine.
See Him to thy help come down,
This excellence divine.

Thee the great Jehovah deigns
To succour and defend;
Thee the eternal God sustains,
Thy Maker and thy Friend;
Israel, what hast thou to dread?
Safe from all impending harms,
Round thee and beneath are spread
The everlasting arms.

God is thine: disdain to fear
The enemy within;
God shall in thy flesh appear
And make an end of sin;
God the man of sin shall slay,
Fill thee with triumphant joy,
God shall thrust him out, and say:
Destroy them all, destroy!

All the struggle then is o'er
And wars and fightings cease;
Israel then shall sin no more,
But dwell in perfect peace;
All his enemies are gone;
Sin shall have in him no part;
Israel now shall dwell alone
With Jesus in his heart.

Blest, O Israel, art thou!
What people is like thee?
Saved from sin by Jesus, now
Thou art and still shalt be;
Jesus is thy sevenfold shield,
Jesus is thy flaming sword;
Earth and hell, and sin shall yield
To God's almighty word.

Psalm 106

¹Praise the LORD. / Hallelujah.
Give thanks to the LORD, for he is good;
his love endures for ever.
²Who can proclaim the mighty acts of the LORD
or fully declare his praise?
³Blessed are they who maintain justice,
who constantly do what is right.
⁴Remember me, O LORD, when You show favour to your people,
come to my aid when You save them,
⁵that I may enjoy the prosperity of your chosen ones,
that I may share in the joy of your nation
and join your inheritance in giving praise.
⁶We have sinned, even as our fathers did;
we have done wrong and acted wickedly.
⁷When our fathers were in Egypt,
they gave no thought to your miracles;
they did not remember your many kindnesses,
and they rebelled by the sea, the Red Sea.
⁸Yet he saved them for his name's sake,
to make his mighty power known.
⁹He rebuked the Red Sea, and it dried up;
he led them through the depths as through a desert.

173

^{10}He saved them from the hand of the foe;
from the hand of the enemy he redeemed them.
^{11}The waters covered their adversaries; not one of them survived.
^{12}Then they believed his promises and sang his praise.
^{13}But they soon forgot what he had done
and did not wait for his counsel.
^{14}In the desert they gave in to their craving;
in the wasteland they put God to the test.
^{15}So he gave them what they asked for,
but sent a wasting disease upon them.
^{16}In the camp they grew envious of Moses
and of Aaron, who was consecrated to the LORD.
^{17}The earth opened up and swallowed Dathan;
it buried the company of Abiram.
^{18}Fire blazed among their followers; a flame consumed the wicked.
^{19}At Horeb they made a calf and worshipped an idol cast from metal.
^{20}They exchanged their Glory
for an image of a bull, which eats grass.
^{21}They forgot the God who saved them,
who had done great things in Egypt,
^{22}miracles in the land of Ham and awesome deeds by the Red Sea.
^{23}So he said he would destroy them—
had not Moses, his chosen one, stood in the breach before him
to keep his wrath from destroying them.
^{24}Then they despised the pleasant land;
they did not believe his promise.
^{25}They grumbled in their tents and did not obey the LORD.
^{26}So he swore to them with uplifted hand
that he would make them fall in the desert,
^{27}make their descendants fall among the nations
and scatter them throughout the lands.
^{28}They yoked themselves to the Baal of Peor
and ate sacrifices offered to lifeless gods;
^{29}they provoked the LORD to anger by their wicked deeds,
and a plague broke out among them.
^{30}But Phinehas stood up and intervened,
and the plague was checked.
^{31}This was credited to him as righteousness
for endless generations to come.

^{32}*By the waters of Meribah they angered the* L ORD,
and trouble came to Moses because of them;
^{33}*for they rebelled against the Spirit of God,*
and rash words came from Moses' lips.
^{34}*They did not destroy the peoples as the* L ORD *had commanded them,*
^{35}*but they mingled with the nations and adopted their customs.*
^{36}*They worshipped their idols, which became a snare to them.*
^{37}*They sacrificed their sons and their daughters to demons.*
^{38}*They shed innocent blood, the blood of their sons and daughters,*
whom they sacrificed to the idols of Canaan,
and the land was desecrated by their blood.
^{39}*They defiled themselves by what they did;*
by their deeds they prostituted themselves.
^{40}*Therefore the* L ORD *was angry with his people*
and abhorred his inheritance.
^{41}*He handed them over to the nations,*
and their foes ruled over them.
^{42}*Their enemies oppressed them and subjected them to their power.*
^{43}*Many times he delivered them,*
but they were bent on rebellion
and they wasted away in their sin.
^{44}*But he took note of their distress when he heard their cry;*
^{45}*for their sake he remembered his covenant*
and out of his great love he relented.
^{46}*He caused them to be pitied by all who held them captive.*
^{47}*Save us, O* L ORD *our God, and gather us from the nations,*
that we may give thanks to your holy name and glory in your praise.
^{48}*Praise be to the* L ORD, *the God of Israel,*
from everlasting to everlasting.
Let all the people say, "Amen!"

Praise the L ORD. */ Hallelujah.*

Reflections:

Unlike, and in contrast to, the author of psalm 105, this psalmist dwells on all the sins of mistrust, complaining and even rebellion against God on the part of the Hebrews both in their journey to the Promised Land and the early days of their dwelling there. The psalmist is not slow to say that "therefore the Lord was angry with His people" (v 40). We have to recognise in the Biblical revelation of the nature of God, especially in the Old Testament but also in the New, "for those who are self-seeking and who reject the truth and follow evil, there will be wrath and anger" (Romans 2 v 8). The Christian revelation is however in Paul's writings that not only the Jews, but also people of all nationalities – the Gentiles – have sinned against God and are under His condemnation (Romans 2 vv 9-16). However, Paul teaches the glorious fact that whilst God must continue to act justly against sinners, yet Jesus, when He died upon the Cross, bore all the righteous anger of a holy God towards sin and every individual sinner. Now therefore that justice has been satisfied God can, of His love and grace, freely pardon all who will put their trust in this great act. Thus God is both just and, at the same time, the justifier of all sinners (Romans 4 vv 5-11). This is the heart of the Christian Gospel as set forth in the hymn of Samuel Davies:

> Great God of wonders! All Thy ways
> Display the attributes divine:
> But countless acts of pardoning grace
> Beyond Thine other wonders shine
>
> *Who is a pardoning God like Thee?*
> *Or who has grace so rich and free?*
>
> In wonder lost, with trembling joy
> We take the pardon of our God:
> Pardon for crimes of deepest dye
> A pardon bought with Jesus' blood!
> Pardon – from an offended God!
> Pardon – for sins of deepest dye!
> Pardon – bestowed through Jesus' blood!
> Pardon – that brings the rebel nigh!

O may this strange, this matchless grace,
This God-like miracle of love,
Fill the wide earth with grateful praise,
As now it fills the choirs above!

Who is a pardoning God like Thee?
Or who has grace so rich and free?

Psalm 107

[1]Give thanks to the LORD, for he is good;
his love endures for ever.
[2]Let the redeemed of the LORD say this—
those he redeemed from the hand of the foe,
[3]those he gathered from the lands,
from east and west, from north and south.
[4]Some wandered in desert wastelands,
finding no way to a city where they could settle.
[5]They were hungry and thirsty, and their lives ebbed away.
[6]Then they cried out to the LORD in their trouble,
and he delivered them from their distress.
[7]He led them by a straight way to a city where they could settle.
[8]Let them give thanks to the LORD for his unfailing love
and his wonderful deeds for men,
[9]for he satisfies the thirsty and fills the hungry with good things.

[10]Some sat in darkness and the deepest gloom,
prisoners suffering in iron chains,
[11]for they had rebelled against the words of God
and despised the counsel of the Most High.
[12]So he subjected them to bitter labour;
they stumbled, and there was no one to help.

¹³*Then they cried to the* LORD *in their trouble,*
and he saved them from their distress.
¹⁴*He brought them out of darkness and the deepest gloom*
and broke away their chains.
¹⁵*Let them give thanks to the* LORD *for his unfailing love*
and his wonderful deeds for men,
¹⁶*for he breaks down gates of bronze*
and cuts through bars of iron.

¹⁷*Some became fools through their rebellious ways*
and suffered affliction because of their iniquities.
¹⁸*They loathed all food and drew near the gates of death.*
¹⁹*Then they cried to the* LORD *in their trouble,*
and he saved them from their distress.
²⁰*He sent forth his word and healed them;*
he rescued them from the grave.
²¹*Let them give thanks to the* LORD *for his unfailing love*
and his wonderful deeds for men.
²²*Let them sacrifice thank-offerings*
and tell of his works with songs of joy.

²³*Others went out on the sea in ships;*
they were merchants on the mighty waters.
²⁴*They saw the works of the* LORD,
his wonderful deeds in the deep.
²⁵*For he spoke and stirred up a tempest that lifted high the waves.*
²⁶*They mounted up to the heavens and went down to the depths;*
in their peril their courage melted away.
²⁷*They reeled and staggered like drunken men;*
they were at their wits' end.
²⁸*Then they cried out to the* LORD *in their trouble,*
and he brought them out of their distress.
²⁹*He stilled the storm to a whisper;*
the waves of the sea were hushed.
³⁰*They were glad when it grew calm,*
and he guided them to their desired haven.
³¹*Let them give thanks to the* LORD *for his unfailing love*
and his wonderful deeds for men.

³²*Let them exalt him in the assembly of the people*
and praise him in the council of the elders.
³³*He turned rivers into a desert, flowing springs into thirsty ground,*
³⁴*and fruitful land into a salt waste,*
because of the wickedness of those who lived there.
³⁵*He turned the desert into pools of water*
and the parched ground into flowing springs;
³⁶*there he brought the hungry to live,*
and they founded a city where they could settle.
³⁷*They sowed fields and planted vineyards*
that yielded a fruitful harvest;
³⁸*he blessed them, and their numbers greatly increased,*
and he did not let their herds diminish.
³⁹*Then their numbers decreased, and they were humbled*
by oppression, calamity and sorrow;
⁴⁰*he who pours contempt on nobles*
made them wander in a trackless waste.
⁴¹*But he lifted the needy out of their affliction*
and increased their families like flocks.
⁴²*The upright see and rejoice, but all the wicked shut their mouths.*
⁴³*Whoever is wise, let him heed these things*
and consider the great love of the LORD.

Reflections:

The theme which is reiterated throughout this psalm is: "Let them give thanks to the Lord" (vv 1,8,15,21,31). The psalmist bids us to give these thanks because of the way the Lord delivers people when they are in dire conditions or situations. These are:

a) When people are lost and our lives are ebbing away through hunger and thirst (v 5).
b) When people are in prison suffering in chains and irons (v 10).
c) When people are sick (v 20). And
d) When they are at sea and a terrible storm arises (vv 25-29).
e)

The instrument God uses for deliverance from sickness is His spoken word (v 20). This is the same way in which the Bible says He created all things: "God said" in Genesis 1.

Though the situations are completely out of man's control or ability to save themselves, yet they are no problem to God who has supreme authority and power to deliver people whatever their need might be. This gives us faith and hope for God's deliverance from any situation or peril we may meet in our daily lives.

The psalmist concludes by pointing out how God reverses or turns upside down the things which mankind regards as 'great'. This theme is reiterated in the Virgin Mary's song of praise – the Magnificat (See Luke 1 vv 46-55) and Paul's assertion that God has chosen the weak things of the world to confound the wise (See 1 Corinthians 1 vv 18 to 2 v 5). There is therefore no place in our Christian lives for haughtiness or false pride.

Psalm 108

(A psalm of David)

> [1]My heart is steadfast, O God;
> I will sing and make music with all my soul.
> [2]Awake, harp and lyre! I will awaken the dawn.
> [3]I will praise You, O LORD, among the nations;
> I will sing of You among the peoples.
> [4]For great is your love, higher than the heavens;
> your faithfulness reaches to the skies.
> [5]Be exalted, O God, above the heavens,
> and let your glory be over all the earth.
> [6]Save us and help us with your right hand,
> that those You love may be delivered.
> [7]God has spoken from his sanctuary:
> "In triumph I will parcel out Shechem
> and measure off the Valley of Succoth.

⁸Gilead is mine, Manasseh is mine;
Ephraim is my helmet, Judah my sceptre.
⁹Moab is my washbasin, upon Edom I toss my sandal;
over Philistia I shout in triumph."

¹⁰Who will bring me to the fortified city? Who will lead me to Edom?
¹¹Is it not You, O God, You who have rejected us
and no longer go out with our armies?
¹²Give us aid against the enemy, for the help of man is worthless.
¹³With God we will gain the victory,
and he will trample down our enemies.

Reflections:

This is a psalm of David when he asserts that the Israelites are God's special people and he speaks of God's word to each of the tribes (vv 6-9). He longs however to be brought by God to his capital, fortified city of Edom (v 10). He feels that God has however rejected His people (v 11). He prays that God will give His people help against their enemies (v 12). He is sure, absolutely confident that with God on their side, God's people will always be victorious (v 13). He can be sure of this help, for God's love is great – "higher than the heavens" (v 4) and this faithfulness "reaches to the skies" (v 4).

I am reminded of a song I learned when I was a student at Cliff Bible College, Derbyshire. When on mission all the students would parade through the streets singing:

> On the victory side
>
> On the victory side
>
> No foe can daunt us
> No fear can haunt us
> On the victory side —
> With Christ within
> The fight we'll win
> On the victory side!

181

Psalm 109

(A psalm of David)

¹O God, whom I praise, do not remain silent,
²for wicked and deceitful men have opened their mouths against me;
they have spoken against me with lying tongues.
³With words of hatred they surround me;
they attack me without cause.
⁴In return for my friendship they accuse me,
but I am a man of prayer.
⁵They repay me evil for good, and hatred for my friendship.

²¹But You, O Sovereign LORD, deal well with me
for your name's sake;
out of the goodness of your love, deliver me.
²²For I am poor and needy, and my heart is wounded within me.
²³I fade away like an evening shadow; I am shaken off like a locust.
²⁴My knees give way from fasting; my body is thin and gaunt.
²⁵I am an object of scorn to my accusers;
when they see me, they shake their heads.
²⁶Help me, O LORD my God;
save me in accordance with your love.
²⁷Let them know that it is your hand, that You, O LORD, have done it.
²⁸They may curse, but You will bless;
when they attack they will be put to shame,
but your servant will rejoice.
²⁹My accusers will be clothed with disgrace
and wrapped in shame as in a cloak.
³⁰With my mouth I will greatly extol the LORD;
in the great throng I will praise him.
³¹For he stands at the right hand of the needy one,
to save his life from those who condemn him.

Reflections:

In this psalm, according to the generally accepted translation, David wishes, even prays to God to render such evils to a man or men who are his enemies that no Christian, in the light of New Testament teaching could possibly utter – so I have omitted that particular section of the psalm from our considerations. However, if you wish to look up the passage in the New International Version of the Bible, you will see that verse 6 can be understood as reading: [They say:] "Appoint ..., closing the quotation marks at the end of verse 19.

The positive key to the psalm lies in verses 30-31 where David says that he will extol the Lord greatly in private and in public, "for he stands at the right hand of the needy one, to save his life from those who condemn him." Christians can be sure that God will uphold them when they are unjustly condemned by people of other religions or those bent on bringing them and their faith to ridicule. Many Christians today are in the position of having to work in close liaison with such people in their daily lives in secular employment. There are hose who will criticise, argue against or even ridicule a Christian who openly and unashamedly witnesses to his faith, in ungodly workplaces or even the armed forces; but they can be sure with David that God will uphold them and vindicate them against their adversaries.

Psalm 110

(A psalm of David)

The LORD says to my Lord:
"Sit at my right hand until I make your enemies
a footstool for your feet."
The LORD will extend your mighty sceptre from Zion;
you will rule in the midst of your enemies.
Your troops will be willing on your day of battle.
Arrayed in holy majesty, from the womb of the dawn
you will receive the dew of your youth.
The LORD has sworn and will not change his mind:
"You are a priest for ever, in the order of Melchizedek."

183

⁵The Lord is at your right hand;
he will crush kings on the day of his wrath.
⁶He will judge the nations, heaping up the dead
and crushing the rulers of the whole earth.
⁷He will drink from a brook beside the way;
therefore he will lift up his head.

Reflections:

This is a Messianic psalm, for in it David foretells the coming of Jesus Christ and the work He would do for man's salvation (v 1). This verse is actually quoted by our Lord in His dispute with the Pharisees about His superiority to King David (Matt 22 vv 41-44, Mark 12 v 36, Luke 20 v 42) and by Peter (Acts 2 v 34) to assert to the crowd which gathered on the day of Pentecost that "Therefore let all Israel be assured of this: God has made this Jesus, whom you crucified, both Lord and Christ" (Acts 2 v 36).

Then David mentions 'Melchizedek', the priest and king of Salem who met Abraham and blessed him and to whom Abraham gave a ttenth of all he possessed (Genesis 14 v 20).

The writer of the Letter to the Hebrews in the New Testament gives a lot of significance to the fact that Melchizedek was a precursor of Jesus Christ especially to the Lord's High Priesthood which role he fulfils in the heavenly realm (Hebrews 5 vv 6-10, 7 vv 1-17). The unknown writer of this letter (formerly erroneously attributed to Paul) teaches that Jesus Christ, by His death on the Cross and subsequent ascension to Heaven, is both victim and priest, offering the perfect sacrifice to God for the sins of humanity and who "always lives to intercede" for us (Hebrews 7 v 25).

This is a Christian's faith and hope. He knows also that every moment of day and night Jesus Christ is praying for him to the Father.

Psalm 111

[1]Praise the LORD. / Hallelujah.
I will extol the LORD with all my heart
in the council of the upright and in the assembly.
[2]Great are the works of the LORD;
they are pondered by all who delight in them.
[3]Glorious and majestic are his deeds,
and his righteousness endures for ever.
[4]He has caused his wonders to be remembered;
the LORD is gracious and compassionate.
[5]He provides food for those who fear him;
he remembers his covenant for ever.
[6]He has shown his people the power of his works,
giving them the lands of other nations.
[7]The works of his hands are faithful and just;
all his precepts are trustworthy.
[8]They are steadfast for ever and ever,
done in faithfulness and uprightness.
[9]He provided redemption for his people;
he ordained his covenant for ever—
holy and awesome is his name.

[10]The fear of the LORD is the beginning of wisdom;
all who follow his precepts have good understanding.
To him belongs eternal praise.

Reflections:

This is a psalm of praise to God for all His wondrous deeds which He has performed for the wellbeing of His people. It is a good thing to praise God as an individual in one's own prayer time but it is even more wonderful when a whole congregation of God's people praise Him together. Such praise certainly reaches the heavenly realm and is pleasing to God. The sacrament of Holy Communion isn't only an act of remembrance for all God has accomplished in Christ for the redemption of His people and a re-enactment of the New Covenant He has established with them through the shedding of Christ's Blood; it is also a great act of thanksgiving and praise for this great act. The

185

Anglican and Catholic liturgies declare that "with angels and archangels and with all the company of heaven we praise and magnify Thy Holy Name."

Like the psalmist we should not only remember this great act of salvation, but 'ponder' (slowly reflect) on all that Christ has done for us recorded in the four Gospels as a daily act of meditation (vv 2-9).

The psalmist also asserts that "the fear of the Lord is the beginning of wisdom" (v 10). This is not a matter of living in some sort of terror of God but rather means 'reverencing' God in our daily lives; then we shall live wisely, living lives which are in communion with God and pleasing to Him. We shall not go wrong in our lives if we live in constant reverence for the laws, especially the law of the love for God and our fellow men and women.

The psalm ends fittingly with the declaration that "to him belongs eternal praise"! (v 10).

Psalm 112

¹Praise the LORD. / Hallelujah.
Blessed is the man who fears the LORD,
who finds great delight in his commands.
²His children will be mighty in the land;
the generation of the upright will be blessed.
³Wealth and riches are in his house,
and his righteousness endures for ever.
⁴Even in darkness light dawns for the upright,
for the gracious and compassionate and righteous man.
⁵Good will come to him who is generous and lends freely,
who conducts his affairs with justice.
⁶Surely he will never be shaken;
a righteous man will be remembered for ever.
⁷He will have no fear of bad news;
his heart is steadfast, trusting in the LORD.
⁸His heart is secure, he will have no fear;
in the end he will look in triumph on his foes.

⁹He has scattered abroad his gifts to the poor,
his righteousness endures for ever;
his horn will be lifted high in honour.
¹⁰The wicked man will see and be vexed,
he will gnash his teeth and waste away;
the longings of the wicked will come to nothing.

Reflections:
:

Once again as in psalm 111 we meet with the mindset of "fearing the Lord" (v 1), which we can remind ourselves means living with a continual reverence and respect for Him, but this time we find that such a person "delights" in His commands (v 1). To live keeping God's commandments is not therefore an irksome task, making life difficult, rather living like this brings a person real happiness (the meaning of 'blessed' v 1). Such a person will find that God meets all his material needs (see Philippians 4 v 19). Jesus promised also that all who follow Him shall not walk in darkness, but have "the light of life" (John 8 v 12). This means that such a person will have real purpose in his life and not live going around in circles, getting nowhere.

The psalmist lists some of the deeds of a righteous man (v 5) and says that such a person will be secure in his life and "be remembered for ever" (vv 6 & 9). It is certainly customary at a funeral service for someone who knew the deceased well to give a 'eulogy' remembering all his or her goodness and good deeds. There are however 'heroes of faith' like William Tyndale, John Wesley, Florence Nightingale and many more whose outstandingly good deeds coming out of their Christian faith are indeed remembered from generation to generation and serve as examples for us in our daily lives. To live the Christian life, in close communion with God is the most secure state to be in and have no fear (v 8). In the light of eternity wickedness is self destructive and is to be avoided at all costs as we walk the Christian way through life.

Psalm 113

¹Praise the LORD. / Hallelujah.

Praise, O servants of the LORD, praise the name of the LORD.
²Let the name of the LORD be praised, both now and for evermore.
³From the rising of the sun to the place where it sets,
the name of the LORD is to be praised.
⁴The LORD is exalted over all the nations,
his glory above the heavens.
⁵Who is like the LORD our God,
the One who sits enthroned on high,
⁶who stoops down to look on the heavens and the earth?
⁷He raises the poor from the dust
and lifts the needy from the ash heap;
⁸he seats them with princes, with the princes of their people.
⁹He settles the barren woman in her home
as a happy mother of children.
Praise the LORD. / Hallelujah.

Reflections:

Verses 1-3 are echoed in the well-known Christian hymn by John Ellerton:

> The day Thou gavest, Lord, is ended,
> The darkness falls at Thy behest;
> To Thee our morning hymns ascended,
> Thy praise shall sanctify our rest.
>
> We thank Thee that Thy church, unsleeping,
> While earth rolls onward into light,
> Through all the world her watch is keeping,
> And rests not now by day or night.
>
> As o'er each continent and island
> The dawn leads on another day,
> The voice of prayer is never silent,
> Nor dies the strain of praise away.

> The sun that bids us rest is waking
> Our brethren 'neath the western sky,
> And hour by hour fresh lips are making
> Thy wondrous doings heard on high.
>
> So be it, Lord; Thy throne shall never,
> Like earth's proud empires, pass away;
> Thy kingdom stands, and grows for ever,
> Till all Thy creatures own Thy sway.

Further the psalmist states that although God is truly transcendent as He "sits enthroned on high", yet He is also omnipresent everywhere, not far from the life of mankind and every individual believer, and His knowledge of this life is absolute (vv 4-6).

Verses 7-9 are again echoed in a Christian hymn, but this time a biblical one – the Magnificat – the song of Mary when it was made known to her that she would give birth to the Son of God:

> My soul proclaims the greatness of the Lord,
> my spirit rejoices in God my Saviour;
> he has looked with favour on his lowly servant.
> From this day all generations will call me blessed;
> the Almighty has done great things for me
> and holy is his name.
> He has mercy on those who fear him,
> from generation to generation.
> He has shown strength with his arm
> and has scattered the proud in their conceit,
> casting down the mighty from their thrones
> and lifting up the lowly.
> He has filled the hungry with good things
> and sent the rich away empty.
> He has come to the aid of his servant Israel,
> to remember his promise of mercy,
> the promise made to our ancestors,
> to Abraham and his children for ever.

189

The fact that God is truly cognisant of all our lives and knows all about what we are doing is a fact in the light of which every Christian life should be lived. And we can rejoice in the fact that, as a perfect Father, His interest in us is for our highest good.

Psalm 114

[1]When Israel came out of Egypt,
the house of Jacob from a people of foreign tongue,
[2]Judah became God's sanctuary, Israel his dominion.
[3]The sea looked and fled,
the Jordan turned back;
[4]the mountains skipped like rams,
the hills like lambs.
[5]Why was it, O sea, that you fled,
O Jordan, that you turned back,
[6]you mountains, that you skipped like rams,
you hills, like lambs?
[7]Tremble, O earth, at the presence of the Lord,
at the presence of the God of Jacob,
[8]who turned the rock into a pool,
the hard rock into springs of water.

Reflections:

The psalmist recalls God's great act in delivering the Hebrew people from slavery in Egypt. He especially remembers the way in which God divided the waters firstly of the Red Sea (v 3a), then secondly of the river Jordan (v 3b) so that His people crossed on dry land. He also recalls how the Lord had used Moses to strike hard rock with his rod and water poured out to quench the thirst of His chosen people (Exodus 14, Joshua 3 and Exodus 17). Christians believe that the great God of the Universe who is Lord over all nature, truly did this, but even more remember and give God thanks daily for the great 'exodus' ('deliverance') which He wrought for them in delivering them from their sins in the life, death, resurrection and ascension of their Lord, Jesus Christ.

Psalm 115

¹Not to us, O LORD, not to us but to your name be the glory,
because of your love and faithfulness.

²Why do the nations say, "Where is their God?"
³Our God is in heaven; he does whatever pleases him.
⁴But their idols are silver and gold,
made by the hands of men.
⁵They have mouths, but cannot speak,
eyes, but they cannot see;
⁶they have ears, but cannot hear,
noses, but they cannot smell;
⁷they have hands, but cannot feel,
feet, but they cannot walk;
nor can they utter a sound with their throats.
⁸Those who make them will be like them,
and so will all who trust in them.

⁹O house of Israel, trust in the LORD—
he is their help and shield.
¹⁰O house of Aaron, trust in the LORD—
he is their help and shield.
¹¹You who fear him, trust in the LORD—
he is their help and shield.

¹²The LORD remembers us and will bless us:
He will bless the house of Israel, he will bless the house of Aaron,
¹³he will bless those who fear the LORD—small and great alike.
¹⁴May the LORD make you increase, both you and your children.

191

15May you be blessed by the LORD, the Maker of heaven and earth.
16The highest heavens belong to the LORD,
but the earth he has given to man.
17It is not the dead who praise the LORD,
those who go down to silence;
18it is we who extol the LORD, both now and for evermore.

Praise the LORD. / Hallelujah.

Reflections:

In every generation there have been those who have denied the existence of a living, active God. In Theological College in the 1950s I was introduced to the 'God is Dead' theology propounded by the German philosopher Nietzsche, who stated that God never existed. In recent times the book by Richard Dawkins, 'The God Delusion' has been a best seller and again states that God does not exist. The psalmist lived in days when the same beliefs were held (v 2). In the days of our Old Testament those who denied belief in a living, spiritual Person Jehovah, turned to the worship of idols, a worship which is scorned by the psalmist (vv 4-7). On the contrary he declares that "our God is in heaven; he does whatever pleases him" (v 3). In our day the belief that there is no God inevitably leads to a life of materialism because there is, in fact, no other reason for living, except to extol what our senses can apprehend.

The psalmist bids his people to worship the true God, Yahweh, to trust Him and reverence Him and then this living God will bless them. He declares that it is not the dead who will praise Him, but those who are alive and therefore can be conscious of Him. Christians, however, expand the beliefs of the psalmist and assert that those who have died in the faith of God are, in fact, still alive and in heaven still sing their praises to God (see Revelation chapter 7).

To live daily with belief in a living, spiritual Person who is our Father in Heaven pervades the whole of the life of Christians for whom to be "absent from the body" is to be "present with the Lord" (see Philippians 1 vv 18-26).

Psalm 116

^{1}*I love the LORD, for he heard my voice;*
he heard my cry for mercy.
^{2}*Because he turned his ear to me,*
I will call on him as long as I live.
^{3}*The cords of death entangled me,*
the anguish of the grave came upon me;
I was overcome by trouble and sorrow.
^{4}*Then I called on the name of the LORD:*
"O LORD, save me!"
^{5}*The LORD is gracious and righteous;*
our God is full of compassion.
^{6}*The LORD protects the simple-hearted;*
when I was in great need, he saved me.
^{7}*Be at rest once more, O my soul,*
for the LORD has been good to you.
^{8}*For You, O LORD, have delivered my soul from death,*
my eyes from tears, my feet from stumbling,
^{9}*that I may walk before the LORD in the land of the living.*
^{10}*I believed; therefore I said, "I am greatly afflicted."*
^{11}*And in my dismay I said, "All men are liars."*
^{12}*How can I repay the LORD for all his goodness to me?*
^{13}*I will lift up the cup of salvation and call on the name of the LORD.*
^{14}*I will fulfil my vows to the LORD in the presence of all his people.*
^{15}*Precious in the sight of the LORD is the death of his saints.*
^{16}*O LORD, truly I am your servant;*
I am your servant, the son of your maidservant;
You have freed me from my chains.
^{17}*I will sacrifice a thank-offering to You*
and call on the name of the LORD.
^{18}*I will fulfil my vows to the LORD in the presence of all his people,*
^{19}*in the courts of the house of the LORD—in your midst, O Jerusalem.*

Praise the LORD. / Hallelujah.

Reflections:

There is nothing in the Bible or Christian experience to suggest that believers will be immune from any of the cares, situations or afflictions which can assail anyone in their journey through life on earth. If it were so then we would not be short of believers! On the contrary Jesus warned that His followers might, along with all this, be subjected to more pain than unbelievers as they could well experience persecution from non-Christians. However, Jesus has promised to be with us at all times, so He will help us as a friend. Peter, in his first Letter, says: "Cast all your anxiety on him because he cares for you" (1 Peter 5 v 7).

This psalmist had been in dire trouble, perhaps having suffered from a terminal illness (v 3). He had cried out to the Lord God for deliverance from his affliction and had been healed. Christians too pray either individually or corporately for God to answer prayer when they are sick, and their experience is that God frequently heals in response to prayer they have offered themselves or when they have called other believers to pray for them and/or when they have received Divine ministry from the elders of their church (James 5) or from one whom God has endowed with a gift of healing (1 Cor 12).

Experience shows how easy it is for Christians who have been healed to forget to do what this psalmist did and thank God from the bottom of their hearts. How then should we express our gratitude to God? The Book of Common Prayer rightly says that we should do so "not only with our lips but also in our lives by giving up ourselves to your service and by walking before You in holiness and righteousness all the days of our lives" (Prayer of General Thanksgiving).

Psalm 117

¹Praise the LORD, all you nations;
extol him, all you peoples.
²For great is his love toward us,
and the faithfulness of the LORD endures for ever.

Praise the LORD. / Hallelujah.

Reflections:

This is a short, simple, yet profound expression of praise which a Christian or Christians can use on any and every occasion of thanksgiving to God. In it the believers look beyond themselves and bid all nations to praise the Lord (v 1) for His love and faithfulness which endure for ever.

Psalm 118

¹Give thanks to the LORD, for he is good;
his love endures for ever.
²Let Israel say: "His love endures for ever."
³Let the house of Aaron say: "His love endures for ever."
⁴Let those who fear the LORD say: "His love endures for ever."

⁵In my anguish I cried to the LORD,
and he answered by setting me free.
⁶The LORD is with me; I will not be afraid. What can man do to me?
⁷The LORD is with me; he is my helper.
I will look in triumph on my enemies.
⁸It is better to take refuge in the LORD than to trust in man.
⁹It is better to take refuge in the LORD than to trust in princes.
¹⁰All the nations surrounded me,
but in the name of the LORD I cut them off.
¹¹They surrounded me on every side,
but in the name of the LORD I cut them off.
¹²They swarmed around me like bees,
but they died out as quickly as burning thorns;
in the name of the LORD I cut them off.
¹³I was pushed back and about to fall, but the LORD helped me.
¹⁴The LORD is my strength and my song;
he has become my salvation.
¹⁵Shouts of joy and victory resound in the tents of the righteous:
"The LORD's right hand has done mighty things!

¹⁶The LORD's right hand is lifted high;
the LORD's right hand has done mighty things!"
¹⁷I will not die but live,
and will proclaim what the LORD has done.
¹⁸The LORD has chastened me severely,
but he has not given me over to death.
¹⁹Open for me the gates of righteousness;
I will enter and give thanks to the LORD.
²⁰This is the gate of the LORD
through which the righteous may enter.
²¹I will give You thanks, for You answered me;
You have become my salvation.
²²The stone the builders rejected has become the capstone;
²³the LORD has done this, and it is marvellous in our eyes.
²⁴This is the day the LORD has made;
let us rejoice and be glad in it.
²⁵O LORD, save us; O LORD, grant us success.
²⁶Blessed is he who comes in the name of the LORD.
From the house of the LORD we bless you.
²⁷The LORD is God, and he has made his light shine upon us.
With boughs in hand, join in the festal procession
up to the horns of the altar.
²⁸You are my God, and I will give You thanks;
You are my God, and I will exalt You.

²⁹Give thanks to the LORD, for he is good;
his love endures for ever

Reflections:

What should we think, what should we do and what should our attitude
be as believers, when, like this psalmist, we are in terrible trouble?

i.   We should remember that however we may be feeling and
     thinking, the objective fact is that God is love (vv 1-4,29).

ii. We should recognise that through this trouble God may be
     chastening us to deepen our hope, faith, our holiness and
     our sympathy for others who are in trouble. As Paul says, "we

also rejoice in our sufferings, because we know that suffering produces perseverance; perseverance character; and character, hope. And hope does not disappoint us, because God has poured out his love into our hearts by the Holy Spirit; whom he has given us" (Rom 5 vv 3-5) (v 18).

iii. We should not be afraid what man can do to us (v 6).

iv. Remember that the Lord and not man ultimately is our helper (vv 7-9).

v. Remember that the Lord is our strength and our song and has indeed become our salvation (v 14).

vi. Trust in the Lord's mighty hand (vv 15-16).

vii. Remember that though man may reject us, God will vindicate us (vv 22-23) (a verse quoted by our Lord about His own rejection (Matt 21 v 42)).

viii. We should receive anyone who truly comes "in the name of the Lord" as our helper i.e. one who is a Christian, God's servant and has faith in God, who is anointed by His Holy Spirit and sent specifically to deliver us.

Then we shall say with the psalmist: "I will not die but live, and will proclaim what the Lord has done".

Psalm 119

A. 1-8

*¹Blessed are they whose ways are blameless,
who walk according to the law of the LORD.
²Blessed are they who keep his statutes
and seek him with all their heart.*

³They do nothing wrong; they walk in his ways.
⁴You have laid down precepts that are to be fully obeyed.
⁵Oh, that my ways were steadfast in obeying your decrees!
⁶Then I would not be put to shame
when I consider all your commands.
⁷I will praise You with an upright heart
as I learn your righteous laws.
⁸I will obey your decrees; do not utterly forsake me.

Reflections:

'Blessed' (vv 1-2) really means 'happy' including 'being fulfilled' and above all 'blessed by God' are those who keep the Law given through Moses as recorded in the first five books of the Bible. Not all the intricate laws and the laws concerning sacrifice apply to Christians. However the Ten Commandments (Exodus 20 vv 3-17) certainly do, as do the great laws of loving God with heart, soul and strength (Deuteronomy 6 v 5) and loving one's neighbour as oneself (Leviticus 19 v 18) still are the goals to which Christians should aspire. These were reiterated and confirmed by our Lord Jesus Christ in Luke chapter 10 verse 27. It is these Laws which Christians should apply to the whole of Psalm 119. The psalmist in vv 1-8 longs through them to seek God with his whole heart and to have the strength of his whole being to keep God's laws, (v 5). Learning and keeping God's laws is not to be considered as irksome but are to be accompanied by praise to God (vv 7-8). This is also the Christian's attitude as he or she lives their daily life with God.

B. 9-16

⁹How can a young man keep his way pure?
By living according to your word.
¹⁰I seek You with all my heart;
do not let me stray from your commands.
¹¹I have hidden your word in my heart
that I might not sin against You.

¹²Praise be to You, O LORD; teach me your decrees.
¹³With my lips I recount all the laws that come from your mouth.
¹⁴I rejoice in following your statutes as one rejoices in great riches.
¹⁵I meditate on your precepts and consider your ways.
¹⁶I delight in your decrees; I will not neglect your word.

Reflections:

Youth is a difficult time as a young person begins to set the goals of his future life. The psalmist asserts that the best advice to a young person is to live according to God's word (for the Christian this means the teaching of the whole Bible which is God's ultimate 'Word' to the whole of the human race) (v 9). It includes seeking God with the whole of one's heart (v 10). The essence of keeping God's laws is not just a matter of outward observance but should emanate from the believer's inner life (v 11). Once again we are told that this is not an irksome task but is accompanied by rejoicing (vv 14 & 16) and is to be the subject not of a cursory activity but of deep meditation (long prayerful reflection) (vv 15-16).

C. 17-24

¹⁷Do good to your servant, and I will live; I will obey your word.
¹⁸Open my eyes that I may see wonderful things in your law.
¹⁹I am a stranger on earth; do not hide your commands from me.
²⁰My soul is consumed with longing for your laws at all times.
²¹You rebuke the arrogant, who are cursed
and who stray from your commands.
²²Remove from me scorn and contempt,
for I keep your statutes.
²³Though rulers sit together and slander me,
your servant will meditate on your decrees.
²⁴Your statutes are my delight; they are my counsellors.

Reflections:

The psalmist refers to himself as a "stranger on earth" (v 19). In other words he can see no ultimate purpose in life unless he knows and keeps God's laws which are "wonderful" (vv 18-20). Those who stray from God's commands are "cursed" and "arrogant" (v 21). Even though people in authority slander him, yet he will meditate on God's statutes which are his "delight" and they also counsel him – that is, they guide him through life. All of this is a very good guide for Christians whom Peter calls "strangers" on earth (I Peter 1 v 17) or "sojourners" (1 Peter 2 v 11 NKJV).

D. 25-32

²⁵I am laid low in the dust; preserve my life according to your word.
²⁶I recounted my ways and You answered me;
teach me your decrees.
²⁷Let me understand the teaching of your precepts;
then I will meditate on your wonders.
²⁸My soul is weary with sorrow;
strengthen me according to your word.
²⁹Keep me from deceitful ways;
be gracious to me through your law.
³⁰I have chosen the way of truth;
I have set my heart on your laws.
³¹I hold fast to your statutes, O LORD;
do not let me be put to shame.
³²I run in the path of your commands,
for You have set my heart free.

Reflections:

The psalmist is sick (v 25) but he has not lost his faith in God or His Word. He asks that, even in his sickness, he may learn even more about God's decrees (v 26). Though his soul is weary with sorrow he will hold fast to God's statutes and he believes that meditating upon them will give him strength (vv 28-31). Although he is very sick and sorrowful, yet, deep down, in his heart he is a free man (v 32). There is much here for a Christian to learn from and an example to follow when sick and in deep distress.

E. 33-40

> [33] Teach me, O LORD, to follow your decrees;
> then I will keep them to the end.
> [34] Give me understanding, and I will keep your law
> and obey it with all my heart.
> [35] Direct me in the path of your commands, for there I find delight.
> [36] Turn my heart toward your statutes and not toward selfish gain.
> [37] Turn my eyes away from worthless things;
> preserve my life according to your word.
> [38] Fulfil your promise to your servant, so thatYou may be feared.
> [39] Take away the disgrace I dread, for your laws are good.
> [40] How I long for your precepts! Preserve my life in your righteousness.

Reflections:

There is a constant here declared by the psalmist between the worthlessness of selfish gain and the delight and fulfilment to be found in the Word of God (vv 33-37), the statutes of which he desires to keep to the end (v 33). Here is a lesson about perseverance in God's ways which is essential for the Christian to learn and put into practice and not be led astray in heart by the seeming attraction of material things or visually seductive but worthless images available on our TV screens..

F. 41-48

> [41] May your unfailing love come to me, O LORD,
> your salvation according to your promise;
> [42] then I will answer the one who taunts me,
> for I trust in your word.
> [43] Do not snatch the word of truth from my mouth,
> for I have put my hope in your laws.

⁴⁴I will always obey your law, for ever and ever.
⁴⁵I will walk about in freedom, for I have sought out your precepts.
⁴⁶I will speak of your statutes before kings
and will not be put to shame,
⁴⁷for I delight in your commands because I love them.
⁴⁸I lift up my hands to your commands, which I love,
and I meditate on your decrees.

Reflections:

There are two important lessons to learn in this portion of psalm 119 which all Christians should learn and apprehend. The first is that following the laws of God does not result in bondage and curtail the freedom which we should always follow as we walk with God (v 45). The Book of Common Prayer speaks about the One "whose service is perfect freedom". When we are young we may find this very difficult to acknowledge; but those of us who have been Christians for many decades can confirm from our experience that it is true.

The second lesson is that we should never be ashamed about our faith, in openly speaking about it, as the psalmist says: "I will speak of your statutes [even] before kings" (v 46). Sometimes God may give us an opportunity to share our faith with unbelievers and we do not take it because we may feel embarrassed. Paul is a great example about sharing the faith to which we hold fast as he did to King Agrippa (Acts 26 vv19-end). In his Letter to the Romans he writes: "I am not ashamed of the gospel, because it is the power of God for the salvation of everyone who believes; first for the Jew, then for the Gentile" (Romans 1 v 16). Let is follow his example in our daily lives.

G. 49-56

⁴⁹Remember your word to your servant, for You have given me hope.
⁵⁰My comfort in my suffering is this: Your promise preserves my life.
⁵¹The arrogant mock me without restraint,
but I do not turn from your law.

[52]I remember your ancient laws, O LORD, and I find comfort in them.
[53]Indignation grips me because of the wicked,
who have forsaken your law.
[54]Your decrees are the theme of my song wherever I lodge.
[55]In the night I remember your name, O LORD,
and I will keep your law.
[56]This has been my practice: I obey your precepts.

Reflections:

The psalmist finds, as we should, that God's word to us gives hope and comfort in suffering despite the attitude of unbelievers who say that God should not let good men and women suffer (vv 49-51). Despite suffering, God's word is such that it is the theme even of our songs, and we remember God's name even during sleepless nights (vv 54-56). As Christians, however, we also remember that Jesus healed those who came to Him for healing; we can rest in Him and believe that He is able and willing to restore us.

H. 57-64

[57]You are my portion, O LORD; I have promised to obey your words.
[58]I have sought your face with all my heart;
be gracious to me according to your promise.
[59]I have considered my ways
and have turned my steps to your statutes.
[60]I will hasten and not delay to obey your commands.
[61]Though the wicked bind me with ropes,
I will not forget your law.
[62]At midnight I rise to give You thanks for your righteous laws.
[63]I am a friend to all who fear You,
to all who follow your precepts.
[64]The earth is filled with your love, O LORD;
teach me your decrees.

Reflections:

There are some precious thoughts here. The psalmist has sought God with all his heart (v 58). So too Christianity should never be on the periphery of our lives or only something which is a sort of 'God slot' into our daily lives. Faith in Christ crucified for us, bearing unimaginable agony physically and spiritually, calls for total commitment as we may sing: "All to Jesus I surrender".

Also Christianity should be a matter of complete obedience to God and His word (see v 60), for Jesus said: "If anyone loves me, he will obey my teaching" (John 14 v 23). Prayer also should not be just for a convenient time, once a day, but should be something to which we can turn at any time, even at midnight (v 62). Another precious thought the psalmist declares is that "the earth is filled" with the Lord's love (v 64).

I. 65-72

⁶⁵*Do good to your servant according to your word, O* LORD.
⁶⁶*Teach me knowledge and good judgment,*
for I believe in your commands.
⁶⁷*Before I was afflicted I went astray, but now I obey your word.*
⁶⁸*You are good, and what You do is good; teach me your decrees.*
⁶⁹*Though the arrogant have smeared me with lies,*
I keep your precepts with all my heart.
⁷⁰*Their hearts are callous and unfeeling, but I delight in your law.*
⁷¹*It was good for me to be afflicted*
so that I might learn your decrees.
⁷²*The law from your mouth is more precious to me*
than thousands of pieces of silver and gold.

Reflections:

Perhaps we shall never fully know in this life why a good, all-powerful God allows good people to suffer. The psalmist has himself suffered but still states his belief which all Christians say, in faith, that God is good (v 68). One fact cannot be denied: that it is in fact personal suffering which has brought people to a place where they turn to God, as happened to me myself when as a suffering teenager I turned to God whom I had never known and found Him to be my healer. See v 71 where the psalmist even states that, for this reason, it was good to be afflicted. Further he has found that the Word of God is more precious than "thousands of pieces of silver and gold" (v 72).

J. 73-80

^{73}Your hands made me and formed me;
give me understanding to learn your commands.
^{74}May those who fear You rejoice when they see me,
for I have put my hope in your word.
^{75}I know, O LORD, that your laws are righteous,
and in faithfulness You have afflicted me.
^{76}May your unfailing love be my comfort,
according to your promise to your servant.
^{77}Let your compassion come to me that I may live,
for your law is my delight.
^{78}May the arrogant be put to shame
for wronging me without cause;
but I will meditate on your precepts.
^{79}May those who fear You turn to me,
those who understand your statutes.
^{80}May my heart be blameless toward your decrees,
that I may not be put to shame.

Reflections:

We have already seen that the author of psalm 119 affirms that believers should never be ashamed to speak out about their faith. However, if their lives do not match up to their confession of belief, then they can rightly be seen as hypocrites. In this portion of the psalm, the author asks God to help him so that unbelievers may be drawn to Him by the quality of his life (vv 74,79). What we are matters in the end as Christians, more than what we say! Jesus said to His disciples, "Let your light shine before men, that they may see your good deeds and praise your Father in heaven" (Matt 5 v 16).

K. 81-88

⁸¹*My soul faints with longing for your salvation,*
but I have put my hope in your word.
⁸²*My eyes fail, looking for your promise;*
I say, "When will You comfort me?"
⁸³*Though I am like a wineskin in the smoke,*
I do not forget your decrees.
⁸⁴*How long must your servant wait?*
When will You punish my persecutors?
⁸⁵*The arrogant dig pitfalls for me, contrary to your law.*
⁸⁶*All your commands are trustworthy;*
help me, for men persecute me without cause.
⁸⁷*They almost wiped me from the earth,*
but I have not forsaken your precepts.
⁸⁸*Preserve my life according to your love,*
and I will obey the statutes of your mouth.

Reflections:

One of the lessons which believers have to learn is that, like the psalmist, God may keep them waiting, even for a long time, before He grants their prayers (vv 81-84). They may even feel they are 'going under' before God visits them. Yet, like the psalmist, this experience should only increase their longing for God to visit them with comfort (v 82). Again, we learn that when suffering, believers should not become bitter or cynical in their attitude to God, but rather never forget His decrees (v 83). To use a modern phrase, we must 'hang in there' when God is keeping us waiting for Him to save us from our affliction.

L. 89-96

⁸⁹*Your word, O LORD, is eternal; it stands firm in the heavens.*
⁹⁰*Your faithfulness continues through all generations;*

You established the earth, and it endures.
⁹¹Your laws endure to this day, for all things serve You.
⁹²If your law had not been my delight,
I would have perished in my affliction.
⁹³I will never forget your precepts,
for by them you have preserved my life.
⁹⁴Save me, for I am yours; I have sought out your precepts.
⁹⁵The wicked are waiting to destroy me, but I will ponder your statutes.
⁹⁶To all perfection I see a limit; but your commands are boundless.

Reflections:

Insecurity is a factor which pervades the whole of the life of mankind in the 21ˢᵗ century. Internationally it is insecurity which causes nations to stockpile weapons, even nuclear weapons, the cause of which politicians state is "national security". In many places of the world people cannot find security in their governments. Insecurity causes marital breakdown and children are reared in situations of insecurity in their homes. Insecurity causes social problems. Security cannot be found even in a lifetime of saving, as we see in collapses of banking institutions in the last few years; the financial world is insecure. On a personal level insecurity causes mental breakdowns and exacerbates other illnesses.

The psalmist, however, declares in these verses that ultimate, certain security can be found in God alone and in His Word which is "eternal" and stands firm in the heavens (v 89). God's faithfulness continues through all generations (v 90) and so God has established the earth and it endures (v 90). God's laws have preserved his life and God's commands are boundless. Christians believe all this and also the many promises of the New Testament, including the words of Jesus in Matthew's gospel chapter 6: "Do not worry, saying, 'What shall we eat?' or 'What shall we drink?' or 'What shall we wear?' For the pagans run after all these things, and your heavenly Father knows that you need them. But seek first his kingdom and his righteousness, and all these things will be given to you as well" (vv 31-33). Christians therefore, in their lives, should be the most secure people on earth.

M. 97-104

^{97}Oh, how I love your law! I meditate on it all day long.
^{98}Your commands make me wiser than my enemies,
for they are ever with me.
^{99}I have more insight than all my teachers,
for I meditate on your statutes.
^{100}I have more understanding than the elders,
for I obey your precepts.
^{101}I have kept my feet from every evil path
so that I might obey your word.
^{102}I have not departed from your laws,
for You yourself have taught me.
^{103}How sweet are your words to my taste,
sweeter than honey to my mouth!
^{104}I gain understanding from your precepts;
therefore I hate every wrong path.

Reflections:

The psalmist extols the wonders of God's laws on which he meditates all day long (v 97). He rejoices in declaring that they make him wiser than his enemies and give him more insight than all his teachers and more understanding than his elders (vv 99-100). God's words are not harsh and condemning, rather they are "sweet" (v 103). He gains understanding from God's precepts, which means he lives a good life, of rich quality, in harmony with God. This is what every Christian can and should find in his or her daily meditation on the words of the Bible.

N. 105 – 112

^{105}Your word is a lamp to my feet and a light for my path.
^{106}I have taken an oath and confirmed it,
that I will follow your righteous laws.
^{107}I have suffered much;

*preserve my life, O L*ORD*, according to your word.*
[108]*Accept, O L*ORD*, the willing praise of my mouth,*
and teach me your laws.
[109]*Though I constantly take my life in my hands,*
I will not forget your law.
[110]*The wicked have set a snare for me,*
but I have not strayed from your precepts.
[111]*Your statutes are my heritage for ever;*
they are the joy of my heart.
[112]*My heart is set on keeping your decrees to the very end.*

Reflections:

The verse 105: "Your word is a lamp to my feet and a light for my path" has been treasured by many Christians for over two thousand years. They portray the world as a dark place in the believer's pilgrimage to heaven. However, God's Word, embodied in the life and teaching of Jesus Christ, and written in the Bible, if followed (v 106) lights up the path on which a believer treads, so that he or she can see where they are journeying and not stumble over obstacles placed in their way by the evil one or be led astray. I remember a remark by my theological professor when I was a young Christian. He said, "the Holy Spirit is like 'cats' eyes' in the road" (the small bulbs which reflect the lights of the car for the next mile or two on a dark night). As we travel life's road we cannot literally see the end of the road but enough for the next small distance and then the next part of the journey opens up before us. So we believers journey on the Christian path, every step of the way being lit up by the Word of God.

O. 113 -120

[113]*I hate double-minded men, but I love your law.*
[114]*You are my refuge and my shield;*
I have put my hope in your word.
[115]*Away from me, you evildoers,*

that I may keep the commands of my God!
[116]Sustain me according to your promise, and I shall live;
do not let my hopes be dashed.
[117]Uphold me, and I shall be delivered;
I shall always have regard for your decrees.
[118]You reject all who stray from your decrees,
for their deceitfulness is in vain.
[119]All the wicked of the earth You discard like dross;
therefore I love your statutes.
[120]My flesh trembles in fear of You; I stand in awe of your laws.

Reflections:

John Bunyan's book "The Pilgrim's Progress" has been a Christian classic for several generations. It tells of the journey of the new Christian endeavouring to reach the heavenly city. Bunyan describes especially the enticement of "Vanity Fair" and of unbelievers who would try to get him to go with them away from his desired destiny. In today's world it is still the same. There are many we meet who would try to entice us to go along with them away from the relatively narrow path on which we must walk as Christians. It is easy to go along with the secular non-Christian crowd and try to experience what they consider to be "living life to the full", consisting of entertainment, even drunkenness and "pleasures". The psalmist has experienced this (v 115) then realises that he needs God's help to resist the evil way (vv 116-7). He understands that all the wicked in the world may have their so-called "pleasures" but God discards them like dross (v 119). Let us, like him, "stand in awe" of God's laws and remember that in the words of the Book of Common Prayer:

"O God, for as much as without Thee
we are not able to please Thee,
grant that Thy Holy Spirit may
in all things direct and rule our hearts."

P. 121 – 128

¹²¹*I have done what is righteous and just;*
do not leave me to my oppressors.
¹²²*Ensure your servant's well-being;*
let not the arrogant oppress me.
¹²³*My eyes fail, looking for your salvation,*
looking for your righteous promise.
¹²⁴*Deal with your servant according to your love*
and teach me your decrees.
¹²⁵*I am your servant; give me discernment*
that I may understand your statutes.
¹²⁶*It is time for You to act, O LORD; your law is being broken.*
¹²⁷*Because I love your commands more than gold,*
more than pure gold,
¹²⁸*and because I consider all your precepts right,*
I hate every wrong path.

Reflections:

In the prayer our Lord taught us He said: "This, then is how you should pray:

> Our Father in Heaven
> Hallowed be your name,
> Your kingdom come
> Your will be done
> On earth as it is in heaven…." (Matt 6 vv 9-10)

This fervent prayer to see God's Kingdom come and so His will be done on earth as it is in heaven expresses the urgent desire of God's people for two thousand years. In the Book of Revelation we further read of Jesus:

"The Spirit and the bride say, 'Come!' And let him who hears say, 'Come!' " (Rev 22 v 17) and again of Jesus it says: "Behold, I am coming soon!" (Rev 22 v 12).

God's people long for the return of the Lord Jesus Christ to bring an end to all wickedness. The psalmist hundreds of years before the

211

Revelation was written had likewise longed in the words: "My eyes are looking for your salvation , looking for your righteous promise" (v 123). "It is time for you to act, O Lord; your law is being broken" (v 126). It is because he considers the Lord's precepts to be right and loves them more than gold or silver that he "hates every wrong path" (v 128). Even so it behoves everyone who loves the things of God to yearn daily for the time when there will be an end to evil and wickedness under the reign of Jesus Christ. And so the Christian prays daily to this end.

Q. 129-136

¹²⁹*Your statutes are wonderful; therefore I obey them.*
¹³⁰*The unfolding of your words gives light;*
it gives understanding to the simple.
¹³¹*I open my mouth and pant, longing for your commands.*
¹³²*Turn to me and have mercy on me,*
as You always do to those who love your name.
¹³³*Direct my footsteps according to your word;*
let no sin rule over me.
¹³⁴*Redeem me from the oppression of men,*
that I may obey your precepts.
¹³⁵*Make your face shine upon your servant*
and teach me your decrees.
¹³⁶*Streams of tears flow from my eyes, for your law is not obeyed.*

Reflections:

When reading these words, I am reminded of a wealthy landowner in the days of the slave trade. He paid an enormous price for a female slave. After the purchase she said to him: "I hate you! I hate you! I will only obey you because I am forced to, otherwise I would be punished."

"No!" he replied. "I bought you to set you free."

Falling at his feet, she cried: "Sir, I will serve you forever!"

In a similar way, this psalmist does not set out to obey God's statutes because he is compelled to, in a legalistic way otherwise he would be punished, but because he finds them "wonderful" (v 129). He opens "his mouth and pants" as if thirsty, longing for God's commands (v

131). It is because of this that he desires always to have his footsteps directed according to God's word (v 133). He does not want sin to govern him but rather God who redeems him (vv 132-134). The fact that others do not obey God's word brings tears to his eyes (v 136).

Christians have been redeemed by God at an incalculable cost – the shed blood of His Son, Jesus. He did that to set us free, therefore we will serve Him forever.

R. 137-144

[137]*Righteous are You, O LORD, and your laws are right.*
[138]*The statutes You have laid down are righteous;*
they are fully trustworthy.
[139]*My zeal wears me out, for my enemies ignore your words.*
[140]*Your promises have been thoroughly tested,*
and your servant loves them.
[141]*Though I am lowly and despised,*
I do not forget your precepts.
[142]*Your righteousness is everlasting and your law is true.*
[143]*Trouble and distress have come upon me,*
but your commands are my delight.
[144]*Your statutes are for ever right;*
give me understanding that I may live.

Reflections:

The heart of this portion of the psalm lies in the words "Your promises have been thoroughly tested, and your servant loves them" (v 140). The Bible in fact is full of promises which God has made to His children. They are especially an essential part of the Covenant God made to His chosen people the Jews. He spoke through Moses and there came into being what Christians call the Old Testament or Old Covenant. In it God stated that if His people kept His laws then He would be their God: a father to them; bringing them into and keeping them in the Promised Land, the land of Canaan, and provide for all their needs (e.g. Exodus 15 v 26; chap 32; Nehemiah 9 vv 15-23). The New Testament which

Jesus brought into being at the Last Supper also promises forgiveness, a supply of all believers' needs and eventually, eternal life. The witness of the Bible is that, whereas men and women have not kept their side of the 'good buy', God has never failed, as the psalmist declares in v 140. He states that God's laws are "right" (v 137), righteous and trustworthy (v 138) and true (v 142). He laments that his enemies ignore God's words (v 139) but although trouble has come upon him God's commands are still his delight (v 143). All of this should be taken to heart by Christians living today who know that if they sin against God they will suffer the consequences; yet, if they repent God will keep His promise and forgive them. (I John 1 v 9)

S. 145-152

¹⁴⁵*I call with all my heart; answer me, O LORD,*
and I will obey your decrees.
¹⁴⁶*I call out to You; save me*
and I will keep your statutes.
¹⁴⁷*I rise before dawn and cry for help;*
I have put my hope in your word.
¹⁴⁸*My eyes stay open through the watches of the night,*
that I may meditate on your promises.
¹⁴⁹*Hear my voice in accordance with your love;*
preserve my life, O LORD, according to your laws.
¹⁵⁰*Those who devise wicked schemes are near,*
but they are far from your law.
¹⁵¹*Yet You are near, O LORD,*
and all your commands are true.
¹⁵²*Long ago I learned from your statutes*
that You established them to last for ever.

Reflections:

The psalmist is in distress and is calling out to God for help (vv 145-6)..
He is putting his trust in God's word (v 147) and is persisting in prayer and meditation even in the night. Here is a lesson for Christians to learn because Jesus Himself taught us that if our prayers do not have an

immediate answer from God, yet we should not give up, but rather we should persevere in prayer. He told us, in prayer, to keep on knocking, keep on asking and to keep on seeking (Matt 7 v 7) – this is the literal meaning of the Greek. In Luke chapter 18 Jesus told a parable about an unjust judge who at first refused to grant a widow's request, but when she kept "bothering" him he agreed to it. Jesus said that even more, God will grant our requests quickly when we persist in prayer. He also taught a similar lesson in a parable of a man who eventually got out of bed in the middle of the night to give a friend three loaves of bread when he kept resolutely asking for this help, even in the night. So Christians should persist in prayer to their heavenly Father.

Another lesson from this part of the psalm is that God, although transcendent 'above' the earth and mankind, is still near to those who trust Him and obey His commandments (v 151). So believers know that Jesus is with them always, to the very end of the age (Matt 28 v 20).

T. 153-160

[153]*Look upon my suffering and deliver me,*
for I have not forgotten your law.
[154]*Defend my cause and redeem me;*
preserve my life according to your promise.
[155]*Salvation is far from the wicked,*
for they do not seek out your decrees.
[156]*Your compassion is great, O LORD;*
preserve my life according to your laws.
[157]*Many are the foes who persecute me,*
but I have not turned from your statutes.
[158]*I look on the faithless with loathing,*
for they do not obey your word.
[159]*See how I love your precepts;*
preserve my life, O LORD, according to your love.
[160]*All your words are true;*
all your righteous laws are eternal.

Reflections:

In these verses the psalmist's main problem is that he is being persecuted because he loves God's precepts. Those who are persecuting him are the "wicked" who do not seek out God's decrees (v 155). The faith of believers is a constant challenge to those who want to believe that God does not exist, so that they can live their lives just as they like without any fear of or regard to the judgment of God. Jesus also predicted that those who believe in Him will suffer persecution if, like the psalmist, they will not compromise their faith. He said, "Blessed are those who are persecuted because of righteousness, for theirs is the kingdom of heaven. Blessed are you when people insult you, persecute you and falsely say all kinds of evil against you because of me. Rejoice and be glad, because great is your reward in heaven" (Matt 5 vv 10-12). There can be no greater test of the reality and depth of our faith than when we hold fast to it when we are being persecuted for it.

U. 161–168

[161] Rulers persecute me without cause,
but my heart trembles at your word.
[162] I rejoice in your promise like one who finds great spoil.
[163] I hate and abhor falsehood but I love your law.
[164] Seven times a day I praise You for your righteous laws.
[165] Great peace have they who love your law,
and nothing can make them stumble.
[166] I wait for your salvation, O LORD,
and I follow your commands.
[167] I obey your statutes, for I love them greatly.
[168] I obey your precepts and your statutes,
for all my ways are known to You.

Reflections:

In these verses the theme of persecution continues but this time the psalmist states that it is the *rulers* who are persecuting him without cause (v 161). He refuses to compromise his obedience and love of God's statutes and he experiences great peace in being aware that God is pleased with him, knowing all his ways (vv 167-8).

The early Christians also experienced persecution by the Roman Emperors Nero and Domitian and many died in horrific ways rather than worship the Emperor. In later centuries Christians were persecuted by the governments of Stalin and Mao Tse Tung because they were seen as a danger to these atheistic states. If Christians do not experience persecution then it can only be because they have converted the nation to Christianity or because they have so compromised their faith that they no longer pose a threat to an ungodly government. Yet we have seen in Western society in our day laws passed permitting abortion and also in some countries gay and lesbian so-called 'marriages'. Even in secular states which do such things the Christian voice of objection should be far more widely heard than it is. It is time for Christians to awaken from their slumbers!

V. 169–176

[169] May my cry come before You, O LORD;
give me understanding according to your word.
[170] May my supplication come before You;
deliver me according to your promise.
[171] May my lips overflow with praise,
for You teach me your decrees.
[172] May my tongue sing of your word,
for all your commands are righteous.
[173] May your hand be ready to help me,
for I have chosen your precepts.
[174] I long for your salvation, O LORD,
and your law is my delight.
[175] Let me live that I may praise You,
and may your laws sustain me.
[176] I have strayed like a lost sheep.

Seek your servant, for I have not forgotten your commands.

Reflections:

The psalmist prays that his lips may "overflow" with praise because:
God teaches him His decrees (v 171)
and   All His commands are righteous (v 172).

He asks that he may live to praise God (v 175). This is obviously, for him, the primary purpose of human life, and it should be of vital importance for every believer; we should follow the example of Paul, who declared, "For me, to live is Christ and to die is gain" (Phil 1 v 21). To praise and worship God is the ultimate, most pure and most noble activity in which a human being can engage. Let us do it often!

Yet, for all his love for the law, the psalmist has to admit that he has strayed like a lost sheep. His prayer is for God to seek him and find him (v 176). This has many echoes in the teaching of Jesus, who said that "the Son of Man came to seek and to save that which was lost" (Luke 19 v 10). His teaching about the joy in heaven when a person who had been lost to God is found, takes up a whole chapter in Luke's Gospel in parables about a lost coin, a lost sheep and a lost son (Luke 15). We can never stray so far away from God that He cannot find us!

Having now come to the end of Psalm 119, let's take a few moments to reflect on the main theme. It is, of course, all about God's law, His righteousness, and how blessed is the person who follows those statutes. As Christians we rejoice with the psalmist, because Jesus came to this earth not to destroy the law, but so that it would be ***fulfilled*** in Him. Jesus has given himself for us; He is our righteousness – in other words, all that the psalmist has been exulting in throughout this psalm and praising God for, is given to us in Jesus. Hallelujah!

Psalm 120

¹I call on the LORD in my distress, and he answers me.
²Save me, O LORD, from lying lips and from deceitful tongues.

³What will he do to you, and what more besides, O deceitful tongue?
⁴He will punish you with a warrior's sharp arrows,
with burning coals of the broom tree.
⁵Woe to me that I dwell in Meshech,
that I live among the tents of Kedar!
⁶Too long have I lived among those who hate peace.
⁷I am a man of peace; but when I speak, they are for war.

Reflections:

This psalm is mainly about the use of the tongue (v 1-4). James in his Letter, gives a lot of teaching on this theme (chapter 3). He teaches how the tongue, though small in itself, can have a huge impact on the person who is speaking and either be destructive or a blessing to those who hear. He teaches that taming the tongue is of immense importance in the life of a believer, but that is not an easy task (James 3 v 8). Jesus stated that a person would be judged, in part at least, by the words he has uttered in his lifetime (Matt 12 v 36-37). Let us ask God to help us so that we shall always bless and not destroy others by the use of our tongues.

Psalm 121

¹I lift up my eyes to the hills—where does my help come from?
²My help comes from the LORD, the Maker of heaven and earth.

³He will not let your foot slip—
he who watches over you will not slumber;
⁴indeed, he who watches over Israel will neither slumber nor sleep.
⁵The LORD watches over you—
the LORD is your shade at your right hand;
⁶the sun will not harm you by day, nor the moon by night.
⁷The LORD will keep you from all harm—
he will watch over your life;
⁸the LORD will watch over your coming and going
both now and for evermore.

Reflections:

The psalmist lifts up his eyes to the hills (v 1). These are a help-aid in his worship. They speak to him of the majesty, the transcendence, the power and the security which is to be found in God. Many people find the world of nature a help-aid in their prayers and meditation on the being of the Lord as expressed in the hymn:

> All things bright and beautiful,
> All creatures great and small,
> All things wise and wonderful
> The Lord God made them all.
>
> He gave us eyes to see them
> And lips that we might tell
> How great is God Almighty
> Who has made all things well.
>
> (Cecil Alexander)

Roman Catholic Christians find a crucifix, the stained glass windows of a church, the altar, candles and the colours worn by the priests a similar help-aid, but evangelical protestants find them a hindrance to their worship. However, help-aids to our worship are common and can be a valuable means for many to come closer in their contemplation of an invisible spiritual God.

The main theme of this psalm, however, is that God 'watches' over

His people. He never sleeps (v 3-4). He watches over His children night and day (v 5). This means that He is constantly aware of the smallest details of a believer's life (v 8). He will protect them from all harm (v 7). Jesus taught that not a sparrow falls from the air without the Creator's knowledge (Matt 10 v 29) and so intimately aware is He of a believer's life that He knows the number of hairs on his head (Luke 12 v 7). Such knowledge is a great comfort to believers in the uncertain world in which we live.

Psalm 122

(A psalm of David)

¹I rejoiced with those who said to me,
"Let us go to the house of the LORD."
²Our feet are standing in your gates, O Jerusalem.
³Jerusalem is built like a city that is closely compacted together.
⁴That is where the tribes go up, the tribes of the LORD,
to praise the name of the LORD
according to the statute given to Israel.
⁵There the thrones for judgment stand,
the thrones of the house of David.
⁶Pray for the peace of Jerusalem:
"May those who love you be secure.
⁷May there be peace within your walls
and security within your citadels."
⁸For the sake of my brothers and friends,
I will say, "Peace be within you."
⁹For the sake of the house of the LORD our God,
I will seek your prosperity.

Reflections:

The psalmist glories in the city of Jerusalem which houses the Temple, the house of God (v 3-5). It is this city and its temple which is the object of pilgrimage for the people of God in the Old Testament. Above all he sees it as a place of security (v 7) and bids his people to pray that it will experience constant peace (v 6-8). Christians transfer all that is said about Jerusalem or 'Zion' to the universal Church of all ages in which as members they find security, in its 2,000 years of history, its beliefs, and its witness to the world expressed in the hymn beginning, "Glorious things of thee are spoken":

> Saviour, if of Zion's city,
> I, through grace, a member am,
> Let the world deride or pity,
> I will glory in Thy name.
> Fading is the worldling's pleasure,
> All his boasted pomp and show;
> Solid joys and lasting treasure
> None but Zion's children know.
>
> . (John Newton 1725-1807)

Being a Christian is not a solitary walk with God. The believer should be conscious that he or she is one of millions of believers past and present who share in his faith and to which fellowship he belongs.

Psalm 123

> [1]*I lift up my eyes to You,*
> *to You whose throne is in heaven.*
> [2]*As the eyes of slaves look to the hand of their master,*
> *as the eyes of a maid look to the hand of her mistress,*
> *so our eyes look to the LORD our God,*
> *till he shows us his mercy.*
> [3]*Have mercy on us, O LORD, have mercy on us,*

for we have endured much contempt.
[4]We have endured much ridicule from the proud,
much contempt from the arrogant.

Reflections:

A constant looking to God for His help and deliverance is the theme of
this psalm. This looking to receive all we need from Him is likened to
the constant and expectant way the eyes of a maid look to the hand of
her mistress and the eyes of a slave look to the hand of their master. It
is easy for a Christian in trouble to be so overwhelmed by his/her
troubles that they are aware of nothing else. It is important however
that the troubled person looks beyond their problems to God who will
sustain, comfort, support and deliver them.

Psalm 124

(A psalm of David)

[1]If the LORD had not been on our side—let Israel say—
[2]if the LORD had not been on our side when men attacked us,
[3]when their anger flared against us,
they would have swallowed us alive;
[4]the flood would have engulfed us,
the torrent would have swept over us,
[5]the raging waters would have swept us away.
[6]Praise be to the LORD,
who has not let us be torn by their teeth.
[7]We have escaped like a bird
out of the fowler's snare;
the snare has been broken,
and we have escaped.
[8]Our help is in the name of the LORD,
the Maker of heaven and earth.

Reflections:

This psalm is ascribed to David who declares that God has saved His people when their situation seemed hopeless. He let them escape from their enemies, "like a bird out of the fowler's snare" (v 7). "The snare has been broken and we have escaped" (v 7). The most important verse is the statement that "our help is in the name of the Lord, the Maker of heaven and earth" (v 8). It is good to be reminded that when we consider that God created heaven and earth, we recognise that He is able to help His people no matter how helpless or hopeless their situation may be.. This is the faith by which today's believer must and can trust.

Psalm 125

¹Those who trust in the LORD are like Mount Zion,
which cannot be shaken but endures for ever.
²As the mountains surround Jerusalem,
so the LORD surrounds his people both now and for evermore.

³The sceptre of the wicked will not remain
over the land allotted to the righteous,
for then the righteous might use their hands to do evil.
⁴Do good, O LORD, to those who are good,
to those who are upright in heart.
⁵But those who turn to crooked ways
the LORD will banish with the evildoers.

Peace be upon Israel.

Reflections:

Again we are taught in this psalm that a believer's trust in the Lord can be like Mount Zion (the Church) which cannot be moved (v 1). This Lord surrounds His people so they cannot be attacked by evil coming from any direction (v 2). The psalmist writes about "the land" allotted to Israel which God will protect. However, for the Christian the "land" represents the whole of his life which God has given him. The Lord is good and will only do good to those who are "upright in heart" (v 4). So God surrounds with His loving power those who trust in Him.

Psalm 126

¹When the LORD brought back the captives to Zion,
we were like men who dreamed.
²Our mouths were filled with laughter, our tongues with songs of joy.
Then it was said among the nations,
"The LORD has done great things for them."
³The LORD has done great things for us,
and we are filled with joy.
⁴Restore our fortunes, O LORD,
like streams in the Negev.
⁵Those who sow in tears will reap with songs of joy.
⁶He who goes out weeping, carrying seed to sow,
will return with songs of joy, carrying sheaves with him.

Reflections:

The psalmist rejoices that the Lord has brought back His people from captivity (in Babylon). This happened in the days of Nehemiah and is described in detail in that book of the Bible.

To return to the Lord when one has gone away from Him is a wonderful cause for rejoicing in any generation. It applies to those who have known God and lived in communion with Him, experiencing all His blessings, but have then gone away from Him through their own fault or the enticement or force of others, and have subsequently returned to the Lord (see Jesus' parable of the prodigal son in Luke 15). It is especially true of those who, for one reason or another, have been compelled to go into a lost state. If they still keep their faith their return will be inevitable as the harvest will definitely be reaped by those who have sown their seed (vv 5-6). Christians, in fact, should be sowing the seeds of faith by their witness and teaching, into the hearts of their children; in Sunday School; or in the hearts of relatives and friends. It is the seed of the Gospel which will bear fruit in the hearer's salvation. Jesus said, "The harvest is plentiful, but the workers are few. Ask the Lord of the harvest, therefore, to send out workers into His harvest field." (Matthew 9 vv 37-38)

Psalm 127

[1]Unless the LORD builds the house,
its builders labour in vain.
Unless the LORD watches over the city,
the watchmen stand guard in vain.
[2]In vain you rise early and stay up late, toiling for food to eat—
for he grants sleep to those he loves.
[3]Sons are a heritage from the LORD,
children a reward from him.
[4]Like arrows in the hands of a warrior
are sons born in one's youth.
[5]Blessed is the man whose quiver is full of them.
They will not be put to shame
when they contend with their enemies in the gate.

Reflections:

This psalm is ascribed to Solomon. It teaches that any project undertaken without prayer and reference to God (even building a house) is insecure (v 1). Again, if a project is finished without trusting for God's protection it is also insecure (v 2). This is true of the building and of our lives. We teach children to sing:

"We are building day by day

226

in our work and in our play."

So the believer does not keep his life with God limited to Sunday worship in church but needs to let God permeate the whole of his or her life endeavours, even relaxation and sleep (v 1-2).

Jesus later taught that a house (life) built upon His words is like one built upon a rock which will withstand the storms of life, whereas a house (life) which is built without reference to His teaching is like one built upon sand which will soon fall (Matt 7 vv 24-27).

The psalmist also teaches what blessings there are in a married couple having children (v 3-5). Having children is thus shown to be the greatest blessing a married man and woman can experience. Those of us who are privileged to have a family must see that each child has to be cherished and loved as a gift from God.

Psalm 128

[1] Blessed are all who fear the LORD,
who walk in his ways.
[2] You will eat the fruit of your labour;
blessings and prosperity will be yours.
[3] Your wife will be like a fruitful vine within your house;
your sons will be like olive shoots around your table.
[4] Thus is the man blessed who fears the LORD.
[5] May the LORD bless you from Zion
all the days of your life;
may you see the prosperity of Jerusalem,
[6] and may you live to see your children's children.

Peace be upon Israel.

Reflections:

The word 'blessed' which the psalmist uses (v 1) is a very precious one. There can be no greater goal or achievement of a human life than to be a blessed man, woman or child, when they are experiencing that they are living a life "blessed" by God. This will be the reward of those who "walk in His ways" (v 1). When the whole of life is lived like this; when the whole of life is surrendered to God in love, then God will bless a believer's work, his business and his family (v 2-4). We cannot pray a more wonderful and precious prayer for others than that they should experience God's blessing "all the days of their life" and that they should live long enough to see God's blessing upon their grandchildren (v 5-6).

Psalm 129

¹They have greatly oppressed me from my youth—let Israel say—
²they have greatly oppressed me from my youth,
but they have not gained the victory over me.
³Ploughmen have ploughed my back
and made their furrows long.
⁴But the LORD is righteous;
he has cut me free from the cords of the wicked.
⁵May all who hate Zion be turned back in shame.
⁶May they be like grass on the roof,
which withers before it can grow;
⁷with it the reaper cannot fill his hands,
nor the one who gathers fill his arms.
⁸May those who pass by not say,
"The blessing of the LORD be upon you;
we bless you in the name of the LORD."

Reflections:

The teaching of this psalm is that wickedness and evil will never have the final say or triumph over a believer's life no matter how it may seem to be at times (v 1-4}. Christians cannot pray with the psalmist that wicked men and women will be "put to shame" (v 5), but the fact is that the believer lives his life in the knowledge that because he trusts in a righteous God, love and peace, not evil and wickedness, will triumph in the end.

Psalm 130

¹Out of the depths I cry to You, O LORD;
²O Lord, hear my voice.
Let your ears be attentive to my cry for mercy.
³If You, O LORD, kept a record of sins,
O Lord, who could stand?
⁴But with You there is forgiveness;
therefore You are feared.
⁵I wait for the LORD, my soul waits,
and in his word I put my hope.
⁶My soul waits for the Lord
more than watchmen wait for the morning.
⁷O Israel, put your hope in the LORD,
for with the LORD is unfailing love
and with him is full redemption.
⁸He himself will redeem Israel from all their sins.

Reflections:

The central and basic message of this psalm is that at the heart of the universe is God, who is a God who forgives to the ultimate all sin whatever and whenever the sinner repents and cries out to Him (v 3-4). God, however, despite the truth is to be "feared", meaning that His love in forgiveness is not sloppy and sentient but He, who is holy, has, throughout one's life to be reverenced and obeyed. It is possible to be too 'slap happy' and to take God's forgiveness for granted, so that we couldn't care less about how we live. Paul taught in his Letter to the Romans that the one who has been forgiven by God's grace will "cease from sin". He declares, "sin shall not be your master" (Rom. 6 v 14). So the forgiven believer never wilfully sins but seeks to live a blameless life. (See Romans 6 vv 8-11.)

Psalm 131

(A psalm of David)

> [1]*My heart is not proud, O LORD, my eyes are not haughty;*
> *I do not concern myself with great matters*
> *or things too wonderful for me.*
> [2]*But I have stilled and quieted my soul;*
> *like a weaned child with its mother,*
> *like a weaned child is my soul within me.*
> [3]*O Israel, put your hope in the LORD both now and for evermore*.

Reflections:

Here David speaks about his humility, and that he has become as a little child in his trust and receptivity to "great matters" and "things too wonderful" for him. This attitude is much practised by Jesus in the New Testament. In Matthew's account of the Sermon on the Mount, he records that Jesus said, "Blessed are the meek, for they will inherit the earth" (Matt 5 v 5). Jesus later taught His disciples that "whoever exalts himself will be humbled, and whoever humbles himself will be exalted" (Matt 23 v 12). He also taught the importance of receiving divine truth with the simplicity and trust of a little child, saying: "I tell you the truth, anyone who will not receive the Kingdom of God like a little child will never enter it" (Luke 18 v 17). He even described Himself as "meek and lowly of heart" (Matt 11 v 29 KJV). Of the truths of the Kingdom of Heaven He said, "I praise you Father, Lord of heaven and earth, because you have hidden these things from the wise and learned and revealed them to little children. Yes, Father for this was your good pleasure" (Matt 11 v 25-26). David's attitude was therefore right by any standards. He spoke before his time. There can be no place for pride and seeking popular praise in the Christian life.

Psalm 132

^{1}O LORD, remember David and all the hardships he endured.
^{2}He swore an oath to the LORD
and made a vow to the Mighty One of Jacob:
^{3}"I will not enter my house or go to my bed—
^{4}I will allow no sleep to my eyes,
no slumber to my eyelids,
^{5}till I find a place for the LORD,
a dwelling for the Mighty One of Jacob."
^{6}We heard it in Ephrathah,
we came upon it in the fields of Jaar
^{7}"Let us go to his dwelling place;
let us worship at his footstool—
^{8}arise, O LORD, and come to your resting place,
You and the ark of your might.
^{9}May your priests be clothed with righteousness;
may your saints sing for joy."
^{10}For the sake of David your servant,
do not reject your anointed one.
^{11}The LORD swore an oath to David,
a sure oath that he will not revoke:
"One of your own descendants I will place on your throne—
^{12}if your sons keep my covenant and the statutes I teach them,
then their sons will sit on your throne for ever and ever."
^{13}For the LORD has chosen Zion,
he has desired it for his dwelling:
^{14}"This is my resting place for ever and ever;
here I will sit enthroned, for I have desired it—
^{15}I will bless her with abundant provisions;
her poor will I satisfy with food.
^{16}I will clothe her priests with salvation,
and her saints will ever sing for joy.
^{17}"Here I will make a horn grow for David
and set up a lamp for my anointed one.
^{18}I will clothe his enemies with shame,
but the crown on his head will be resplendent."

Reflections:

David was hailed by the Jews, in successive generations, to have been the ideal king. So much so that they believed that when the Messiah came he would be "of the line of David" (v 11-12). In the New Testament genealogies Matthew and Luke trace Jesus back to David.

However, Jesus questioned the accuracy of this belief in an argument with the Pharisees. He said if David called the Messiah "Lord", how then could he be his son (Matt 22 v 41-45). He seems to have been hinting at His Divine sonship in this discussion. His mother was the cousin of Elizabeth, who was a descendant of Aaron (Luke 1 v 5) who was, together with Moses, the son of Levi. So Mary was from the priestly tribe of Levites. We can interpret the phrase "of David's line" as referring to David's dedication to God's righteousness, faithfulness, truth, compassion and justice, which would be everlasting.

The psalm may have been written at the time of the dedication of the Temple, and although David did not himself build the Temple but was instructed by God to leave this task to his son Solomon, he had wanted the ark, holding God's special presence, to be given a "resting place", so he had it brought to Jerusalem and placed in the Tabernacle (2 Sam 6 v 17). In David's time worship and sacrifices were offered in the Tabernacle.

The psalmist extols David as the epitome of a king who really worshipped and served God (v 1-12) and saw Zion (Jerusalem) which David conquered from the Jebusites, as God's dwelling place and "resting place for ever and ever", declaring that Zion will be abundantly and in every way blessed by God (vv 15-17).

The truth we can learn from this psalm is that, like David, we should live to *serve* the Lord as our ultimate purpose in life. We can do this in many ways. Like Mother Theresa we can seek to improve the lot of the poor especially those in the Third World, or like the priests (v 9) serve Him in and through His Church. In Matthew chapter 25 Jesus sets out those who enter into their inheritance in the Kingdom prepared for them since creation as those who had fed the hungry; clothed the naked; given drink to the thirsty; cared for strangers and looked after the sick and visited prisoners (vv 34-39). In our daily lives believers have been saved to serve.

Psalm 133

(A psalm of David)

¹How good and pleasant it is when brothers live together in unity!
²It is like precious oil poured on the head,
running down on the beard, running down on Aaron's beard,
down upon the collar of his robes.
³It is as if the dew of Hermon were falling on Mount Zion.
For there the LORD bestows his blessing, even life for evermore.

Reflections:

The first verse of this psalm of David gives the theme of the two verses
that follow. "How good and pleasant it is when brothers live together in
unity". David is not teaching, for instance, about divisions between
nations, although that too would be wonderful for the human race which
has been torn by wars throughout the whole of history. He is, in fact,
making a statement about 'brothers', those who should have a natural
affinity which makes them belong together. This, of course, can be
applied to the Christian Church (the redeemed people of God) who are
bound together by the one act of salvation: the shedding of Jesus' blood
on the Cross. On the evening before this happened Jesus prayed
fervently that His disciples might be <u>one</u> (John 17 vv 20-26). He prayed:
"May they be brought to complete unity to let the world know that You
sent me and have loved them even as You have loved me" (v 23).
Despite this urgent and vital prayer there were soon divisions in the
Church, for instance, at Corinth (1 Corinthians 1 vv 10-17). Paul
appealed to this church for unity amongst those who were brothers in
Christ. Church unity is therefore vital and every believer must pray and
work for the ending of our+ scandalous divisions. And for peace
amongst different races and nations. Christians must never cause
division but work for peace and harmony at all times. Jesus said,
"Blessed are the peacemakers, for they will be called sons of God"
(Matt 5 v 9).

Psalm 134

¹Praise the LORD, all you servants of the LORD
who minister by night in the house of the LORD.
²Lift up your hands in the sanctuary and praise the LORD.
³May the LORD, the Maker of heaven and earth, bless you from Zion.

Reflections:

This is a simple psalm, teaching us that as we praise the Lord, then He will bless us. We differ from the psalmist in that we do not believe this blessing today will come from present-day Jerusalem but from the heavenly realm where the spiritual being of God today is seen to be.

We can be assured, however, that when we gather with true believers to worship our Lord, we are blessed in Zion, which is the Church, the heavenly Jerusalem.

Psalm 135

¹Praise the LORD. / Hallelujah.

Praise the name of the LORD;
praise him, you servants of the LORD,
²you who minister in the house of the LORD,
in the courts of the house of our God.
³Praise the LORD, for the LORD is good:
sing praise to his name, for that is pleasant.
⁴For the LORD has chosen Jacob to be his own,
Israel to be his treasured possession.
⁵I know that the LORD is great,
that our Lord is greater than all gods.
⁶The LORD does whatever pleases him,
in the heavens and on the earth,

in the seas and all their depths.
⁷He makes clouds rise from the ends of the earth;
he sends lightning with the rain
and brings out the wind from his storehouses.
⁸He struck down the firstborn of Egypt,
the firstborn of men and animals.
⁹He sent his signs and wonders into your midst, O Egypt,
against Pharaoh and all his servants.
¹⁰He struck down many nations and killed mighty kings—
¹¹Sihon king of the Amorites,
O king of Bashan and all the kings of Canaan—
¹²and he gave their land as an inheritance,
an inheritance to his people Israel.
¹³Your name, O LORD, endures for ever,
your renown, O LORD, through all generations.
¹⁴For the LORD will vindicate his people
and have compassion on his servants.
¹⁵The idols of the nations are silver and gold,
made by the hands of men.
¹⁶They have mouths, but cannot speak,
eyes, but they cannot see;
¹⁷they have ears, but cannot hear,
nor is there breath in their mouths.
¹⁸Those who make them will be like them,
and so will all who trust in them.
¹⁹O house of Israel, praise the LORD;
O house of Aaron, praise the LORD;
²⁰O house of Levi, praise the LORD;
you who fear him, praise the LORD.
²¹Praise be to the LORD from Zion,
to him who dwells in Jerusalem.

Praise the LORD. / Hallelujah.

Reflections:

Here we have an assertion of the attribute of God which theologians call the 'omnipotence' of God – that He is **all-powerful.** There is nothing or no one in the universe who is more powerful than Him (v 5). "The Lord does whatever pleases Him in the heavens and on the earth, in the seas and all their depth" (v 6). The psalmist goes on to describe the mighty acts of God in delivering His chosen people, "Israel", from the hand of their enemies (vv 8-12), and this the psalmist contrasts with the inability of idols to do anything at all (vv 15-18).

Christians certainly believe in the omnipotence of God and Father of our Lord Jesus Christ. However, it is important to state and believe that the mighty acts of God are not of an arbitrary nature. They are not just unpredictable fads and fancies. God does indeed do what pleases Him in heaven and earth but He always acts according to His nature, which in essence, is *His love*, as the psalmist says, "the Lord is good" (v 3) and His power is always for the ultimate benefit of those who believe and trust in Him (cf Romans 8 v 28). For this reason God's people continually praise Him and the voice of praise rings through the whole of this psalm (v 4-5). God's ultimate power for the Christian is the deliverance of His people from the power of sin and the devil through the life, death, resurrection and ascension of His Son, the Lord Jesus Christ. It is ultimately for this reason that Christian worship, whether corporate or individual, is filled with songs and expressions of praise.

Psalm 136

[1]Give thanks to the LORD, for he is good.

His love endures for ever.

[2]Give thanks to the God of gods.

His love endures for ever.

[3]Give thanks to the Lord of lords:

His love endures for ever.

[4]to him who alone does great wonders,

His love endures for ever.

[5]who by his understanding made the heavens,

His love endures for ever.

[6]who spread out the earth upon the waters,

His love endures for ever.

[7]who made the great lights—

His love endures for ever.

⁸the sun to govern the day,

His love endures for ever.

⁹the moon and stars to govern the night;

His love endures for ever.

¹⁰to him who struck down the firstborn of Egypt

His love endures for ever.

¹¹and brought Israel out from among them

His love endures for ever.

¹²with a mighty hand and outstretched arm;

His love endures for ever.

¹³to him who divided the Red Sea asunder

His love endures for ever.

¹⁴and brought Israel through the midst of it,

His love endures for ever.

¹⁵but swept Pharaoh and his army into the Red Sea;

His love endures for ever.

¹⁶to him who led his people through the desert,

His love endures for ever.

¹⁷who struck down great kings,

His love endures for ever.

¹⁸and killed mighty kings—

His love endures for ever.

¹⁹Sihon king of the Amorites

His love endures for ever.

²⁰and Og king of Bashan—

His love endures for ever.

²¹and gave their land as an inheritance,

His love endures for ever.

²²an inheritance to his servant Israel;

His love endures for ever.

²³to the One who remembered us in our low estate

His love endures for ever.

²⁴and freed us from our enemies,

His love endures for ever.

²⁵and who gives food to every creature.

His love endures for ever.

²⁶Give thanks to the God of heaven.

237

His love endures for ever.

Reflections:

This psalm was probably written to be sung in the Temple. The refrain, "His love endures for ever", was probably sung by the choir of the Levites, or perhaps by the general congregation in response. Recalling some of the words from Psalm 135, the whole assembly rehearses the mighty acts of God in creation (v 1-9) and His deliverance of Israel throughout what Christians call the Old Testament. It is a very good thing for Christians to look through their history as a whole to appreciate the survival of the Church, despite frequent persecution and sometimes error, through over two thousand years. Believers as individuals can go through very difficult times in their lives when their faith is tested to the ultimate and they may be tempted to doubt that "God's love endures for ever". However, this is a statement of faith to which he or she must hold fast when their experience of their own life or the wider life of mankind seems to contradict it. The believer must look beyond himself to the God who is revealed in the New Testament of the Bible. The statement will then be seen to be true *objectively* despite the subjective contradiction of present events. They must interpret such events in the light of God's love which has shone through the past and is present in every moment however difficult it may be to believe. The message of the Bible and human experience is that God's love is invincible in its power to turn seeming evil into good.

Psalm 137

*[1]By the rivers of Babylon we sat and wept
when we remembered Zion.
[2]There on the poplars we hung our harps,
[3]for there our captors asked us for songs,
our tormentors demanded songs of joy;
they said, "Sing us one of the songs of Zion!"
[4]How can we sing the songs of the LORD while in a foreign land?*

238

⁵If I forget you, O Jerusalem, may my right hand forget its skill.
⁶May my tongue cling to the roof of my mouth
if I do not remember you,
if I do not consider Jerusalem my highest joy.
⁷Remember, O Lᴏʀᴅ, what the Edomites did
on the day Jerusalem fell.
"Tear it down," they cried, "tear it down to its foundations!"
⁸O Daughter of Babylon, doomed to destruction,
happy is he who repays you for what you have done to us—
⁹he who seizes your infants and dashes them against the rocks.

Reflections:

Christians can learn from this psalm by *contrast* to the psalmist's beliefs and statements rather than by imitating them. The psalmist is a captive, resulting from the Babylonian destruction of Jerusalem and their policy of weakening nations they conquered by forcing them from their home country to Babylon. There it seems the Israelites were required by their captors to sing their songs of worship to Jehovah (v 3). The psalmist responded by lamenting, "How can we sing the songs of the Lord while in a foreign land?" (v 4). It was a rhetorical question for, in effect, he was saying that singing like this was impossible.

Christians, by contrast, have sung their songs of worship whilst they had to do it in secret, in the face of possible execution. They did this at the beginning of the Church in the Roman Empire where Christianity was designated an illegal religion to follow. They have done so throughout the Church's history and do so today in Islamic countries, as they did also in Stalin's Russia and Mao Tse Tung's China. A foreign land can also apply in any situation ehere Christians are called to maintain their faith when isolated from places of Christian worship or from fellow believers. Further, whilst Christians are free to worship, for instance in Britain or other Western countries, yet the secular, materialistic, non-Christian society there makes maintaining a Christian witness ever more difficult. Yet Christians do continue to maintain their faith and worship.

Again by contrast, rather than wishing ill to enemies of one's faith, even to dashing their children's heads against a wall, we believers follow the instruction of Jesus: "Love your enemies and pray for those who persecute you, that you may be sons of your Father in heaven"

(Matt 5 v 43-end). Our land is getting ever more secular, even anti-Christian – let us sing our songs of worship and love our enemies.

Psalm 138
(A psalm of David)

¹I will praise You, O LORD, with all my heart;
before the "gods" I will sing your praise.
²I will bow down toward your holy temple
and will praise your name
for your love and your faithfulness,
for You have exalted above all things
your name and your word.
³When I called, You answered me;
You made me bold and stouthearted.
⁴May all the kings of the earth praise You, O LORD,
when they hear the words of your mouth.
⁵May they sing of the ways of the LORD,
for the glory of the LORD is great.
⁶Though the LORD is on high, he looks upon the lowly,
but the proud he knows from afar.
⁷Though I walk in the midst of trouble, You preserve my life;
You stretch out your hand against the anger of my foes,
with your right hand You save me.
⁸The LORD will fulfil his purpose for me;
your love, O LORD, endures for ever—
do not abandon the works of your hands.

Reflections:

This is a song of praise to the Lord who is seen by David to have exalted His name and His word above all things (v 2). David praises God for His love and faithfulness (v 2). When a person has such a view and experience of God it is inevitable that he desires "all the kings of the earth" to know and praise God. This has been the driving force of

Christian missionaries for over two thousand years. They sing: "Let all the world in every corner sing: My God and King" (George Herbert). This theme is continued by David in verses 7-8.

Christians today who exult in their experience of God should want to share this wonderful blessing of their faithfulness and love of God.

David takes up the theme of God's disdain of those who are proud and His love for those who are lowly (v 6,8). This is a teaching which runs right through the Bible and is sublimely expressed by Mary, the mother of Jesus in her song of praise which is called the 'Magnificat'.

David declares that he is sure the Lord will fulfil His purpose for him (v 8). Christians believe that God has a definite purpose for the life of every one of His children and that this was planned by Him before the creation of the world (see Ephesians 1 v 1-4). Every believer should turn away from feeling that their life is going round in circles getting nowhere and cherish the thought that their life is full of purpose which God will surely bring to pass.

David's assertion that the Lord has made him bold and stouthearted ((v 3) is important for Christians in their daily lives. Christians are called upon to be bold, especially in their witness for the Lord. See Acts 4 v 13 – the boldness of Peter and John when on trial before the Sanhedrin. Paul also was bold in later sharing his testimony to his experience of the risen Christ before hostile Jews and then King Agrippa (See Acts Chapters 21-26).
Christian – be bold, be daring, for your God is with you: cf Joshua 1 v 6.

Psalm 139

(A psalm of David)

*[1]O Lord, You have searched me and You know me.
[2]You know when I sit and when I rise;
You perceive my thoughts from afar.
[3]You discern my going out and my lying down;
You are familiar with all my ways.
[4]Before a word is on my tongue You know it completely, O Lord.*

241

⁵*You hem me in—behind and before;*
You have laid your hand upon me.
⁶*Such knowledge is too wonderful for me,*
too lofty for me to attain.
⁷*Where can I go from your Spirit?*
Where can I flee from your presence?
⁸*If I go up to the heavens, You are there;*
if I make my bed in the depths, You are there.
⁹*If I rise on the wings of the dawn,*
if I settle on the far side of the sea,
¹⁰*even there your hand will guide me,*
your right hand will hold me fast.
¹¹*If I say, "Surely the darkness will hide me*
and the light become night around me,"
¹²*even the darkness will not be dark to You;*
the night will shine like the day,
for darkness is as light to You.

¹³*For You created my inmost being;*
You knit me together in my mother's womb.
¹⁴*I praise You because I am fearfully and wonderfully made;*
your works are wonderful, I know that full well.
¹⁵*My frame was not hidden from You*
when I was made in the secret place.
When I was woven together in the depths of the earth,
¹⁶*your eyes saw my unformed body.*
All the days ordained for me were written in your book
before one of them came to be.
¹⁷*How precious to me are your thoughts, O God!*
How vast is the sum of them!
¹⁸*Were I to count them, they would outnumber the grains of sand.*
When I awake, I am still with You.
¹⁹*If only You would slay the wicked, O God!*
Away from me, you bloodthirsty men!
²⁰*They speak of You with evil intent;*
your adversaries misuse your name.
²¹*Do I not hate those who hate You, O LORD,*
and abhor those who rise up against You?

²²I have nothing but hatred for them; I count them my enemies.
²³Search me, O God, and know my heart;
test me and know my anxious thoughts.
²⁴See if there is any offensive way in me,
and lead me in the way everlasting.

Reflections:

In psalm 135 we read about the omnipotence (all-powerful attributes) of God. In this psalm we have teaching about the 'omnipresence' (God is everywhere) and 'omniscience' (God knows everything) attributes of God. So God is present and knows everything about us – even our innermost thoughts:

❖ when we sit and when we stand (v 2)
❖ when we go out or lie down (v 3)
❖ behind and before (v 5)
❖ when we are in heaven or in the depths (v 8)
❖ when in the far parts of the sea (v 9)
❖ when in the darkness or the light (v 11)
❖ when we are asleep or awake (v 18)

God knew us before we were born and was active in our being made and all our days were ordained for us from that time (vv 13-16). All this truth is a source of wonderment to the psalmist and to each one of us.

Verses 19-21 cannot be uttered by a Christian.

However, no wonder David asks God to search him and know his heart as well as his anxious thoughts (v 23). This is a Christian's prayer – that God will search not only his deeds but his innermost heart to reveal to him anything that may be there which is unworthy of his calling, and will lead him "in the way everlasting" (v 23-24).

The words, "For You created my inmost being

You knit me together in my mother's womb,

I praise You because I am fearfully

And wonderfully made"

came home to me with extra poignancy when my grandson and his wife put them alongside a photograph which they circulated of their newly born son. They are true of us all.

Psalm 140

(A psalm of David)

¹*Rescue me, O* LORD*, from evil men;*
protect me from men of violence,
²*who devise evil plans in their hearts*
and stir up war every day.
³*They make their tongues as sharp as a serpent's;*
the poison of vipers is on their lips.

⁴*Keep me, O* LORD*, from the hands of the wicked;*
protect me from men of violence who plan to trip my feet.
⁵*Proud men have hidden a snare for me;*
they have spread out the cords of their net
and have set traps for me along my path.

⁶*O* LORD*, I say to You, "You are my God."*
Hear, O LORD*, my cry for mercy.*
⁷*O Sovereign* LORD*, my strong deliverer,*
who shields my head in the day of battle—
⁸*do not grant the wicked their desires, O* LORD*;*
do not let their plans succeed, or they will become proud.

⁹*Let the heads of those who surround me*
be covered with the trouble their lips have caused.
¹⁰*Let burning coals fall upon them;*
may they be thrown into the fire, into miry pits, never to rise.
¹¹*Let slanderers not be established in the land;*
may disaster hunt down men of violence.

¹²*I know that the* LORD *secures justice for the poor*
and upholds the cause of the needy.
¹³*Surely the righteous will praise your name*
and the upright will live before You.

Reflections:

In this psalm David prays that God will deliver him from his enemies. There is nothing wrong with that from a Christian perspective. Believers certainly prayed for such deliverance in the Second World War when the Nazis had conquered the whole of Europe except Britain, which then faced the imminent threat of invasion. However, Christians cannot join David in praying such a dreadful fate for their enemies as he does in this psalm. Perhaps the best Christian commentary on verse 10 are the words of Paul in his Letter to the Romans:

> "Love must be sincere.
> Hate what is evil, cling to what is good" (12 v 9).

And   "If your enemy is hungry, feed him;
> if he is thirsty, give him something to drink.
> In doing this, you will heap burning coals on his head.
> Do not be overcome by evil, but overcome evil with good"
> (12 v 20-21).

Paul was quoting from Proverbs 25 v 21-22 (most of which are attributed to Solomon). It is thought that the "burning coals" refers to an Egyptian ritual in which a guilty person carried a basin of red-hot coals on his head as a sign of his repentance. In this context the kindness shown is likely to help towards repentance.

Once again in this psalm we see that God is the helper of the poor and needy (v 12) who should be the concern of every Christian today as he or she champions the cause of justice. Jesus Himself taught:

"Blessed are you who are poor, for yours is the Kingdom of God." (Luke 6 v20).

Psalm 141

(A psalm of David)

¹O Lᴏʀᴅ, I call to You; come quickly to me.
Hear my voice when I call to You.
²May my prayer be set before You like incense;
may the lifting up of my hands be like the evening sacrifice.

³*Set a guard over my mouth, O LORD;*
keep watch over the door of my lips.
⁴*Let not my heart be drawn to what is evil,*
to take part in wicked deeds
with men who are evildoers;
let me not eat of their delicacies.
⁵*Let a righteous man strike me—it is a kindness;*
let him rebuke me—it is oil on my head.
My head will not refuse it.
Yet my prayer is ever against the deeds of evildoers;
⁶*their rulers will be thrown down from the cliffs,*
and the wicked will learn that my words were well spoken.
⁷*They will say, "As one ploughs and breaks up the earth,*
so our bones have been scattered at the mouth of the grave."
⁸*But my eyes are fixed on You, O Sovereign LORD;*
in You I take refuge—do not give me over to death.
⁹*Keep me from the snares they have laid for me,*
from the traps set by evildoers.
¹⁰*Let the wicked fall into their own nets,*
while I pass by in safety.

Reflections:

Prayer is an intrinsic part of a believer's life. When he or she turns their thoughts towards God, then they are praying.

> Prayer is the soul's sincere desire,
> Uttered or unexpressed,
> The motion of a hidden fire
> That trembles in the breast.   (James Montgomery)

Prayer can be silent as one expresses one's thoughts or, as here with David, spoken aloud. He prays that his prayer may rise up as incense into the presence of God (v 2). Prayer would be a fruitless exercise unless we believed, with him, that God hears and answers prayers.

David prays that God will set a guard over his mouth and keep a watch over the "door of his lips" (v 3-4). Christians are again reminded

246

of the teaching of James in his Letter, of the importance for a believer of the right and sanctified use of the tongue (James 3). We cannot be people of prayer and, at the same time, use our tongue in everyday life to hurt, gossip, lie or speak in an evil way.

He accepts that a righteous man may at times have to hurt him so that he can progress in his spiritual life (v 5-6) and the same is true for us today: we should listen and act on, say, a word of criticism from a fellow believer.

Despite the attacks from evildoers David's heart looks beyond them, their words and deeds, and he fixes his heart upon God (v 6-7). A prayer from the Book of Common Prayer should be a believer's constant attitude that

"amid all the fleeting changes and chances of this fleeting world,
our hearts may truly there be fixed where true joys are to be found"
– *fixed* on God.

Psalm 142

(Of David)

¹I cry aloud to the LORD;
I lift up my voice to the LORD for mercy.
²I pour out my complaint before him;
before him I tell my trouble.
³When my spirit grows faint within me,
it is You who know my way.
In the path where I walk
men have hidden a snare for me.
⁴Look to my right and see;
no one is concerned for me.
I have no refuge; no one cares for my life.
⁵I cry to You, O LORD;
I say, "You are my refuge,
my portion in the land of the living."

> *⁶Listen to my cry, for I am in desperate need;*
> *rescue me from those who pursue me,*
> *for they are too strong for me.*
> *⁷Set me free from my prison,*
> *that I may praise your name.*
> *Then the righteous will gather about me*
> *because of your goodness to me.*

Reflections:

David is again in trouble. He is trapped by his enemies and there seems to be no way of escape. In like manner a believer may feel there is no escape, not from physical enemies, but from problems of life which have come upon him and he cannot see a way out. Then, like David, he must realise that there is no situation which God cannot overcome and he too must pray and trust in God.

David poured out his complaint before the Lord and told him about his trouble (v 2). Of course, the all-knowing and caring God knows all about our troubles but what we are taught in this psalm is that, in our prayers we must be *absolutely honest* with God. Like David we too should lay our situation before Him even to the minutest detail. We must be <u>real</u> with God as also the tax collector was in the parable that Jesus told to His hearers as recorded in Luke chapter 18 vv 9-14. The tax collector, unlike the Pharisee in the parable, poured out his heart to God and cried aloud: "God, have mercy on me, a sinner" (v 13). Jesus said that this man, unlike the Pharisee who reminded God of his right-eousness, really met with God, and his prayer was answered. So too, every believer must be honest with God at all times, especially in his prayers, and he too will find that God respects his honesty and delivers him from his problems.

Psalm 143

(A psalm of David)

*[1]O LORD, hear my prayer, listen to my cry for mercy;
in your faithfulness and righteousness come to my relief.
[2]Do not bring your servant into judgment,
for no one living is righteous before You.
Show me the way I should go,
for to You I lift up my soul.
[3]The enemy pursues me, he crushes me to the ground;
he makes me dwell in darkness like those long dead.
[4]So my spirit grows faint within me;
my heart within me is dismayed.
[5]I remember the days of long ago;
I meditate on all your works
and consider what your hands have done.
[6]I spread out my hands to You;
my soul thirsts for You like a parched land.*

*[7]Answer me quickly, O LORD; my spirit fails.
Do not hide your face from me
or I will be like those who go down to the pit.
[8]Let the morning bring me word of your unfailing love
for I have put my trust in You.
Show me the way I should go,
for to You I lift up my soul.
[9]Rescue me from my enemies, O LORD,
for I hide myself in You.
[10]Teach me to do your will,
for You are my God;
may your good Spirit lead me on level ground.
[11]For your name's sake, O LORD, preserve my life;
in your righteousness, bring me out of trouble.
[12]In your unfailing love, silence my enemies;
destroy all my foes, for I am your servant.*

Reflections:

Here David is at prayer again, in the midst of his troubles. He does not rely on any righteousness in himself to merit God's deliverance and carefully states: "no one living is righteous before You" (v 2). So, realising, as we all should, that we cannot deserve God's deliverance, we like David should throw ourselves upon and trust in *God's* faithfulness and righteousness. This, in fact, is the basis on which all Christian prayer too is offered to God, and it is because we know the love of God for each of His children as the basis of all our petitions, so we can be sure that He will act for us in His mercy.

Once again David also teaches us that we should not allow troubles to overwhelm us, but rather look back in our lives and in the revelation of God's great acts in the Bible for encouragement, so that as we "praise Him for all that is past" so we can "trust Him for all that's to come" (Charles Wesley).

This psalm also teaches us that as we reflect upon God's past mercies, we should ask Him to guide us in our future way our decisions and our actions, so that they may be in accordance with His will (v 8-10).

Psalm 144

(Of David)

¹Praise be to the LORD my Rock,
who trains my hands for war, my fingers for battle.
²He is my loving God and my fortress,
my stronghold and my deliverer,
my shield, in whom I take refuge,
who subdues peoples under me.

³O LORD, what is man that You care for him,
the son of man that You think of him?
⁴Man is like a breath; his days are like a fleeting shadow.

⁵Part your heavens, O LORD, and come down;
touch the mountains, so that they smoke.
⁶Send forth lightning and scatter [the enemies];
shoot your arrows and rout them.
⁷Reach down your hand from on high;
deliver me and rescue me
from the mighty waters,
from the hands of foreigners
⁸whose mouths are full of lies,
whose right hands are deceitful.

⁹I will sing a new song to You, O God;
on the ten-stringed lyre I will make music to You,
¹⁰to the One who gives victory to kings,
who delivers his servant David from the deadly sword.
¹¹Deliver me and rescue me from the hands of foreigners
whose mouths are full of lies,
whose right hands are deceitful.
¹²Then our sons in their youth will be like well-nurtured plants,
and our daughters will be like pillars
carved to adorn a palace.
¹³Our barns will be filled with every kind of provision.
Our sheep will increase by thousands,
by tens of thousands in our fields;
¹⁴our oxen will draw heavy loads.
There will be no breaching of walls,
no going into captivity, no cry of distress in our streets.
¹⁵Blessed are the people of whom this is true;
blessed are the people whose God is the LORD.

Reflections:

The twentieth century saw a great spread of humanism, the belief that human beings are able to overcome all their problems unaided by any reference to a Divine Being. It was, and today still is, conceived that through science, technology and education man would be able to say "glory to man in the highest for man is master of all things" and this viewpoint has been held despite two bloody world wars and conflicts, like that in Afghanistan which still rage today. How different from the attitude of David in this psalm, who ascribes all his abilities and victories to the mighty power of the Lord God (vv 1-2, 9-10). He trusts God to bring him future wellbeing and prosperity (vv 12-14).

David, in this psalm reiterates the teaching of Psalm 8 and Psalm 98 as he points to the weakness, the transience and finitude of mankind (v 3-4) and, at the end of this psalm he concludes with the triumphant: "blessed are the people whose God is the Lord" (v 15).

Christians do not deny that progress has been made in the realm of, say, medical science, which means that at least in the Western part of the world, people are living longer lives, but recall to mind that also things like new forms of crime have, in fact, increased and that man still goes to war with more sophisticated and deadly weapons.   Unlike humanists, Christians ascribe all real progress ultimately to God's guidance, love and power and look to Him to further the wellbeing and prosperity of the human race. They trust in God, not only for blessings of mankind in this life but also have a view of human destiny in the light of eternity and share with David, for themselves and all believers world-wide, that "Blessed are the people whose God is the Lord".

Psalm 145

(A psalm of David)

[1] I will exalt You, my God the King;
I will praise your name for ever and ever.
[2] Every day I will praise You
and extol your name for ever and ever.
[3] Great is the LORD and most worthy of praise;
his greatness no one can fathom.
[4] One generation will commend your works to another;
they will tell of your mighty acts.
[5] They will speak of the glorious splendour of your majesty,
and I will meditate on your wonderful works.

⁶They will tell of the power of your awesome works,
and I will proclaim your great deeds.
⁷They will celebrate your abundant goodness
and joyfully sing of your righteousness.
⁸The LORD is gracious and compassionate,
slow to anger and rich in love.
⁹The LORD is good to all;
he has compassion on all he has made.
¹⁰All You have made will praise You, O LORD;
your saints will extol You.
¹¹They will tell of the glory of your kingdom
and speak of your might,
¹²so that all men may know of your mighty acts
and the glorious splendour of your kingdom.
¹³Your kingdom is an everlasting kingdom,
and your dominion endures through all generations.
The LORD is faithful to all his promises
and loving toward all he has made.
¹⁴The LORD upholds all those who fall
and lifts up all who are bowed down.
¹⁵The eyes of all look to You,
and You give them their food at the proper time.
¹⁶You open your hand
and satisfy the desires of every living thing.
¹⁷The LORD is righteous in all his ways
and loving toward all he has made.
¹⁸The LORD is near to all who call on him,
to all who call on him in truth.
¹⁹He fulfils the desires of those who fear him;
he hears their cry and saves them.
²⁰The LORD watches over all who love him,
but all the wicked he will destroy.
²¹My mouth will speak in praise of the LORD.
Let every creature praise his holy name for ever and ever.

Reflections:

In this psalm David is full of praise to God for all he has learnt about Him, especially in His dealings with His people. So, through David's experience of God we learn that God is

  1. Great (v 3)
  2. Glorious in splendour (v 5, v 12)
  3. All-powerful (v 6)
  4. Full of abundant goodness (v 7)
  5. Righteous (v 7, v 17)
  6. Gracious (v 8)
  7. Compassionate (v 8, v 9)
  8. Mighty (v 11)
  9. Good (v 9)
  10. Faithful (v 13)
  11. Loving (v 13).

He also: upholds all who fall (v 14)

lifts up all who are bowed down (v 14)

gives people food at the proper time (v 15)

satisfies the desires of every living thing (v 16)

is near to all who call upon Him in truth (v 18)

hears people's cries and saves them (v 19)

watches over all who love Him (v 20).

With all this everlasting truth no wonder David concludes:

"My mouth will speak in praise of the Lord.
Let every creature praise his holy name
for ever and ever."

Jesus later said, "Now this is eternal life: that they may know You, the only true God, and Jesus Christ, whom You have sent." (John 17 v 3)

Do you know Him? Because when we do, our everyday life is completely transformed.

Psalm 146

¹Praise the LORD. / Hallelujah.
Praise the LORD, O my soul.
²I will praise the LORD all my life;
I will sing praise to my God as long as I live.

³Do not put your trust in princes, in mortal men, who cannot save.
⁴When their spirit departs, they return to the ground;
on that very day their plans come to nothing.

⁵Blessed is he whose help is the God of Jacob,
whose hope is in the LORD his God,
⁶the Maker of heaven and earth, the sea, and everything in them—
the LORD, who remains faithful for ever.
⁷He upholds the cause of the oppressed
and gives food to the hungry.
The LORD sets prisoners free,
⁸the LORD gives sight to the blind,
the LORD lifts up those who are bowed down,
the LORD loves the righteous.
⁹The LORD watches over the alien
and sustains the fatherless and the widow,
but he frustrates the ways of the wicked.
¹⁰The LORD reigns for ever,
your God, O Zion, for all generations.
Praise the LORD. / Hallelujah.

Reflections:

The heart of this psalm is about trust, which is an integral factor in human life. Husbands and wives must trust each other, otherwise a proper relationship is impossible. Likewise children and parents must trust each other. Business dealings are also based on trust. We must be able to trust our friends and fellow human beings. Religious congregations must be able to trust their leaders to guide them right in their spiritual lives. Patients must be able to put their trust in their doctors and, as in this psalm, people must be able to trust their governments or other forms of national governance, or as in the days of the psalmist, able to trust their kings or their princes. It is to the degree that we trust that we feel let down or even devastated when that trust is betrayed.

This psalmist, however, tells us not to put our **absolute** trust in princes (v 3). He reminds us that all human beings are finite, fallible and destined one day to die. What he is teaching is that, whilst we are alive in our everyday life, the only one who will never let us down or fail us is God alone, as He has revealed Himself to mankind by His Holy Spirit (v 5). He, the maker of heaven and earth, the sea and everything in them, remains faithful for ever (v 6). He has proved Himself also to be the helper of the afflicted and able to frustrate the ways of the wicked (v 7-9). So, as we live our lives on earth and where trust is essential to human life, let us put our absolute trust in God alone – for "Blessed is he whose help is the God of Jacob, whose hope is in the Lord his God".

Psalm 147

[1]Praise the LORD. / Hallelujah.

How good it is to sing praises to our God,
how pleasant and fitting to praise him!
[2]The LORD builds up Jerusalem;
he gathers the exiles of Israel.
[3]He heals the broken-hearted
and binds up their wounds.
[4]He determines the number of the stars
and calls them each by name.
[5]Great is our Lord and mighty in power;
his understanding has no limit.
[6]The LORD sustains the humble
but casts the wicked to the ground.
[7]Sing to the LORD with thanksgiving;

make music to our God on the harp.
⁸He covers the sky with clouds;
he supplies the earth with rain
and makes grass grow on the hills.
⁹He provides food for the cattle
and for the young ravens when they call.
¹⁰His pleasure is not in the strength of the horse,
nor his delight in the legs of a man;
¹¹the LORD delights in those who fear him,
who put their hope in his unfailing love.
¹²Extol the LORD, O Jerusalem; praise your God, O Zion,
¹³for he strengthens the bars of your gates
and blesses your people within you.
¹⁴He grants peace to your borders
and satisfies you with the finest of wheat.
¹⁵He sends his command to the earth; his word runs swiftly.
¹⁶He spreads the snow like wool and scatters the frost like ashes.
¹⁷He hurls down his hail like pebbles.
Who can withstand his icy blast?
¹⁸He sends his word and melts them;
he stirs up his breezes, and the waters flow.
¹⁹He has revealed his word to Jacob,
his laws and decrees to Israel.
²⁰He has done this for no other nation;
they do not know his laws.

Praise the LORD. / Hallelujah.

Reflections:

God, by definition, is pure spirit; Man is flesh and blood, limited in his experience of reality to his five senses. How then can a human being apprehend the Being and the Nature of God? There have been attempts to prove the existence of God by the use of human reason, for instance by Anselm in what is called by philosophers the 'ontological' argument. Kant tried also, much later, to point to the conscience of human beings and their sense of 'I ought', but Richard Dawkins has recently shown, in his book "The God Delusion" that it is an impossible task to prove God's existence one hundred percent. Christians do not deny this, although there are innumerable 'near-proofs'. How then can human beings like ourselves, living in the 21st century, be sure that we know God? The answer is that we could not, except for the wonderful fact, as this psalmist declares, that "He has *revealed* his word to Jacob, his laws and decrees to Israel" (v 19). Christians share in Israel's knowledge as recorded in our Old Testament but declare that the fullness of this revelation is to be found in the life, death and resurrection of His Son, Jesus Christ. They also see God's acts for His chosen people the Jews (v 2, 12-14) and in nature (v 4, 7-9, 15-18) but go beyond this in their belief in Jesus, who gives us the ultimate understanding of God..

In our daily lives, in this scientific and technological age, the Lord delights in those who fear [respect] Him, who put their hope in His unfailing love (v 11).

Psalm 148

¹Praise the LORD. / Hallelujah.

Praise the LORD from the heavens,
praise him in the heights above.
²Praise him, all his angels,
praise him, all his heavenly hosts.
³Praise him, sun and moon,
praise him, all you shining stars.
⁴Praise him, you highest heavens
and you waters above the skies.
⁵Let them praise the name of the LORD,
for he commanded and they were created.
⁶He set them in place for ever and ever;

he gave a decree that will never pass away.
⁷Praise the LORD from the earth,
you great sea creatures and all ocean depths,
⁸lightning and hail, snow and clouds,
stormy winds that do his bidding,
⁹you mountains and all hills,
fruit trees and all cedars,
¹⁰wild animals and all cattle,
small creatures and flying birds,
¹¹kings of the earth and all nations,
you princes and all rulers on earth,
¹²young men and maidens, old men and children.
¹³Let them praise the name of the LORD, for his name alone is exalted;
his splendour is above the earth and the heavens.
¹⁴He has raised up for his people a horn,
the praise of all his saints, of Israel, the people close to his heart.

Praise the LORD./ Hallelujah.

Reflections:

This is a psalm of undiluted praise from the first verse to the last. Verses 1-8 call forth praise from the "heavens" and from the "heights above" while verses 7 -11 call forth praises from all that is on the earth, for "his name alone is exalted." "His splendour is above the earth and the heavens" (v 13) and finally he calls forth praise from Israel "the people close to his heart" (v 14). This is a wondrous conception of all creation joined in praise to the Lord. We are called individually and corporately to join in this universal chorus of praise.

Psalm 149

¹Praise the LORD. / Hallelujah.

Sing to the LORD a new song,
his praise in the assembly of the saints.
²Let Israel rejoice in their Maker;
let the people of Zion be glad in their King.
³Let them praise his name with dancing
and make music to him with tambourine and harp.
⁴For the LORD takes delight in his people;
he crowns the humble with salvation.
⁵Let the saints rejoice in this honour
and sing for joy on their beds.
⁶May the praise of God be in their mouths
and a double-edged sword in their hands,
⁷to inflict vengeance on the nations and punishment on the peoples,
⁸to bind their kings with fetters, their nobles with shackles of iron,
⁹to carry out the sentence written against them.
This is the glory of all his saints.

Praise the LORD. / Hallelujah.

Reflections:

I once overheard a man in a restaurant sitting with his friend near to me express his sentiments about religion by saying: "I would be interested in becoming a Christian except that there have been so many wars in religion". And he was speaking the truth.

In our day there are Islamic terrorists carrying out often suicide missions, killing and maiming scores of innocent people in the name of their religion. This psalmist also seems to be implying war and religion go hand in hand when he states "may the praise of God be in their mouths (the saints) and a double-edged sword in their hands to inflict vengeance on the nations and punishment on the peoples" – see the whole of verses 6-9. A superficial reading might see these verses as justifying war. But it is **"the praise of God"** which is to achieve these results. Perhaps the psalmist is remembering how Jehoshaphat's army marched out **praising the Lord** – and the enemy was routed (2 Chronicles 20).

Christians have fought in wars but this has in recent centuries tended to be in defence of their nation and they do not believe that they should ever be the aggressor. Christian chaplains also serve in the armed forces and have been called upon, for instance, to bless war planes. Other Christians however are pacifists and feel that war, under any circumstances, does not cohere with their Christian faith. In the church where I attend there are always prayers for those serving in the armed forces. Individual Christians must prayerfully decide if war is ever justifiable and pray and act accordingly, many hundreds of years after this psalm was written, which could be interpreted as expressing similar thoughts to those of the apostle Paul in his 2nd Letter to the Corinthians, chapter 10 v 3,4: "For though we live in the world, we do not wage war as the world does. The weapons we fight with are not the weapons of the world. On the contrary, they have divine power to demolish strongholds." Whatever our decision we must pray for peace in all the world and support all that makes for peace and furthers the common good.

Psalm 150

[1]Praise the LORD. / Hallelujah.

Praise God in his sanctuary;
praise him in his mighty heavens.
[2]Praise him for his acts of power;
praise him for his surpassing greatness.
[3]Praise him with the sounding of the trumpet,
praise him with the harp and lyre,
[4]praise him with tambourine and dancing,
praise him with the strings and flute,
[5]praise him with the clash of cymbals,
praise him with resounding cymbals.
[6]Let everything that has breath praise the LORD.

Praise the LORD. / Hallelujah.

Reflections:

The Book of Psalms fittingly ends with a call to "Praise God in His sanctuary" (v 1) and to praise Him for *who He is* and what He has done throughout history for His children, indeed for all mankind. Every instrument known at that time is called upon to accompany these songs of praise and we end with these sentiments:

"Let everything that has breath praise the Lord. Hallelujah!"

CPSIA information can be obtained at www.ICGtesting.com
Printed in the USA
LVOW081835201112

308212LV00007B/10/P

9 780956 178794